Farhad Malekian

Barrels of Justifications Violating International Criminal Responsibility

nova
science publishers
www.novapublishers.com

DOI: https://doi.org/10.52305/UJER2708

Library of Congress Cataloging-in-Publication Data

ISBN: 979-8-89530-495-2 (Softcover)
ISBN: 979-8-89530-523-2 (eBook)

Published by Nova Science Publishers, Inc. † New York

To the milestone labour
of UN Special Rapporteur

Francesca Albanese

Contents

Abstract

The legal discipline of international criminal justice has followed a trajectory that has failed to facilitate a genuine and comprehensive exploration of current realities. These issues are often obscured and serve as major causes of the violations of the fundamental principles of international human rights law and international criminal justice. The prevailing narrative suggests that human rights and criminal justice are akin to a barrel in the possession of oppressive governments that masquerade as advocates of humanitarian norms while showing little regard for the traditional legal and moral rights of victims. This barrel is used to perpetuate deceptive regulations, falsehoods, convoluted metaphors, and empty promises in international criminal courts. A wide array of prominent theories addresses the system of international criminal law without uncovering the underlying truths, while the concept of international criminal responsibility for rogue governments is frequently stripped of its intended meaning. The goal of this book is to provide a thorough examination of the animosity exhibited by Western governments and highlight the dangers of their inextricable judgmental outbursts and dishonest military protection of major criminals from official arrest warrants issued by the ICC. This book will offer support to the rights of victims through promoting the moral truth and imperative legal reasoning.

Introduction

This book does not include arguments from readers or the perspectives of others regarding the nature of genocide, nor does it address the fundamental concept of international criminal responsibility of states or its underlying principles.[1] Instead, it presents a standalone argument concerning how we have been guided in a direction that does not provide any true to faithful analysis of the facts that are deliberately being hidden from us and are the major reasons for the principles of international human rights law and international criminal justice not being valued. *It would have been less controversial and more desirable to avoid saying the truth if I had continued to promote the wishes and wills of those who have the law of the governments, the courts, or even of the faculties of law under their control. However, it would have weakened the argument of the book and undermined the theory of appropriate justice if I had just continued to quote and reconstruct the same theoretical or juridical discussions that have been circulating. Doing this is seen as more desirable for many writers, professors, and even politicians. Obviously, if I did this, I would lose my personal integrity and become a vassal of those who promote the positive law of the political powers by painting the lies as truths and truths as lies.*

In fact, a number of prominent theories address the system of international criminal law, and particularly the framework of international criminal justice. However, there has been little progress made in uncovering the truth or empowering the body of international criminal law. We refer here to the true body of international criminal law that has not been regulated and subjugated to the unjustified, immoral regulations and interpretations of the big powers. Moreover, I have in no way compromised my position by discussing contemporary theories or the philosophies of a number of other writers in order to convey and support my thoughts, as I do have full respect for the works of others. I hope my strategy guides readers to become more conscious of their

[1] Farhad Malekian, *System of International Law: Formation, Treaties, Responsibility* (Uppsala, 1987).

thinking and help them decide which portions of my arguments to accept or reject entirely. The latter outcome is part of the natural process since a work that is never rejected will not grow and will die in its infancy. The strength of a piece increases when it is subjected to scrutiny, which is essential in fostering meaningful debates in the pursuit of truth.

Readers who are already certain that moral principles do not exist or those who believe that scepticism is itself a substantive moral position will surely encounter a number arguments that may or may not suit the frame of their legal bodies. Acknowledging such arguments is the reader's personal choice and is dependent on their ability to either recognise the true power behind the system of criminal justice or ignore it. They can linger on the arguments that are integral to the understanding of the true nature of international criminal justice. Between all of my arguments, I will try to show a roadmap of the entire body of international criminal justice and international criminal law. We will come together to recognise the problems within international criminal justice and identify the reasons why it has not functioned properly throughout this bloody period of history. Of the utmost importance is identifying why it is handicapped and continues to perpetuate a chain of serious human rights propagations. This is one of the most essential reasons for the miscarriage of the system of international criminal justice and the commission of numerous international crimes using very cruel new methods and advanced technology.

As a general rule, when the philosophy of morality or the notion of a united value of man is not respected, violations of the provisions of international human rights become a dangerous partisan custom or a method of existence for those who hold political power under the control of the system of arms.[2] Consequently, the plea for the rights and respect for the integrity of others turns out to be of little or no value. Subsequently, pursuing gluttonous or materialist cravings becomes the primary motivation for the existence of international human rights. As a result of this, the commission of international violations can no longer be seen as a violation, but rather as the method by which the intentions of the political or economic powers are achieved. As we will see and reference, the entire system of international human rights and the features of justice presented within it are under the control of political foxes who only care about what advantages they can gain through their decisions.

In the end, whether intentionally or unintentionally, we change the direction of the objectives of the body of international criminal law and fail to

---

[2] Farhad Malekian, *Tour de force of Moral Virtue in International Criminal Justice* (New York: Nova Science Publishers, 2022).

enforce the international criminal responsibility of states. Our view is that the outside goals are so large and exalting that violating the legal provisions of the international criminal justice system becomes less important than it being seen and protected. As long as we interpret the system of law as a tool of political power and not justice, proxy interests will continue to drive our political morality.[3] However, the situation indicates that we must stand up to any violation that infringes upon the rights of others and undermines the system of moral values for the good of all humankind. I will try to illustrate all these matters within the different paragraphs of the book and present ethical and moral values to the broken systems of human rights and international criminal justice, even though the nature of international criminal responsibility of states will not be enforced.

My depiction of the system of international criminal justice is not about finding a way to cure it, since the system is so ill and damaged that it cannot be treated with the expression of rules or theories. The only alternative to the reestablishment and application of a healthy system of international criminal justice is to achieve an understanding of its sickness and to place weight on ethical and moral values, which in turn could potentially affect the respect of its intentions. As we know, the system is a large and complex piece of legislation that consists of different parts and expresses a broad variety of philosophical issues that should not be treated generally by argumentation, but rather by the *theory of wisdom and tolerance*. I shall try to identify the roots of these shortcomings of international criminal law within the system along with the best way to address the relevant mainstream issues in the philosophy of moral truth and legal truth. These issues are of practical importance both in terms of the potential consequences of non-respect or violations and what can be seen from the consequences of understanding and respecting the united values of human civilisation. The potential existence of the requisite binding norms of international criminal responsibility in the realm of the barrel of international criminal justice will be scrutinised to honour the memory of those who have suffered injustices at the hands of our own criminal governments.

This book is not limited to the current Holocaust in the Middle East; it addresses all crimes committed on an international scale. Due to political considerations, influential governments around the world consistently appoint chiefs, prosecutors, and judges to the international courts. This has been

[3] Consult Farhad Malekian, *The Mirage of International Criminal Law, Kant Metaphysics of Mens Rea* (Cambridge Scholars Publishing, 2018).

demonstrated frequently. Consequently, the fact that a significant number of judges and prosecutors in international courts are monopolised and compromised is an issue we must not ignore. Their connections with the intelligence agencies of powertionism governments are extensive, and they are often influenced by the covert manipulation strategies of certain governments.[4]

With a pure theory of love for humanity
Farhad Malekian
Uppsala, Sweden,
3rd March; 4th June
23rd June; 12th September 2024
f.malekian.in.crim.l@telia.com
f.malekian.in.crim.l@gmail.com

[4] Consult also Professor Norman Finkelstein, *How Israel Employs the 'Dark Arts' to Evade International Justice* https://www.youtube.com/watch?app=desktop&v=pBm6-M3kD1E.

Chapter 1

Incapacitating International Criminal Responsibility

1. Missing Qualification of Criminal Justice

As a general principle of international criminal justice, no rule is legitimate unless it subscribes to the two governing principles of international criminal justice. These are *equal treatment* concerning their subjects and the notion of international *criminal responsibility* for those who violate the principle of equality by one means or another.[5] This is precisely how the barrel of international criminal justice should sound and function.[6] We mean jus cogens norms.[7] However, the reality is somewhat different, and having fate tied to the barrel of justice is much more problematic than it seems.[8] There has been a long struggle for the recognition of the barrel of international criminal responsibility of states without any true progress—even though there have been some codified movements to identify the criminal responsibility of states.[9] The aforementioned principles are the guiding principles of the system

---

[5] Farhad Malekian, *Concreting Righteousness in International Criminal Justice* (New York: Nova publishers, 2024).

[6] *Id.*

[7] On *jus cogens*, see A. Verdross, 'Jus dispositivum and jus cogens in international law,' 60 *American Journal of International Law* (1966), 55-63; E. Suy, 'The concept of *jus cogens* in public international law,' in *Lagonissi Conference on International Law* (1967), 17-77; A. Gomez Robledo, "Le ius cogens international: sa genèse, sa nature, ses fonctions," *III RCADI* (1981), 9-217; R. St. J. Macdonald, 'Fundamental norms in contemporary international law,' 25 *Canadian Yearbook of International Law* (1987), 115-149; L. Alexidze, "Legal nature of *jus cogens* in contemporary international law," *III RACADI* (1981), 223-268; G. Gaja "Jus cogens beyond the Vienna Convention," III RACADI (1981), 271-31; G. A. Christenson, '*Jus cogens*: Guarding interests fundamental to international society,' 28 *Virginia Journal of International Law* (1988), 585-628; G. M. Danilenko, 'International *jus cogens*: Issues of law-making,' 2 *European Journal of International Law* (1991), 42-65.

[8] *Id.*

[9] Farhad Malekian, *International Criminal Responsibility of States: A Study on the Evolution of International Responsibility of States with particular Emphasis on the Concept of Crime and Criminal Responsibility* (Stockholm, 1985); Farhad Malekian, *System of International Law: Formation, Treaties, Responsibility* (Uppsala, 1987); Farhad Malekian, 'International Criminal Responsibility: International Criminal Responsibility of Individuals' in M. Cherif

of international criminal justice and the reasons for the value of appropriate theories of equivalent international criminal justice and preventing the notion of selectivity of judgments. This indicates that justice must respect these two basic principles if other principles or provisions of the international criminal law system are also going to be respected and valued by all nations across the globe.[10] All these principles, elements, provisions, and rules stipulate the resources and opportunities that the subjects of the system of international criminal justice should respect if the theory of international criminal justice is to persist and be recognised as valid.[11] Consequently, the notion of the international criminal responsibility of states must be given qualified legal support.

We treat the subject based on our own wills and circumstances and therefore deny the possible respect that must be given to the responsibility of its subjects. Governments have learned to omit their natural and moral responsibilities that are supposed to be upheld at all times. As a result, we are missing the qualities necessary for justice and the various forms of moral convictions. I refer here to convictions that exert some sort of control over what we recognise as the basic principles of justice, particularly when the international criminal responsibility of high authorities is involved. The harm caused by our criminal conduct to the victims cannot be justified by our insincere convictions or moral justifications. Based on our individualistic reasoning, our judgements may often lack the necessary qualifications for justice. Contradictory justifications to escape criminal responsibility may therefore take root and affect how our convictions are analysed. Due to this, the effective convictions on the rights of others are reduced and we practically systematise our convictions against others. International criminal responsibility requires truth, and any other influence on its character should be strictly prevented.

I would like to discuss the issue of justice in judicial proceedings as part of the purpose of the international criminal law system. Justice should be tolerated by all states if the value of our international legal personalities is to be highly respected in international human rights law and if the very essence of the highly significant theory of '*somebodiness*' is going to be implemented

Bassiouni, *International Criminal Law,* Vol. *Crimes* (2[ed], ed., New York: Transnational Publishers, 1999).

[10] Farhad Malekian, *International Criminal Law: The Legal and Critical Analysis of International Crimes* (Almqvist & Wiksell International, 2 vols. 1991).

[11] Georg Schwarzenberger, 'The Problem of an International Criminal Law,' 5 *Current Legal Problems* (1950).

against the very harmful theory of '*nobodiness.*' Thus, we must respect the personal qualities and talents of every individual in the world. The theory of human rights law actually goes beyond just respecting the rights of individuals. Normally, any victim of international criminal law is reliant on the appropriate implementation and respect of the international criminal justice system and whether its provisions are respected by the primary subjects of the system of international law. In this case, the primary subjects are states, since states are the only subjects of international law that are authorised to codify, modify, and ratify the most significant principles of international criminal justice. This is regardless of the fact that the principle of international criminal responsibility is only imposed on individuals, and despite the fact that the international criminal responsibility of states is a settled principle that, unfortunately, does not function.

Therefore, every theory concerning the system of international criminal justice is lacking the essential subject of international criminal responsibility.[12] This means that the system of international criminal justice does not show equal concern for the essential subjects of states but rather for the subjects of states, and thus individuals are more often the targets of accusations under the procedures of international criminal justice instead of states. This indicates that insincere convictions and justifications cannot play a good role in the system of international criminal justice and in fact only serve to destroy its moral and legal truth. The basic preamble of effective convictions on the essence of justice plays a significant role in the rights of victims and the application of the notion of international criminal responsibility. This is because the rights of victims are very important, and therefore their protection cannot be guaranteed without prioritising their needs. The elements of preventative protection of the rights of victims can only be reached in the context of contradictory convictions, and not through what the criminals interpret and present.

[12] Examine Georg Schwarzenegger, 'The Problem of an International Criminal Law,' 5 *Current Legal Problems* (1950) 265; Edward M. Wise, 'Prolegomenon to the Principles of International Criminal Law,' 16 *New York University Law Review* (1970) 562; Farhad Malekian, *International Criminal Law: The Legal and Critical Analysis of International Crimes* (2 vols. 1991); Farhad Malekian, *Principles of Islamic International Criminal Law: A Comparative Search* (2011); See Farhad Malekian, *The Monopolization of International Criminal Law in the United Nations, A Jurisprudential Approach* (Stockholm: Almqvist Wiksell International, 1st ed., 1993, 2nd ed., 1995); M. Cherif Bassiouni (ed.), *International Criminal Law* (5 vols., 1999); Farhad Malekian, *International Criminal Responsibility,* in M. Cherif Bassiouni (ed.), *International Criminal Law*, (1999), p. 155.

The previous statement is particularly significant as it concerns decisions that may be issued by the Office of the Prosecutor of the International Criminal Court. A clear example thereof is that the ICC issued arrest warrants for Russian authorities in a timely fashion, but failed to do the same for the State of Israel until they had killed over 45,000 people. This shortcoming of the ICC certainly runs counter to the work of the International Law Commission concerning its draft proposal dealing with the concept of international criminal responsibility of states, which we will examine in the following sections. The question then is, how can the ICC Prosecutor claim that the system of international criminal justice under his authority shows equal concern for the two essential principles of international criminal law: accountability and equality? *It is certainly not appropriate to say that the Court has already dealt with the arrest of heads of state of Israel and pressing the notion of international criminal responsibility of the State of Israel is not necessary, although Chamber I of the International Criminal Court has issued arrest warrants for Israeli Prime Minister Benjamin Netanyahu and former Defence Minister Yoav Gallant, their government still bears criminal responsibility for encouraging the commission of crimes. This is what we have discussed under the principle of our moral responsibility in order to evaluate the convictions in the houses of the prosecutor and judges of the Court.*

2. Extreme Opposite of Moral Choice

The notion of international criminal responsibility applies to any individual, organ, government, or state involved in the commission of international crimes.[13] One of the main circumstances that gives rise to the notion of

---

[13] M. Koskenniemi 'Solidarity Measures: State Responsibility as a New International Order?' 72 *BYIL*, (2001), pp. 337–56 ; Farhad Malekian, '*International Criminal Responsibility,*' in *International Criminal Law* (M. Cherif Bassiouni, 2^{ed}, ed., 1999); Gracia-Amador, 'The Crime of Apartheid: Responsibility and Reparations,' *Review of Contemporary Law* (1981), pp. 31-38 ; Jørgensen, *The Responsibility of States for International Crimes* (OUP Oxford 2000) ; A. de Hoogh *Obligations Erga Omnes and International Crimes: A Theoretical Inquiry into the Implementation and Enforcement of the International Responsibility of States* (Kluwer The Hague, 1996) ; A. Bellamy, *Responsibility to Protect: the Global Effort to End Mass Atrocities* (Polity Press, Cambridge, 2009) ; R. Bellamy (ed.), *C Beccaria, On Crimes and Punishments*. (1995) ; J. Crawford, S. Olleson, 'The Continuing Debate on a UN Convention on State Responsibility,' 54 *ICLQ*, (2005), 959–71 ; J. Hoover *Moral Practices: Assigning Responsibility in the International Criminal Court*, 76 *Law and Contemporary Problems* (2014), pp. 263-86 ; F. Malekian, 'Armenian Genocide and the Questions of Responsibility of the Turkish Government,' *House of*

international criminal responsibility is the use of state resources by a government to commit international crimes. The military organs of a state bear international criminal responsibility for supporting the plans of their governments and their leaders. Nations are responsible for the crimes carried out by their leaders who use the legal, political, and military powers of the international legal personality of their states to harm other nations. If a government makes a choice that represents the extreme opposite of the will of its nation, then that government has civil or criminal responsibility according to the nation's constitution.

The existence of the notion of the international criminal responsibility of states is contingent upon the existence of the notion of civil or criminal responsibility of a government under a national constitution. This is regardless of what crimes have been committed by a government under its political authority. In other words, governments are not criminally responsible unless they commit crimes such as genocide and crimes against humanity at the international level. Therefore, the question of equivalent international criminal justice is important and calls for the prevention of crime in order to hinder the commission of international crimes that, in the end, call upon the international criminal responsibility of states, governments, and individuals. All these concepts of criminal responsibility have arisen since the end of the Second World War.

Henceforth, we must try to find a solution that complements both the reigning principles of equality in the system of international criminal justice as well as the principle of international criminal responsibility. That should be the goal of the final characterisation of the system of international criminal law, or international criminal justice. Thus, when a prosecutor ignores this

---

Commons Conference on the Armenian Genocide, Armenian Solidarity, British-Armenian All-Party Parliamentary Group, No Security Publication (2007), pp. 31-9. T. G. Weiss, *Military-Civilian Interactions: Humanitarian Crises and the Responsibility to Protect* (2nd ed., Rowman & Littlefield Publishers Inc., Lanham (MD), 2005) ; N. Roht-Arriaza, State Responsibility to Investigate and Prosecute Grave Human Rights Violations in International Law, 78 *California Law Review* 451 (1990) ; R. Rosenstock, 'An International Criminal Responsibility of States?,' in United Nations/International Law Commission (ed.), *International Law on the Eve of the Twenty-First Century: Views from the International Law Commission* (United Nations New York, 1997), pp. 265–85 ; Farhad Malekian, *International Criminal Responsibility of States: A Study on the Evolution of International Responsibility of States with particular Emphasis on the Concept of Crime and Criminal Responsibility* (Stockholm, 1985); Farhad Malekian, *System of International Law: Formation, Treaties, Responsibility* (Uppsala, 1987); Farhad Malekian, 'International Criminal Responsibility: International Criminal Responsibility of Individuals' in M. Cherif Bassiouni, *International Criminal Law,* Vol. *Crimes* (2[ed], ed., New York: Transnational Publishers, 1999).

significant and necessary principle of international criminal responsibility of states in its application concerning the commission of genocide by the superior leaders of Israel, it violates the notion of natural and equal justice.[14] This is not an accusation directed at the Israeli government, rather a fact that must be seen and respected if the theory of international criminal justice is impartial and does not seek to eliminate the consequences of its judicial system in favour of a biased one. *International criminal justice requires liberty to be free from threat and fear in addition to requiring equality among all subjects of the law concerning their resources and responsibilities before the jurisdiction of international criminal courts.*

We must also remember that victims have the right to ethical and legal equality, and this right should be respected at all times. Victims also have the right to speak freely and truthfully about what they have suffered through and the rights that were violated by barbaric military powers. Our reference is to the proposed legal, cultural, political, and moral values that are supposed to be upheld during all conflicts between nations. When a nation does not respect the rights of other nations and infringes upon those rights to the fullest extent by committing serious international crimes, it bears international criminal responsibility, and the state of the relevant government becomes responsible for providing reparations to the victims of violations of international criminal law as well as of the moral and legal values of international human rights law.

We refer to a government that has violated the equal voice of international criminal justice and created conflicts between justice, victims, and the law. We should remember that nothing can guarantee that our international criminal justice procedures are just when they are always unjust in practice and do not respect the rights of victims concerning the concept of international criminal responsibility of the state of the offender. Normally, special moral requirements are needed in order to identify the truth. Our selfish position cannot be the true face of international criminal justice because judgements have no special value. These judgements also cannot be true when they lack true virtue and applicability, thereby demonstrating the hidden lies that caused the massacre of millions.[15]

---

[14] Spooner Lysander, *Natural Law; or the Science of Justice: A Treatise on Natural Law, Natural Justice, Natural Rights, Natural Liberty, and Natural Society; showing that all Legislation whatsoever is an Absurdity, a Usurpation, and a Crime.* Part First. [1882], available at http://oll.libertyfund.org/titles/spooner-natural-law-or-the-science-of-justice-1882 (Accessed 2023).

[15] A clear example of this is the Iraq War and the involvement of major powers in the name of bringing justice to the region, with the sole intention of modifying the entire politics of the region and occupying oil and gas resources. That is also true in the case of Syria, when the

The moral realm is thus the realm of argument, at least for those who know how to ignore the system of international criminal responsibility of their governments. Furthermore, it is incorrect to say that governments and states escape their international criminal responsibility. The fact is that governments negotiate their own responsibility for international criminal matters along with that of other governments. *Therefore, it is obvious that a more fundamental unity of value in the system of international criminal justice is required if we wish to see more substantive results in the implementation of the notion of the international criminal responsibility of governments and states. We are thus compelled to ask—in which philosophical pigeonholes do we hide our international crimes and baptise them with the norms of international human rights law and justice?* This is why whenever we hear the barrel of justice under the authority of the big political parties, it sounds very strange with the war slogans of powertionist governments.[16] It is actually a barrel of eels instead of a barrel of honesty. These are the established bitter facts of the system of criminal responsibility.

3. The Main Actors of Criminal Responsibilities

Regarding the subject currently at hand, it is necessary to emphasise that the suggestions of the International Law Commission of the United Nations are plausible to the extent that the boundaries of military violations are so high and unrealistic that the system of international criminal justice cannot be comprehensive without the application of the international criminal responsibility of States. This is particularly essential concerning the American, British, and the Israeli governments' international criminal responsibility for the occupation of Palestine and the barbaric international crimes that have been committed throughout said occupation. This also includes the international criminal responsibility of Germany for its serious complicities in

---

powertionist governments committed the most serious crimes and, at the same time, received impunity. We have reached the same conclusions about the problems in Lebanon. The very simple question is: What do the governments of the United States want in the completely other part of the globe? Are these the same historical kindnesses of the British colonial governments against the Chinese population that exterminated and destroyed a longstanding culture of the nation? Consult Christopher Black: The Criminalisation of International Justice (World Public Forum, Dialogue of Civilizations) https://www.youtube.com/watch?v=u8NHawXaOPc.

[16] Farhad Malekian, *Powertionism in International Criminal Justice* (New York: Nova Science Publishers, 2022).

the commission of genocide against Palestinians. Thus, what might be called procedural international criminal justice, the morality of fair prosecutors, the proceedings of fair criminal courts, and impartial judges are necessary requirements of the system of justice.[17] This is how the healthy barrel of international criminal justice should sound. However, it does not.

Moreover, it is also necessary to understand that morality generally has several elementary structures. As a result, international criminal justice is a branch of political morality, which, in its own terms, developed out of the general concept of governmental morality, and the morality grew out of the attitudes of nations concerning certain matters. This necessitates that we pursue a thorough coherence of values within our convictions regarding the concept of international criminal responsibility. It also requires us to pursue validity in the arguments connected to the notion of criminal responsibility. The notion of the international criminal responsibility of states is closely related to the notions of natural and national morality, which in turn place high value on the integrity of human beings as a whole. Furthermore, this subdivision of many universal principles calls upon all human beings to respect each other and not destroy the rights of nations and nature.

A more general goal of criminal law is to prevent wrongful conduct on the part of individuals, groups, organisations, governments, and states. This is not my own understanding, rather the main reason why we drafted and codified national, regional, and international criminal laws. The intention of all these bodies is to identify criminals and bring them before the relevant national or international criminal courts. This is why the principle of international criminal responsibility of states plays a significant role in the prevention of the commission of crimes, as well as in the prosecution and punishment of offenders at international level. I do not plan to subject states or governments to the procedures of international criminal courts. However, we must acknowledge the fact that they are the only ones committing international crimes. There is no doubt about this.

An act of barbarism is an international crime perpetrated under the authority of a government. Such acts violate the basic principles of

[17] On morality role in justice examine Fuller Lon Luvios, *The Morality of Law* (Virginia: Yale Law University, 2nd, ed., 1969); A. R. C. Duncan, *Practical Reason and Morality* (Nelson, 1957); M. J. Detmold, *The Unity of Law and Morality: A Refutation of Legal Positivism* (Canada: Law Book Co. of Australasia, 1984); Lea Brilmayer, *American Hegemony: Political Morality in a One Superpower World* (1994); Ahmad Haque Adil, *Law and Morality at War* (2017); Himma Kenneth and Brian Bix (eds), *Law and Morality* (2005); David Lyons, 'Moral Aspects of Legal Theory' in Kenneth Himma and Brian Bix (eds) *Law and Morality* (2005).

international criminal justice and go against the main principles of international human rights law—the respect for which has not only been necessary, but also essential during times of war. Therefore, states that directly or indirectly contribute to the commission of the crimes bear international criminal responsibility for said crimes. These crimes can be committed with the assistance, support, aid, cooperation, collaboration, conspiracy, collusion, intrigue, consent, knowledge, complicity, approval, partnership, agreement, plotting, trickery, or fraud in the omission of international crimes by the main actor.

A clear example thereof is the commission of barbaric crimes in Palestine by the Zionist government with the complicity of several governments and states including the United States, the United Kingdom, France, Germany, Canada, Turkey, the Netherlands, Sweden, Australia, Norway, and New Zealand. Indubitably, these governments and states have committed international crimes and omitted their responsibilities and duties by referring to the plea of self-defence granted to the Israeli government on 7 October 2023. They have also ignored all of the serious international crimes committed since October 1946. We can thus assert that they view all of the criminal conduct of the Zionist government as legitimate acts of defence. However, the fact is that the decisions of the International Court of Justice and the International Criminal Court in The Hague, along with reports from numerous international bodies, prove that the international crimes committed against Palestinians have been seriously and aggressively committed by the Israeli government and with the support of its Western allies.[18] Based on this, the system of international criminal justice calls upon the international criminal responsibility of the aforementioned states concerning the level and gravity of their participation in the commission of crimes.

---

[18] The criminal acts are against The Four Geneva Conventions of 12 August 1949 and the First Additional Protocol. The Vienna Convention on Diplomatic Relations; The Vienna Convention on Consular Relations; The Convention on the Rights of the Child and the Optional Protocol to the Convention on the Rights of the Child on the involvement of children in armed conflict. The Convention on the Elimination of All Forms of Discrimination against Women; The Hague Convention (IV) respecting the Laws and Customs of War on Land and its annex: Regulations Concerning the Laws and Customs of War on Land; The Convention on the Rights of Persons with Disabilities: The Vienna Convention on the Law of Treaties; The International Convention on the Elimination of All Forms of Racial Discrimination; The Convention against Torture and Other Cruel, Inhuman or Degrading Treatment or Punishment; The United Nations Convention against Corruption; The Convention on the Prevention and Punishment of the Crime of Genocide; The International Convention on the Suppression and Punishment of the Crime of Apartheid; The International Covenant on Civil and Political Rights; The International Covenant on Economic, Social and Cultural Rights.

4. The Policy of the Compartmentalisation of Responsibility

The body of international criminal law deals with international criminal violations. This is the nature and legal characterisation of international criminal law. Naturally, the focus should not be on particular states, such as African states and their governments, but rather on all states in the world and their governments. How can we be certain that the international criminal law system has not been violated when the notion of international criminal responsibility is only applied to African leaders? If the nature of the crimes is associated with the massacre, denial, and slaughter of all civilians, then how can powertionist governments escape from their international criminal responsibility?[19] This includes for international crimes such as genocide, aggression, piracy, robbery, savagery, rape, torture, burglary, looting, plundering, crimes against humanity, crimes against cultural heritage, war crimes, apartheid, exploitation, and forced immigration, as well as serious violations of humanitarian law during armed conflicts.[20] Such crimes have all been committed with the full intention of expelling various nations from their own states and their traditional historical territories. In a manner similar to the Palestinians, who have consistently been compelled to relocate and become refugees due to aggressive force, the brutal attacks were primarily executed by the British criminal government.[21]

That is why the physical act of committing international crimes is classified as the *actus reus,* which in Latin refers to the guilty acts. Under the system of international criminal law, *actus reus* refers to and covers any criminal behaviour, which means acting physically like the British, Israeli or United States militaries do. [22] It also covers actions that do not directly result

---

[19] Farhad Malekian, *Powertionism in International Criminal Justice* (New York: Nova Science Publishers, 2022).

[20] Examine Antonio Cassese, (ed.), *The New Humanitarian Law of Armed Conflict* (Naples: Editoriale Scientifica, 1979); Karima Bennoune, 'As-Salamu 'Alykum? Humanitarian Law in Islamic Jurisprudence,' 15 *Michigan Journal of International Law*, (1994), pp. 605-643; Kesolofetse Lefenya, 'Use of Explosive Weapons in Densely Populated Areas: Implications for International Humanitarian Law,' *African Yearbook on International Humanitarian Law* (2014), pp. 68–86; Thomas G. Weiss, *Military-Civilian Interactions: Humanitarian Crises and the Responsibility to Protect* (2nd ed., Rowman & Littlefield Publishers Inc, Lanham (MD), 2005).

[21] Francesca Albanese. P. and Lex Takkenberg, *Palestinian Refugees in International Law* (2nd Edition, 2020).

[22] *Mens rea* and *actus reus* are both essential elements of a crime, whether committed abroad or domestically. *Mens rea* speaks about the mental state of offenders at the time of the commission of an international crime and can be used by perpetrators to defend their crimes

in the commission of international criminal crime, but which instead count as conspiracy. All this speaks to the international criminal responsibility of the relevant governments or their states under the system of international criminal justice as formulated by the Italian professor and judge of the International Court of Justice in The Hague, Roberto Ago, as well as earlier by Professor Garcia Amador from Latin America.[23]

Here, I am not relying on the assumption that the theory of the international criminal responsibility of states is the sole solution for preventing the commission of international crimes by states. However, I am aiming to say that while the other theories developed and integrated into the system of international responsibility are comprehensive and seem right, they are not useful when it comes to dealing with Western states that commit international crimes. This means that the convictions of governments that have committed crimes have only hurt the victims. This situation implies the statements made by those governments have been inconsistent, and the reality is that compartmentalisation regarding the main basic principles is effectively filtered.

Through this policy of compartmentalisation, these governments judge their actions as lawful and the actions of others as unlawful. This implies that there is a deep inconsistency in the ideas of moral justification between those considered to allies and those considered deserving of being murdered. *As a result, the concept of genuine respect for the rights of victims does not exist, and the further examination of fair justice falters. Consequently, when we talk about the system of international criminal responsibility of states, we do not intend to view the justice system as a barrel of eels and the sounds of its rooted norms. Slithering over rough ground or in water is accomplished by snakes through lateral undulation. The norms of human rights and justice are applied by powertionist governments in this exact manner.*[24] *The aim is, for example, to present the plight of a nation suffering from political intrigues within the State of Israel for over seven decades before the International Criminal Court in The Hague.*

---

as acts of self-defence. The term "*actus reus*" concerns the physical criminal acts committed by the suspect, offender, or the state under the scope of criminal justice. Both terms, "*mens rea*" and "actus reus," give the barrel of justice the correct sound and norms that usually must be heard at the right time. Examine Farhad Malekian, *The Mirage of International Criminal Law*: Kant Metaphysics of *Mens Rea* (Cambridge: Cambridge Scholars Publishing, 2018).

[23] https://www. jstor. org/stable/1286469? seq=4.

[24] Farhad Malekian, *Powertionism in International Criminal Justice* (New York: Nova Science Publishers, 2022).

Therefore, I present an independent, ethical, and powerful fact that has existed in a state of neglect in certain states. Throughout this manuscript, I argue that the systems of international criminal justice and international human rights law should not ignore the principles of international criminal responsibility under any circumstances. The reality of natural morality should not be overshadowed by political power or the actions of governments that ignore the principle of natural morality and the barbaric human suffering caused by military aid, voting assistance, or veto support for the conduct of certain criminal governments.[25] The body of the formation of international criminal responsibility of states, which is clearly outlined in Article 19 of the Draft Articles on International Criminal Responsibility of States presented by the International Law Commission on state crimes, should not be driven away from its practical reasoning and implementation. Vespasian Pella, the Romanian professor, although not involved in drafting the article, long ago predicted the contemporary situation of the world in his work concerning the international criminal responsibility of states for violations of the principles of international criminal law and justice. Therefore, Article 19 clarifies that:

> International crimes and international delicts.
>
> 1. An act of a State which constitutes a breach of an international obligation is an internationally wrongful act, regardless of the subject-matter of the obligation breached.
> 2. An internationally wrongful act which results from the breach by a State of an international obligation so essential for the protection of fundamental interests of the international community that its breach is recognized as a crime by that community as a whole, constitutes an international crime.
> 3. Subject to paragraph 2, and on the basis of the rules of international law in force, an international crime may result, *inter alia,* from:
>   (a) a serious breach of an international obligation of essential importance for the maintenance of international peace and security, such as prohibiting aggression;

[25] On morality examine P. M. S. Hacker and J. Raz, (eds.), Law, *Morality and Society: Essays in Honour of H. L. A. Hart* (1977); Farhad Malekian, *Classical Morality in International Peremptory Criminal Law* (Newcastle: Cambridge Scholars Publishing, 2021); Joseph Raz, *Ethics in the Public Domain: Essays in the Morality of Law and Politics* (Oxford: Oxford University Press, 1994); Joseph Raz, *The Morality of Freedom* (1986); Robert Vischer K., *Martin Luther King Jr. and the Morality of Legal Practice: Lessons in Love and Justice* (2014).

(b) a serious breach of an international obligation of essential importance for safeguarding the right of self-determination of peoples, such as that prohibiting the establishment or maintenance by force of colonial domination;
(c) a serious breach on a widespread scale of an international obligation of essential importance for safeguarding the human being, such as those prohibiting slavery, genocide and apartheid;
(d) a serious breach of an international obligation of essential importance for the safeguarding and preservation of the human environment, such as those prohibiting massive pollution of the atmosphere or of the seas.

4. Any internationally wrongful act which is not an international crime in accordance with paragraph 2, constitutes an international delict.[26]

Finally, I do not support persuasive conceptions of the framework of international criminal responsibility of states. I instead base my writing on the very existence of the concept of international criminal responsibility of states, which is required by the provisions of the system of international law and is the real value of international criminal law. I am also aware of the fact that it is the fox or the criminal state and its allies who easily win by using their artillery against the victims of war crimes, crimes against humanity, and genocide.[27] Consequently, the first step in preventing the commission of international crimes and protecting victims is to impose serious prohibitions against the heavy trade of weapons by Western powers. This can only be solved through the presentation or integration of truth within the vocabulary of international criminal justice. Regrettably, this is exactly what criminal governments avoid doing.

5. The Noisy Barrel of Criminal Responsibility

I am not here to present a series of claims about the true meaning of the system of international human rights law or international criminal justice. However, our moral convictions should apply to everyone and be strong enough to see

[26] Text of Article 19; Report of the ILC on the work of its forty-eight session, A/51/10 (1996), 60.

[27] A major impediment to the system of international criminal responsibility is that the American Parliament vigorously celebrated this evil victory of criminals by applauding beyond measure, which demonstrated the reality of a hollow barrel sounding loud but being fully empty.

the injustices against the populations of Vietnam, Syria, Afghanistan, Lebanon, Libya, and Palestine at the hands of the powerful governments be addressed. The notion of responsibility requires us to critically consider our approach to questions of international criminal responsibility with the goals of promoting integrity and respect for all civilisations. The variety of aggressive political movements proves that the concepts of equality and responsibility have been seriously violated in the system of international criminal justice, and these violations have intensified in Gaza since October 2023.

The fact is that the criminal ally states are providing assistance through different means and are much more aggressive than the Israeli government. If these states did not support the barbaric acts of the Zionist government, then the Israeli state would not have been successful in committing a massacre against Palestinians. Therefore, we must not hesitate to bear witness to the atrocities being committed against victims. Otherwise, we approve the commission of all these atrocities and agree that the commission of international crimes is permitted under the system of international criminal law, and that their commission is legitimate for certain states and illegitimate for other states. This also proves that any serious breach of the norms of international human rights is permitted.

If the system of international human rights law is not supported by the system of international criminal justice, then what is the true function of the latter? My claims about the best understanding of the system of international criminal justice are not based on the concept of international criminal responsibility of states alone. However, the fact is that the criminal responsibility of governments is the most essential reason for the promotion of the system of international human rights law and the protection of the rights of victims who have been the targets of serious international crimes due to the complicity of other governments. I propose using certain terms of international criminal justice, not because they are strong and powerful, but because they largely lack a legal function and their weakness is so obvious that the noisy barrel of international criminal courts has been unable to arrest criminals.[28]

---

[28] J. Holmes Armstead, 'The International Criminal Court: History, Development and Status', 38 *Santa Clara Law Review* 745-835 (1998); John E Ackerman and Eugène O'Sullivan, *Practice and Procedure of the International Criminal Tribunal for the Former Yugoslavia with selected material from the International Criminal Tribunal for Rwanda* (2000); Michael Akehurst, *Jurisdiction in International Law*, 1972-1973 BYIL 145; Bienvenido C. Ambion, 'Organization of a Court of International Criminal Jurisdiction', 29 *Philippine Law Journal* 345 (1954); D. M. Amann and M. N. S. Sellers, 'The United States of America and the International Criminal Court', *American Journal of Comparative Law* 381-404 (2002); Kofi Annan, 'Advocating for an International Criminal Court', 21 *Fordham*

The criminals we are referring to here are states that have supported the Israeli government, such as the United States, the United Kingdom, France, Germany, Canada, Turkey, the Netherlands, Sweden, Australia, Norway, Denmark, and New Zealand. If governments or states share the idea of the concept of criminal responsibility, then their agreements and disagreements do not prove that they are genuine criminals. This is because sincerity does not equate to agreement with the theory of international criminal responsibility of states. Instead, it reflects the fact that certain governments take measures against the criminal conduct of criminal states. For our example, one can simply refer to the South African government and its involvement in the protection of the rights of victims and the prevention of various *blackboard-barbarian* crimes against Palestinians at the international level.[29] The South African government asked the International Court of Justice to condemn the gruesome genocide committed by Israel.[30]With those observations, South Africa requested the Court to order that Israel:

> (a) immediately withdraw and cease its military offensive in the Rafah Governorate; (b) immediately take all effective measures to ensure and facilitate the unimpeded access to Gaza of United Nations and other officials engaged in the provision of humanitarian aid and assistance to the population of Gaza, as well as fact-finding missions, internationally mandated bodies or officials, investigators, and journalists, in order to assess and record conditions on the ground in Gaza and enable the effective preservation and retention of evidence, and shall ensure that its military does not act to prevent such access, provision, preservation or retention; and to (c) submit an open report to the Court: (a) on all measures taken to give effect to these provisional measures within one

---

International Law Journal 363 (1997); Allmand Warren, 'The International Criminal Court and the Human Rights Revolution', 46 (1) *McGill Law Journal* (2000).

[29] The South African government condemns the Israeli genocide and *inter alia* declares that "[t]he current situation and the risks that Israel's military assault on Rafah pose to the very survival of Palestinians in Gaza as a group do not represent a mere escalation of the already extreme pre-existing situation before the Court on 12 February 2024 when the Court issued its previous decision relating to the threat of a military offensive against Rafah. In attacking Rafah, Israel is attacking the 'last refuge' in Gaza, and the only remaining area of the Strip which has not yet been substantially destroyed by Israel. With Rafah's destruction, the destruction of Gaza itself will be complete." Application of the Convention on the Prevention and Punishment of the Crime of Genocide in the Gaza Strip (South Africa v. Israel), Urgent request for the modification and indication of provisional measures pursuant to Article 41 of the Statute of the International Court of Justice and Articles 75 and 76 of the Rules of Court of the International Court of Justice (10 May 2024), para 16.

[30] *Id.* See also https://www.icj-cij.org/case/192.

> week as from the date of this Order; and (b) on all measures taken to give effect to all previous provisional measures indicated by the Court within one month as from the date of this Order.[31]

Naturally, we may share some perceptions of serious violations of the theory of international criminal responsibility of states or governments under the system of international criminal justice. We do this because we are in agreement—except in cases where we believe that our government or state must support a war in order to avoid becoming a target of the warring parties. This indicates that we support the criminal conduct of the Zionist government with the hope that we will receive some support in settling our own issues of international criminal justice in the future. Some may argue that committing international crimes is wrong, depending on who we consider an ally and who we consider an enemy. How do we protect our own positions? We delve into our dreams and bring them into existence through our personal moral attitudes. Achieving the goal of international criminal responsibility would be impossible if we pursued personal or national gains. This means that even if we consciously set out to achieve something, we may not succeed because of the strong connection between the political wills of our governments and the powertionist criminal governments.[32]

The bottom line is that most states see the systems of international human rights law and international criminal justice as two systems that can be the cargos of dealing with interests in certain situations, such as in the case of Palestine for Germany and Turkey. This means that most states draw certain boundaries concerning what criteria they use in recognising the criminal conduct of criminal governments or failing to do so to protect themselves. Germans committed the most serious international crimes against Jews, and now they are assisting in the killing of Palestinians for their own gain because they are one of the most vulnerable nations in the world. Thus, we mainly agree about how far or not we should go. This indicates that governments do not always agree on identifying criminality or the lack thereof because their criteria sometimes differ.

[31] *Id.*, para. 25.

[32] Farhad Malekian, *Powertionism in International Criminal Justice* (New York: Nova Science Publishers, 2022).

6. Violating the Mechanisms of True Justice

In the development of the international criminal justice system, it is important to consider the concept of moral truth and how it can be justified. *Simply put, were the genocidal acts committed against millions of Jews correct according to certain governments? Let us examine the criminal reaction of the German Nazi government towards the innocent Jews during the Second World War and the extermination that has been accompanying the ongoing holocaust that has been carried out against the Palestinian population by Nazi Zionist governments over the past eight decades. Does the system of international criminal justice permit crimes against children?*[33] *We should question the legal and moral validity of such acts and whether the system of international criminal justice is being violated.*[34]

However, we fully understand that moral realism may be criticised and/or have different forms of recognition. Due to this, we should refer to the theory of our international courts and examine the case under their legal procedures. For example, when the International Criminal Court in The Hague, the International Court of Justice, and international human rights organisations say that moral justice, criminal justice, human rights, and natural justice have all been violated, then contradictory arguments within moral realism lose their basis.[35] *This means that we are forced to follow the views of our international courts and other bodies. We should not espouse anti-realism and go against the metaphysical theory of international criminal justice. We*

---

[33] Examine Farhad Malekian, *International Criminal Law of Children* (New York: Nova Science Publishers, 2021); Farhad Malekian, 'The Child as an Autonomous Subject of Justice' in Farhad Malekian and Kerstin Nordlöf, *Sovereignty of Children in Law* (Cambridge: Cambridge Scholars Publishing, 2012), pp. 2-55;

[34] Consult Farhad Malekian, *International Criminal Law of Children* (New York: Nova Science Publishers, 2021); Farhad Malekian, *Prohibition Governing Child Soldiers Constituting an Integral Part of Jus cogens and Obligatio Erga Omnes*, XVII *World Congress of the International Association of Youth and Family Judges and Magistrates*, Belfast, Northern Ireland, 27 August – 2 September (2006); Farhad Malekian, 'Conundrums of *Jus cogens:* In Case Law' (Part II), No. 13 *Вісник Південного регіонального центру Національної академії правових наук України,* [No. 13 *Journal of the South regional Center of National Academy of Legal Sciences of Ukraine*] (2017), pp. 12-21; Farhad Malekian, 'Conundrums of *Jus cogens*: in International Criminal Law' (Part I), *Вісник Південного регіонального центру Національної академії правових наук України* [*No.12 Journal of the South regional Center of National Academy of Legal Sciences of Ukraine*] (2017), pp. 8-16.

[35] Consult significant views of Spooner Lysander, Natural Law; or the Science of Justice: A Treatise on Natural Law, Natural Justice, Natural Rights, Natural Liberty, and Natural Society; showing that all Legislation whatsoever is an Absurdity, a Usurpation, and a Crime. Part First. [1882], available at http://oll.libertyfund.org/titles/spooner-natural-law-or-the-science-of-justice-1882 (Accessed: on 18 December 2017).

should not perpetuate false assumptions about a situation that is already clear and spread speculation or lies. This is how we look at the value of the judgements of our international criminal courts instead of hiding the truth in pigeonholes.

Therefore, our disagreement regarding the special scope applied to the international crimes committed by the Palestinian population may be illusory, based on the fact that we are worried about being hunted and abandoned by authoritarian governments. Even though we have seen that the crimes committed by the Zionist government are aggressive in nature and violate the basic principles of international criminal justice, we still prefer to remain silent and pretend to busy ourselves with other matters. This means that we neither really agree or disagree with the political and criminal situations in Palestine and instead choose the side that benefits us the most. This is what most Western governments, particularly Germany and Sweden, always do when following in the footsteps of the American and the British governments.

The system of international criminal justice and the other systems of international law therefore cannot show their real functions, and their functions are paralysed by our governments. As a result of this, crimes against innocent victims continue to be committed. This indicates that governments do not disagree about whether progressive international crimes against victims should be prevented, and therefore, the offender, with full support and assurance from the Security Council, continues to commit such crimes.

However, as a show of solidarity, governments staunchly disagree in some cases by expressing their belief that crimes against children must be prevented. But in reality, the criteria for certain decisions are merely political propaganda used to pretend that their policies overlap with the maintenance of human rights principles or rights of children—which they do not. Consequently, they continue to provide financial assistance and military equipment in addition to continuing all trade with criminal governments. Consequently, we must accept that delivering some of our understanding is not harmful to the policies of powertionist governments.

Therefore, we ignore the brutality of the crimes being committed against victims, which are in violation of the provisions of international criminal justice, and give rise to the imposition of Article 19 of the International Law Commission concerning the international criminal responsibility of states and governments. This is how the system of international criminal justice functions—by ignoring reality not only in the practice of certain governments, such as the British, Swedish, and Canadian governments, but also under the Statute of the International Criminal Court, which is supposed to attribute the concept of international criminal responsibility to the offenders of international criminal law.

7. Criminal Responsibility for Complicity

Governments often claim to support international human rights law. While they incorporate human rights norms into their legislation to reflect these values, their actions frequently contradict their commitments and obligations. This discrepancy arises from differing interpretations of international criminal law, which in turn lead to varied approaches to international human rights law, especially when it is most needed. Consequently, the critical concept of state criminal responsibility is significantly overlooked due to these misleading political tactics.

These interpretations and disagreements create significant tension within the framework of international human rights law and international criminal justice. They also lead to conceptual disputes regarding the provisions of international criminal justice and, in some cases, to a complete rejection of the notion of state responsibility for international crimes. Consequently, there are profound disagreements concerning the prosecution of international crimes committed by states. This indicates that the standard interpretations of the international criminal justice system and its ability to provide reparations for victims are ultimately ineffective and encounter substantial biases in their implementation.

The concept of international criminal responsibility for states is increasingly being viewed as lacking significance within the framework of international criminal justice. This perception is likely to disappear over time. Disputes among states regarding various legal issues—such as morality, human rights standards, and the inherent and traditional rights of nations—are primary factors that contribute to the absence of peace and the violations of international criminal laws by military forces, which in turn often justify their actions by claiming that their arguments are valid. The situation represents the initial stage of disregarding the principle of international criminal responsibility.

Additionally, violations committed by military forces are consistently overlooked in the arguments presented by governments, while their aggressive actions are often framed as moral. This is exemplified by the claims of the criminal leaders of the Israeli government, who asserted, "the Israeli army is the most moral army in the world." Such statements highlight a serious infringement on the system of international criminal justice and undermine the fundamental concept of international criminal responsibility for states. It suggests that a viable theory of justice and the principles of morality can be conveniently disregarded by the representatives of criminal states.[36]

Any significant disagreements regarding the theory and its judgments are systematically suppressed until the plans for the massacre of the Palestinians are executed. The situation implies that there is no metaphysical foundation upon which the system of international criminal responsibility—particularly concerning states or governments—can be established. The theory of force, akin to Hitler's own during the Second World War, has become dominant and exerted control over the power of international criminal justice. That is why we ought to pay close attention to the basic facts and elements that have been concealed by the Zionist government over the course of several decades. The point we are discussing is not about agreeing or disagreeing, but rather about the crimes that have already been committed by various means. Regrettably, governments are misdirecting the real noise of the barrel of international human rights law.

The situation indicates that defending a specific conception of a political and criminal principle, like equality, responsibility, prosecution, judgement, reparation, and punishment, causes them to lose the value of their character of internationalisation and become simple rules and provisions within the vocabulary of justice that lack any particular force or standard of recognition in the system of international criminal justice. Although we are aware that the provisions of the system of international criminal law must be integrated and imposed on criminals, they are not.

Governments should also interpret these provisions to the same standard of identification—which they fail to do. This implies that governments that have less military or political power cannot defend criminal justice and its implementation because the system of justice is already imprisoned within and beyond our national and international interests. These imprisonments are equivalent to the imprisonment of the principles of international criminal responsibility and their demands for the accountability of those who have violated the basic structure of international criminal justice with the plea of self-defence.

[36] Joseph Raz, *Ethics in the Public Domain: Essays in the Morality of Law and Politics* (Oxford: Oxford University Press, 1994); Joseph Raz, *The Morality of Freedom* (1986); Farhad Malekian, *Classical Morality in International Peremptory Criminal Law* (Newcastle: Cambridge Scholars Publishing, 2021).

I am describing here the interpretive concepts of international criminal justice and not just conventional concepts, which means that any of these notions of justice may coincide with the savagery of criminal conduct carried out by criminal governments, and our criminal governments or criminal states ignore those acts. For example, these governments have participated in the massacre of Palestinians and continue to defend their actions by referring to the events of October 2023. It is in this way that the system of international criminal justice is ignored, and the notion of international criminal responsibility of states loses its value. That is how we make a ruckus about the broken barrel of human rights provisions, as we did in Vietnam, Cuba, Iraq, Afghanistan, Syria, Libya, and a considerable number of other places across the globe.

The notion of international criminal responsibility is appropriate in circumstances where the commission of international crimes has reached the level of a massacre. In the case of the crimes in Gaza, many strong states have participated in the commission of international crimes alongside the Israeli government during their 78 years of occupation. The situation is indeed even more ridiculous and unjust when the crimes are carried out with the assistance of weapons provided by the German government. The German government is directly contributing the massacre of the Palestinian population by the Israeli government. The fact that German lawyers were judges of international criminal tribunals like the International Criminal Tribunal for the former Yugoslavia that dealt with war crimes and genocide in the former Bosnia Herzegovina. That means that they should know what constitutes genocide.

The situation is more critical when one looks back at the history of the Second World War, when the German government unlawfully and brutally committed the Holocaust, carrying out genocide against the innocent Jewish population. Historical records document that several million Jews were killed under the legal and political power of the Nazi government of Germany. Ironically, similar crimes are now being committed against Palestinians with the help of the visible and invisible aid granted by the German government. This is similar to the acts of the Nazi government of Germany between 1939 and 1944. Where are we going, and is there any respect for Article 19 of the International Law Commission? Our reference is obviously to the questions of the responsibility of states and their accountability for the systematic violations of international criminal justice.

The aid given by the German government is contributing to the consolidation of the notion of international criminal responsibility of states, and here our finger is pointed at the current German government and its international criminal responsibility for the assistance given by the criminal allies of NATO as well. The European Union has essentially contributed to the commission of genocide. It is indeed a serious tragedy to witness the German government working again with the most criminal governments in the world, including the United States, the United Kingdom, France, the Netherlands, and Israel. This indicates that the German government is seriously violating the basic principles of international criminal justice, and is thus a serious violator of international humanitarian criminal law.[37]

The fact is that the blood of the Jewish victims of the Second World War was fading because of the regret of the German government and particularly because of the court that was established to try the German government under the authority of the Nuremberg International War Crimes Tribunal. Moreover, the present direct involvement of the German government in the Holocaust and genocide of the Palestinian population in Gaza and the West Bank harkens back to the Nazi crimes of the Second World War. This is how the magical barrel melody of Ludwig van Beethoven's classical music has been destroyed by the noise of the German government's weapons.

8. Mysterious Faculty of Apprehension

In this work, our intention is obviously not to condemn or defend any specific governments for any reason. All states have equal international legal personalities and their governments carry out the implementation of those personalities until a new government comes into power. However, a considerable number of relevant governments of Western countries and NATO have intentionally violated the system of international human rights law, the system of international criminal law, the body of international criminal justice, and the consolidated body of international humanitarian law for armed conflicts that was codified and ratified over one hundred years ago.[38] These significant agreements were expanded upon by the Geneva Conventions of 1948 and their Protocols of 1977 in order to renew their humanitarian and moral intentions.[39]

---

[37] Examine Antonio Cassese, (ed.), *The New Humanitarian Law of Armed Conflict* (Naples: Editoriale Scientifica, 1979); Thomas G. Weiss, *Military-Civilian Interactions: Humanitarian Crises and the Responsibility to Protect* (2nd ed., Rowman & Littlefield Publishers Inc, Lanham (MD), 2005).

[38] *Id.*

[39] *Id.*

Without hesitation, a number of governments, such as the German government, bear international criminal responsibility for abetting, cooperating, participating, and encouraging the commission of barbaric crimes, not only in Palestine, but also in Ukraine. We must recognise the right to enforce the established value of the system of international criminal justice, which in turn calls upon the international criminal responsibility of individuals, superiors, governments, organisations, and states. These scopes of responsibility are based on the general theory concerning accountability for those who commit serious international crimes. The question then is, if the killing and genocide of thousands of civilians is not a crime, then what is it? If such acts are called self-defence against the right to resistance of the occupied population by the German government, then we are entirely rejecting and denying the existence of international human rights and international criminal justice.

We should not undermine the fact that the interpreters of the system of international human rights law and international criminal justice are responsible for the statements they make. The value of interpreting the system of international criminal justice, including the law of the United Nations Charter under Article 51 and Article 2(4), does not depend on political theory, but rather on natural moral theory, which is also based on moral truth and legal truth. The principles of the system of international criminal justice are similar to those for the maxim of an epoch that calls for the true future of evidence and not for lies presented as the truth. The best interpretation of the system of international criminal justice does not rest on individualistic interpretations or specific deductions, but rather on a comprehensive analysis of the relevant laws, treaties, and practices. A correct interpretation assumes that the truthful values and interests of international human rights have been presented, and does not divide international politics. It also aims to enforce the invisible essence of international criminal justice in defence of the rights of victims.[40] However, interpreters of international criminal law may disagree about their responsibility to realise appropriately and accurately because their own private interests could be in threatened.

There will be a few lawyers who will attack and condemn their government's criminal conduct and assistance given to the Nazi-Zionist regime. *The silence of greedy lawyers worldwide is the most powerful weapon*

---

[40] Farhad Malekian, *Imperative Philosophy of International Criminal Justice: Visible Power – Invisible Essence* (New York: Nova Science Publishers, 2022); Farhad Malekian, *Tour de force of Moral Virtue in International Criminal Justice* (New York: Nova Science Publishers, 2022).

used by the Israeli criminal government to commit genocide. The proof of the international criminal responsibility of states then becomes complicated and, as a result, controversial. However, this does not mean that the system of international criminal justice and the International Criminal Court should ignore the assistance given by certain governments to Israeli criminals. *Truth and its potential value in international criminal justice, including enforcement, must take absolute priority over the aggressive political morality of the governments of the allies. This means that the scope of our interpretations unfortunately depends on certain matters that will not harm our national or personal interests. However, as I have emphasised elsewhere, the system of international criminal justice is not, and will never be, a private academic institution.* This is because it has become obvious now that truly achieving the objective of international criminal justice is neither individualistic nor collective, but rather serves to protect the rights of victims and reveal the truth, thereby separating it from the web of lies orchestrated by the evil arguments of politicians. Regrettably, because of these reasons, the governments of the United States hold authority over the system of international criminal justice.[41]

Although I believe that there are certain objections to my statements, it is also true that those objections may be exaggerated in certain instances because nothing indicates that the entire system of international criminal justice is not playing a game under the full protection of those powertionist governments.[42]

---

[41] Concerning the United States criminal policy, Professor Christopher Black in one of his presentations asserts that "So I am going to talk about the Rwanda tribunal because it is the most familiar to me and because the *war in Rwanda is used time and again by the United States in its propaganda to justify its wars of intervention*, so-called. The US claims that the violence that occurred in Rwanda in 1994 would not have happened if only America and others had acted instead of standing by and doing nothing. But now, after 15 years of trials and investigations, we know that the America and its allies did directly intervene. It was they who controlled that war and it was they who unleashed violence of an unprecedented magnitude and savagery simply in order to overthrow a regime that was an obstacle to greater conquests and riches in the Congo. Their forces, we now know, did most of the killing and Bill Clinton's lie that the US was not involved is one of the great lies of history. As Boutros-Ghali told the Canadian writer on Rwanda, Robin Philpot, in 2004, "The Americans are 100% responsible for what happened in Rwanda." Clinton's big lie has been accepted and acted on because of the propaganda campaign that accompanied it in the media and the key to that propaganda campaign are the show trials at the Rwanda Criminal Tribunal, set up and financed by the same NATO countries and corporations and Soros connected NGOs as control the Yugoslav, Sierra Leone and Hariri tribunals." Christopher Black: The Criminalisation of International Justice (26/09/2014), https://milosevic.co/532/christopher-black-the-criminalisation-of-international-justice/.

[42] Consult Farhad Malekian, *Powertionism in International Criminal Justice* (New York: Nova Science Publishers, 2022).

This *means that the system of international criminal justice is the institution of powertionism in international criminal justice, and its provisions have been colonised by authoritarian terrorist governments.*[43] *This indicates that the contrary view concerning the system of international criminal justice and its preliminary intentions is now considered common. It seems absurd to many international criminal lawyers and international human rights supporters to speak about the fake face of international criminal justice on the platforms created by terrorist governments, and their interpretations are seen as normal. This is very natural and a common sickness of the system of justice, based on the fact that many lawyers of international criminal justice and human rights are the vassal lawyers of certain governments.*

This situation concerns many governments such as the German government and certain Scandinavian governments. *For example, in Sweden lawyers follow the orders of their masters, i.e., those who have the political power under their control and decide how Swedish lawyers should write and act in order not to jeopardise the political ambitions of the politicians. Although the Swedish government, like the German government, has been deeply involved in the commission of crimes against the Palestinian population in Gaza and the West Bank, it is the government that has not been condemned by Swedish international lawyers for committing these international crimes. As a result, the state will not recognise their own international criminal responsibility. We must remember that the concept of the international criminal responsibility of states under Article 19 of the Draft Articles on State Responsibility carries a universal morality message. This message also applies to the Swedish lawyers. Why do certain Swedish lawyers*

[43] "Powertionism relates to the preferences, desires, inclinations, and predispositions of individual governments which form the basis for these governments to pursue their malicious intentions by killing and destroying other nations. Powertionism also relates to the powerful desires of governments to reduce the power of other governments indirectly, even if it means putting another nation in danger of facing death and devastation in order to aggressively pursue their interests and take power away from another powertionist government. Some of the most notorious powertionists of the world work collectively to promote the interests of their strongest leader in the name of working for NATO. This does not mean that all NATO members are strong on their own, however they wish to be seen as strong by standing alongside governments which have a long history of promoting devastation, genocide and death in the world. Such governments are green, or as the Germans say: one can certainly see the *grün hinter den Ohren* of certain NATO members. Only a simpleton would believe that any word out of the mouth of a powertionist government is correct. The elephant here is primarily the United States and NATO and other countries are their puppets. The greed, lies, cheating, and theft carried out by powertionist governments have no sovereign boundaries." Farhad Malekian, *Powertionism in International Criminal Justice* (New York: Nova Science Publishers, 2022).

not accept the basic philosophy of international criminal responsibility arising from the moral substance of law is indeed a conundrum?[44] *Their inability to perceive value in the concept of reality is unfortunately acknowledged when it comes to serious violations of the international criminal justice system. This is evident concerning their silent position on the ongoing genocide against the Palestinian people.*

---

[44] Examine Farhad Malekian, *Conscience of Lawyers in International Criminal Law, the Burden of Doppelgängers* (New York: Nova Science Publishers, 2021); Farhad Malekian, *Conscience of Judges in International Criminal Law, the Heart of Judgements* (New York: Nova Science Publishers, 2021); Farhad Malekian, *Conscience of Prosecutors in International Criminal Law, the Heart of the Matter* (New York: Nova Science Publishers, 2021).

Chapter 2

Barrel of the Evolution of International Criminal Responsibility

1. Harvesting Criminal Responsibility

I may think further or agree about the provisions of responsibility after promoting thoughts that can demonstrate how the system of international criminal responsibility may be harnessed using the variety of norms that can be understood by international lawyers, with the hope of not ignoring the significant validity of the element of responsibility. The fact is that the political situation facing the system of international criminal justice in the offices of governments is quite different from that in the Statute of the International Criminal Court. This is because powerful governments do not harvest their interpretations from the Statute of the ICC, but rather from the Statute of their own needs. Political officials have different understandings of the notion of criminal responsibility when it comes to their own conduct, and their conclusions are always akin to the former Statute, even if they have killed millions of people.

Their treatment of their own aggressive terrorist conduct is cowardly and they reject the fact that they even committed any international crimes. The assumptions of their private, harsh moral personality, which is essentially equivalent to aggressive barking could greatly impact their theory of justice.[45] The conflicting convictions between their different distinguishing principles and the principles of justice are so deep that the question of self-preservation overrides the rights of victims. In other words, the political powers use the power of victims to defend themselves or protest. Here, with the rights of victims and their powers, we mean the mobilisation of the victims for their specific cause. If the rights of victims are not properly guided by moral judgment and moral truth, harvesting rights will not be possible. Our aim is not to portray passive inaction, but to demonstrate a viable form of rights that are not just visually appealing in different laws.

---

[45] Consult Farhad Malekian, *The Mirage of International Criminal Law, Kant Metaphysics of Mens Rea* (Cambridge Scholars Publishing, 2018).

The most significant aspect of the international criminal justice system is not its provisions, judges, prosecutors, or lawyers, but its purpose of achieving an appropriate implementation of justice against all those accused of committing international crimes. Here, the traditional concept of criminals refers only to individuals. However, that is the very old notion of offenders and other notions have also existed. The intention of justice has always been to call upon the international criminal responsibility of individuals alone, although this has changed throughout history. When significant crimes are committed, the individuals, groups, clans, governments, and states themselves can come under scrutiny. Thus, the notion of international criminal responsibility of states is rather new. The question of state responsibility has consistently been the first question in the case of attribution of punishment and reparation. Those judgements have varied based on the military and political power of our governments.

In short, we must understand the value of our international criminal judgements in the context of the conditions at the relevant time. We have to determine whether states and their governments were and are prepared to deal with the concept of international criminal responsibility of governments and their states. Without any hesitation, international crimes, particularly those of a genocidal character, are committed under the supervision of governments, and these crimes cannot be carried out without the direct and indirect political, military, and economic contributions of the state or government in question. It is on this account that the various discussions finally brought recognition to the theory of international criminal responsibility. For instance, between the World Wars, the Romanian Professor Vespasian Pella challenged the notion of both the international criminal responsibility of individuals and the international criminal responsibility of states.

The theory was primarily discussed by Romanian Professor Pella after the events of the First World War, to little fanfare. The theory re-entered discussions during the procedures of the International Military Tribunal in Nuremberg. However, it was not given any particular legal standing since the powerful or victorious states, which controlled the gavel of the jurisdiction of the Nuremberg Tribunal, were not interested in their governments or states being judged by an international criminal tribunal. Consequently, the notion of international criminal responsibility of states was not developed under the legal proceedings of the Tribunal, and another generation was saddled with tackling the notion of the crimes of states. It must be noted that the Dutch diplomat Pieter Drost discussed the idea in his book *Crimes of States*. His theory concerned the crimes of both individuals and states. Therefore, the concept of international criminal responsibility had still not yet been attributed to the state itself. He was a positivist moralist, critical of the political authorities of the time.

2. Misleading Epistemology of Knowledge

We must accept that there is no objective truth about the value of the system of international criminal justice. This is because the International Criminal Court (ICC) has not yet been successful in proving a single instance of international criminal responsibility on the part of states. All cases brought before the ICC have concerned the notion of international criminal responsibility of individuals and not states. Still, we must remember that all of the cases brought before the jurisdiction of the ICC have dealt with the notion of international criminal responsibility of African leaders or superiors, and therefore, speaking about the international criminal responsibility of the leaders of Western states is just an illusion and itself a violation of the Convention on Terrorism. *This is because Western governments continue to believe that they never violate the system of international criminal justice, and that any statement to the contrary is false. We must remember that we should not wait for an accident in order to arrive at the true face of the illegal morality of the big governments.*[46]

We might describe a theory of international criminal responsibility of individuals, states, or governments using the term 'epistemology', therein implying its particular approach and description of the hidden truth. This means revealing who the real criminals are. We should not approach the reality

[46] Consult also Joseph Raz, Ethics in the Public Domain: Essays in the Morality of Law and Politics (Oxford: Oxford University Press, 1994). Consult also Roland Dworking, *Justice for Hedgehogs* (2011). For a deep analysis of morality consult P. M. S. Hacker and J. Raz, (eds.), *Law, Morality and Society: Essays in Honour of H. L. A. Hart* (1977); Farhad Malekian, *Classical Morality in International Peremptory Criminal Law* (Newcastle: Cambridge Scholars Publishing, 2021); Joseph Raz, *Ethics in the Public Domain: Essays in the Morality of Law and Politics* (Oxford: Oxford University Press, 1994); Joseph Raz, *The Morality of Freedom* (1986); K. Robert Vischer, *Martin Luther King Jr. and the Morality of Legal Practice: Lessons in Love and Justice* (2014); Fuller Lon Luvios, *The Morality of Law* (Virginia: Yale Law University, 2nd, ed., 1969); A. R. C. Duncan, *Practical Reason and Morality* (Nelson, 1957); M. J. Detmold., *The Unity of Law and Morality: A Refutation of Legal Positivism* (Canada: Law Book Co. of Australasia, 1984); Lea Brilmayer, American Hegemony: *Political Morality in a OneSuperpower World* (1994); Adil Ahmad Haque, *Law and Morality at War* (2017); Kenneth Himma and Brian Bix (eds), *Law and Morality* (2005); David Lyons, 'Moral Aspects of Legal Theory' in Kenneth Himma and Brian Bix (eds) *Law and Morality* (2005).

of the criminal conduct carried out by our governments against other nations with pivotal reasons for explanations. *When the victims retaliate, they are called terrorists, and making this designation is the greatest criminal behaviour of the criminal states.* The systems of international criminal justice and international human rights law are actually responsible for touching upon the moral, legal, and criminal truths, which are carried out by our governments in the name of the implementation of humanity. Of course, we may nonetheless reason about the high quality of our governments' moral truth, albeit with full prejudice when the nature of our crimes has already been proven and demonstrated in our criminal conduct and the demolishing of other classical rights of a nation.

Our moral judgements concerning interpretations based on the systems of international criminal justice and human rights law should be based on the basic moral concepts of the unity of humankind and not on the 'nasty diplomacy' of aggressive, brutal, powertionist governments.[47] Normally, what constitutes right and wrong is itself a moral question, and the mass killing of children and individuals cannot be called moral epistemology. This is because the notion of international criminal justice should not be ignored due to the overestimation of our decisions and their correctness when the commission of crimes, e.g., in Gaza and the West Bank, is obvious and can be seen by everyone.

As a result, we must understand the ICC's political position and its strong ties to the provisions dictated by the protectionist governments. Here, with the powertionist governments, we refer to governments or states with control over the provisions of the law and the power of the Court.[48] Thus, the question of what is just or unjust, right or wrong, saintly or wicked, depends on the power and influence of the powertionist governments in the jurisdiction of the Court. These governments decide when a case is opened or not.[49] This simply means that the judges or prosecutors of the ICC should follow the attitudes or emotions of the big powers. Chamber I of the Court issued an arrest warrant for Israeli leaders six months into the conflict and after the murder of over 50,000 Palestinians. The fact is that the Prosecutor and three judges of the Chamber I were and are shaking. Their recommendations for arrest indicated that their government's friends were responsible for the crimes.

---

[47] Farhad Malekian, *Powertionism in International Criminal Justice* (New York: Nova Science Publishers, 2022).

[48] *Id.*

[49] *Id.*

In the end, governments totally ignore the notion of international criminal responsibility of individuals of Israel. In addition, if such a notion arises in practice, the judges and prosecutors of the ICC are threatened with death. This is precisely the current situation of the case regarding the arrest warrant issued against the Israeli authorities by the ICC. The American government has threatened the prosecutor of the ICC and his family with arrest. This situation demonstrates that the victims can only exercise and demand their rights through political associations. This means the distinct capacity of human rights norms. To also be a member of such a political association for the victims means losing the integrity of somebodiness and being placed in the position of nobodiness.[50]

I have already previewed my core statements about the international criminal responsibility of individuals, governments, and their states elsewhere in this book. All my statements indicate that the systems of international criminal justice and international human rights law are the barrels of the big political powers of the world, who use them to sound great, but the reality is that they are orchestrating crimes, terrorist acts, and the destruction of other nations to their benefit. This is also known as morality, equality, and the establishment of peace within the provisions of human rights of criminal governments in Western countries.

3. Barrel of Criminal Epistemological Reasoning

The philosophy of international human rights says that we should never ignore our international criminal responsibilities. In particular, the notion of international criminal responsibility demands that we never forgive our governments for their international crimes. It is our duty to ensure that our actions and votes are objectively true and to hold our own governments

[50] Read Farhad Malekian, *International Criminal Law, the Law of Somebodiness, the Law of Nobodiness* (New York: Nova Science Publishers, 2021); Farhad Malekian, *International Criminal Law: The Legal and Critical Analysis of International Crimes* (2 vols. 1991); See Farhad Malekian, *The Monopolization of International Criminal Law in the United Nations, A Jurisprudential Approach* (Stockholm: Almqvist Wiksell International, 1st ed., 1993, 2nd ed., 1995); Farhad Malekian, *Jurisprudence of International Criminal Justice* (Introduction by Professor Benjamin B. Ferencz, the former Prosecutor of the Nuremberg Tribunal (Cambridge: Cambridge Scholars Publishing, 2014); Farhad Malekian, *Paralysing International Criminal Justice* (New York: Nova Science Publishers, 2021); Farhad Malekian, *Orchestrating Diversity in International Criminal Justice* (New York: Nova Science Publishers, 2021).

accountable for their actions—not to condemn other states. It is also not recommended for a government to kill individuals in other nations, commit expansive and aggressive genocide, or release itself from their international criminal responsibility by referring to the legal statute of self-defence. If acts of genocide and crimes against humanity are categorised under self-defence, then the system of international criminal justice is intentionally obliterated, and the notion of self-defence is employed to justify the massive killing of civilians with the claim that the perpetrators are fighting against terrorist groups.

This theory about the statute of reasoning of self-defence is humiliating to the population of any victim nation and represents a full rejection of the concept of international criminal responsibility of governments with reference to ill-defined concepts of self-defence. This is precisely what happened during the Vietnam War and the Gulf Wars. The instigators killed innocent civilians in the name of defending the political rights of the United States within the sovereign borders of another nation. Similarly, the hundreds of years of occupation of Palestine have led to the loss of so many lives and continue to threaten the very existence of the Palestinian population. *Powerful governments ignore the Palestinians and label acts of self-defence conducted by Palestinians as acts of terror. This means that the acts of state terrorists are viewed as legitimate forms of self-defence. This is how the systems of international criminal justice and international human rights law mislead the population of the international legal community—simply by labelling any acts of resistance against the aggressive Israeli government as acts of terrorism.*[51]

Most of the philosophy of international criminal responsibility and international criminal justice is linked to the question of who-knows-who. However, states should be prosecuted and punished for committing international crimes against the world. For example, the crimes of British Prime Ministers such as Churchill and Blair are beyond any criminal imagination and seriously violated any notion of morality, legality, or the philosophy of the epistemological knowledge of mankind. These criminals succeeded in escaping the notion of international criminal responsibility of their governments and states as well as their individual criminal responsibility. The British and American governments fought for the establishment of the International Military Tribunal in Nuremberg and the punishment of the

[51] https://forward.com/news/615961/theodor-meron-international-criminal-court-amal-clooney-netanyahu-khan/.

German government for its crimes against the Jewish population of Europe.[52] They washed the blood of millions from their own hands, barrelling through international human rights norms.

This is how international criminal justice functions and why the system is hindered when it comes to attributing the concept of international criminal responsibility to revisionist governments today. This is why serious violations of the system of international criminal law and international human rights law continue to this day in full force. Therefore, if we give up the myth of an objective and autonomous moral standard, then we can do whatever we want with our guns, as the aforementioned states did and the protectionist governments continue to do today. The massive genocide that has been committed by the Israeli government and its allies against the Palestinian population over the course of 78 years is a clear example of this. [53] These crimes were carried out in the name of truth, but were actually characterised by a false religious mentality.

One of the most visible forces behind these crimes is the British government, which has provided all kinds of assistance to the Israeli government over the course of several decades. A very clear example of this is the direct contribution of the British military power to Israeli military activities in Gaza and the West Bank at present. The British government is accused of aiding in the extermination of all Palestinians, pushing them out of their sovereign state, and directly contributing to their massacre. Obviously, our politics, more than any other aspect of social tools, help the Israeli government succeed in the extermination of the Palestinian population.

This means that making the lives of British citizens is connected to the blood of other nations, as it has always been. Obviously, the ICC cannot bring

---

[52] Jean Dautricourt, 'The Concept of International Criminal Court Jurisdiction – Definition and Limitations of the Subject', in vol. I, *A Treatise on International Criminal Law* 656 (M. C. Bassiouni & V. P. Nanda, eds, 1975); 'La Création d'une Juridiction Pénale Internationale et la Coopération Internationale en Matière Pénale', 45 *Revue Internationale de Droit Penale* 455 (1974); Louis Kos-Rabcewicz-Zubrowski, 'The Creation of an International Criminal Court', in *International Terrorism and Political Crimes* 519 (M. Cherif Bassiouni, ed, 1975); Ferencz Benjamin, *International Criminal Court* (2 vols. 1980); M. Cherif Bassiouni & Daniel Derby, 'Final Report on the Establishment of an International Criminal Court for the Implementation of the Apartheid Convention and Other Relevant Instruments', 7 *Hofstra Law Review* 525 (1981); Benjamin N. Schiff, *Building the International Criminal Court* (Cambridge; Cambridge University Press, 2008); William A. Schabas, *An Introduction to the International Criminal Court* (Cambridge University Press, 2011).

[53] Moreover, President Lula De Silva of Brazil on the Genocide in Gaza emphasises "this is a war of a well-trained and armed army against women and children." Then as Israeli journalist Gideon Levy asserts "If this isn't genocide in Gaza, then what is it?".

the British government and its leaders under the jurisdiction of the Court in order to prosecute and punish them for their international criminal responsibility as individuals, the government, or the state. While this is a sad truth about justice, the British government and its relevant players, including the British state, remain guilty of serious violations of the system of international criminal justice. The guilt is not limited to their actions in Palestine, but also to crimes committed against other nations of the world, such as Iran, Afghanistan, India, Iraq, Syria, Lebanon, China, and many other nations in Africa.

4. Lacking a Scheme of Subjectivity

The theory of international criminal justice, and particularly the theory of international human rights, which we believe will bring criminals under their jurisdiction, lacks both a scheme of decency and enforceable principles of natural morality.[54] This indicates that the truthfulness of the rights of man and, therefore, judgements are not complete. Alternatively, the system of powertionist governments deliberately presents their conduct and statements as accurate representations of the situation in the occupied lands. The fact is that criminals escape international criminal responsibility by presenting false accusations and attitudes all while intending to obliterate the victims' rights in the occupied lands. Here, the political principles of criminals are drawn from their criminal traditions, so they do not present the true facts, but rather flaunt their authority or hypocrisy as it concerns international criminal justice.

Clear examples of this include the historical records concerning certain Western governments occupying the African continent and initiating the slave trade of Africans. Another example is the criminal conduct of the British government in China, where they got the majority of the population addicted to opium.[55] The British government was certainly involved in the commission

[54] Consult Ruth Gavison, ed., *Issues in Contemporary Legal Philosophy: The Influence of H. L. A. Hart* (1987); Heidi Hurd, 'Challenging Authority,' 100 *Yale Law Journal* 1611 (1991); G. Hughes, 'Validity and the Basic Norm,' 59 *California Law Review* 695 (1971); H. L. A. Hart, Essays in Jurisprudence and Philosophy (1983); Joseph Raz, *The Morality of Freedom* (1986); J. W. Harris, *Legal Philosophies* (2nd edition, 1997); John Austin, *The Province of Jurisprudence Determined and the Uses of the Study of Jurisprudence* (1954); Gerald J. Postema, *Bentham and the Common Law Tradition* (1986); Julie Dickson, *Evaluation and Legal Theory* (2001); H. L. A. Hart, *The Concept of Law* (1961).

[55] The Opium Wars of the mid-19th century represent a significant turning point in the modern history of China. The First Opium War occurred between China and Great Britain from

of international crimes and terrorist conduct against the Chinese population.[56] The British criminal governments organised a similar policy of monopolisation and hypocrisy against the Iranian population as well.[57]

Of course, a number of nations may disagree about which form of terrorism we are referring to, but the real terrorists are the ones directing and ordering the massacre of nations such Palestine. However, the theory of international criminal justice is clearly understood by those who control the occupation. The norms of international human rights law are an integral part of the same political and legal system and should be fully respected by all governments and states. However, the power of ethical judgements and jurisdiction in the United Nations system does not follow the fundamental logic of law and is instead controlled by the authoritarian power of terrorist states. *Eventually, the concept of international criminal responsibility becomes a dream of the victims who are waiting for wars to end.*

All of these interpretations, documentations, and reinterpretations of the vocabulary of the system of international criminal justice indicate that there exists a system of international criminal responsibility that is attributable to the governments such as the British and American criminal governments along with the German, Dutch, French, and Belgian governments, among others, that have carried out the most inhuman criminal conduct and genocide against generations of human beings all over the world.

We must always ask about where these immoral notions of criminality originate and why we condemn the criminal activities of the British and American governments relating to crimes they committed in Africa, China,

---

1839 to 1842. During the Second Opium War, which took place from 1856 to 1860, an exhausted China confronted both Great Britain and France. In both conflicts, China experienced substantial defeats. The conditions imposed upon China following its capitulation were particularly severe: it was obligated to cede the territory of Hong Kong to British governance, open treaty ports for trade with foreign nations, and extend special privileges to foreigners operating within these ports. Additionally, the Chinese government was compelled to accept an increase in opium sales by the British to the Chinese population. The British rationalized these actions under the guise of free trade, while disregarding the adverse impacts on the Chinese government and its population. The Opium Wars in China, https://asiapacificcurriculum.ca/learning-module/opium-wars-china. See also Frank Dikötter, Lars Laamann, Zhou Xun, Narcotic Culture: A History of Drugs in China (2004).

56 *Id.*

57 The Persian population was subjected to one of the most barbaric genocides by the British, much heavier than any other genocides. The British criminal governments deliberately destroyed and concealed almost all documents. Mohammad Gholi Majd, The Great Famine & Genocide in Iran 1917-1919 (2nd edition, University Press of America, 2013); Mohammad Gholi Majd, A Victorian Holocaust: Iran in the Great Famine of 1869–1873 (Hamilton Books, 2017); Mohammad Gholi Majd, Iran Under Allied Occupation In World War II: The Bridge to Victory & A Land of Famine (University Press of America, 2016).

Iraq, Afghanistan, Syria, and Palestine. I am also not here to laud the bloody politics of the Union of Soviet Socialist Republics. All this indicates that we are dealing with immoral criminality or moral criminality of the superpower colonial powers, which have control over the mallet of the barrel. The fact is that we are playing with the provisions of the system of international criminal responsibility like notes that are sung by the voice of the barrel of eels that prove our immoral face and reveal our disrespect of international law in the name of humanity.

This phenomenon has been consistently observed in the realm of foreign political diplomacy conducted by the United States. The objective of this policy has been to persuade other nations that the American government possesses a superior understanding of political matters and legal frameworks compared to other governments and entities. For instance, the belief that the international criminal justice system is unjust, as presented through the prosecutor's actions regarding the arrest of Israeli leaders, has been propagated by President Biden and Secretary of State Antony Blinken. They characterised the decision made by the Prosecutor of the International Criminal Court (ICC) as "outrageous" and "shameful." Israeli officials have accused the ICC of being anti-Semitic, a claim that parallels prior allegations of anti-African bias.

This exemplifies how issues related to international human rights and criminal justice are interpreted when over 60,000 individuals from a particular nation—predominantly women and children—are exterminated as a result of policies enacted by American governments. This illustrates how subjectivity is reinforced by a government that has historically denied any acknowledgment of its international criminal responsibility for its leaders, superiors, and governing bodies. This is the entire philosophy of monopolisation, even when all evidence of the criminality of Israel has been obvious for several decades. A crucial question is: under which circumstances will the system of international criminal justice function concerning international crimes committed at the behest of greedy powertionist governments?[58]

[58] See Farhad Malekian, *The Monopolization of International Criminal Law in the United Nations, A Jurisprudential Approach* (Stockholm: Almqvist Wiksell International, 1st ed., 1993, 2nd ed., 1995).

5. Paradox of Criminal Responsibility

The theory of moral objectivity within the system of international law is responsible for trying to stay on the side of the victims as much as possible and defend the most radical view or its interrelation with the system of international criminal justice in favour of true justice and the victims. We must believe that there are some forms of moral subjectivity that are more plausible than the false statements of the Zionist government.[59] Regardless of whether we trust it or not, moral subjectivity actually connects with the norms of justice and human rights law that are more realistic than those presented to professional criminals.

Although we understand that moral subjectivity is a self-referential or self-ethical theory, it is still objective since the crimes of the Zionist government are so grave and severe that they can be proven within the system of the International Criminal Court, the International Court of Justice, and in the reports of many international organisations and governments. Thus, although moral judgments are based on individual feelings, this is not a question of feelings. Rather, it is a question concerning visible facts that have been proven thousands of times in the pursuit of achieving objective truths.

Accordingly, certain matters are so clear and obvious that they do not need to be considered "right" or "wrong" because of the gravity of the commission of the crimes. This indicates that no universal legal or moral proof is needed when over 20,000 children have been killed. This threshold indicates the undebatable violations of the provisions of the system of international criminal justice. In particular, one should highlight serious violations of the provisions of international law regarding children. It is the spirit of the norms of human rights that calls upon the criminal responsibility of the accused, i.e., Israel and its allies. The system of international criminal responsibility of states prompts us to consider whether the notions of human rights law and the rights of victims are a chimeric dream or actually the truth. This means that we are required by the system of international criminal justice to recognise whether human rights norms have a quasi-moral character and if independent moral claims are actually true.

The paradox of political power philosophy can result in more crime and massacres than anyone could imagine. It indicates that the presence of fashionable bombastic international human rights principles alongside the

[59] Also Farhad Malekian, *Allegations by Political Laundering* (Cambridge Scholars Publishing, 2019).

killings is itself evidence. Moreover, there are certain principles that should be respected and should not be violated during any conflict. This is particularly evident when populations of occupied territories are involved.[60] It is a moral fact that the occupation and killing of the populations of occupied territories are always wrong, and such populations should not be massacred by the authorities of the occupying forces or their allies.[61] However, trouble arrives when the philosophy of international criminal justice, and particularly international human rights law, is interpreted as the elimination of the rights of an occupied country.[62] This causes the debates around the notion of international criminal responsibility of states to be reopened in the corridors of the United Nations and particularly in the building of international criminal courts, which include national, regional, and *ad hoc* courts/tribunals.[63]

All of the above aim to bring innocent victims together and give them the opportunity to submit an initial moral claim based on the metaphysical aspects of moral atoms or elements. Thus, in the end, we may be able to legally force the ICC, to initiate a case concerning the international criminal responsibility of states based on the provisions of the system of international criminal justice. In our case, this includes Israel and all other governments, such as the American and British governments, which have aided, helped, assisted, participated, associated, and offered massive support for the international crimes being committed against the populations of Gaza and the West Bank. These interpretations are not theoretical perspectives on the law, but instead reflect the principles of international criminal law that have been undermined by criminals. All of this also prompts several questions within the system of international criminal justice and threaten to confuse all sides of the question of justice and its legal efficacy.

Realists within the international human rights system must recognise that presenting a positive case is necessary to promote the implementation of its norms. Furthermore, there is no need to reconcile practical and theoretical points of view of the system if the principles of moral arguments regarding the truth are respected. This indicates that the notion of the international criminal responsibility of states can be imposed correctly if the ICC and its prosecutor just dare to address it. Otherwise, saying that those who help the Israeli government commit international crimes against the Palestinian population

---

[60] Consutl Farhad Malekian, 'Judging International Criminal Justice in the Occupied Territories,' 12 *International Criminal Law Review* (2012), pp. 627-869.

[61] *Id.*

[62] *Id.*

[63] *Id.*

are not accountable for their international crimes is equivalent to saying that the system of international human rights law does not exist and is a *fata morgana*. At the present moment, the system has a *fata morgana* character and is just like a barrel that sounds like it is just the presentation of justice, but in reality, it only echoes a symphony of empty words.

The phenomenon is that the theories of moral knowledge, moral truth, and international criminal responsibility have strong connections to the theories of human rights law. These theories are drawn from natural law. Moreover, respecting the morality of the rights of various nations and groups is imperative and should not be taken away by the force of guns under the power of the United Nations Charter in the Security Council.[64] All of this indicates that we are concluding our statements based on legal and moral judgments. This is what the definition of freedom and independence within the moral philosophy of human rights means. The right to one's own country and protection from the violations of the system of international criminal justice are also natural and protected views that have to be respected and supported by their values.

Circular arguments concerning the principle that human beings should not be moved by the force of powertionist governments from one location to another cannot be accepted.[65] In fact, any agreement that includes the elimination of the rights of any population is invalid. Therefore, any distinction between questions of imperative morality and arms by the imperative legislative character of natural law cannot be denied with friendly discussions or by rejecting the requirements of justice for the universal support of the rights of victims.[66] A clear example is the use of aggressive and criminal force, supported by Israeli Zionist criminals and the brutal regime, to increase the number of settler properties in the West Bank with the ultimate goal of annexing the West Bank and seizing full control of it, including even now the whole Golan Heights.[67] Based on its own terroristic interpretations, the Zionist government views all this criminal conduct as being legitimate and proper in

---

[64] Consult also Farhad Malekian, *Imperative Philosophy of International Criminal Justice: Visible Power – Invisible Essence* (New York: Nova Science Publishers, 2022).

[65] Farhad Malekian, *Powertionism in International Criminal Justice* (New York: Nova Science Publishers, 2022).

[66] *Id.*

[67] The buffer zone between Syria and the Golan Heights was invaded by Israel on December 8, 2024. An aerial campaign was conducted to target the military capabilities of the Syrian Army following the downfall of the Assad regime.

their quest to obtain the promised biblical lands. [68] They place their criminal arguments in a larger framework of value for their artificial rights, which contradicts the norms of proper moral or legal justification.[69]

6. Veto Rights Blocking Criminal Responsibility

Within international criminal responsibility and its evaluation, it is necessary to keep the objectivity of the principles of safety in mind, and no interests should be given priority over the rights of the victims. The members of the Security Council, particularly the permanent members, must take their moral and ethical responsibilities seriously—if they have any. This is not a matter of choice, but rather an imperative duty of any member of the United Nations.

---

[68] Anatomy of a Genocide: Report of the Special Rapporteur on the situation of human rights in the Palestinian territories occupied since 1967, p.3, https://www.ohchr.org/sites/default/files/documents/hrbodies/hrcouncil/sessions-regular/session55/advance-versions/a-hrc-55-73-auv.pdf (visited 03/11/2024). Footnotes omitted.

[69] Francesca Albanese underlines that:

"93. The overwhelming nature and scale of the Israeli assault on Gaza and the destructive conditions of life it has inflicted reveal an intent to physically destroy Palestinians as a group. The present report finds that there are reasonable grounds to believe that the threshold indicating the commission of the following acts of genocide against Palestinians in Gaza has been met: killing members of the group; causing serious bodily or mental harm to groups' members; and deliberately inflicting on the group conditions of life calculated to bring about its physical destruction in whole or in part. Genocidal acts were approved and given effect following statements of genocidal intent issued by senior military and government officials.

94. Israel has sought to conceal its eliminationist conduct of hostilities by defending the commission of international crimes as abiding with international humanitarian law. By distorting customary rules of international humanitarian law, including distinction, proportionality and precautions, Israel has de facto treated an entire protected group and its life-sustaining infrastructure as "terrorist" or "terrorist-supporting", thus transforming everything and everyone into either a target or collateral damage, hence killable or destroyable. In this way, no Palestinian in Gaza is safe by definition. This has had devastating, intentional effects, costing the lives of tens of thousands of Palestinians, destroying the fabric of life in Gaza and causing irreparable harm to its entire population. It constitutes a pattern of conduct from which the only reasonable inference to be drawn is that there is a State policy of genocidal violence against the Palestinian people in Gaza.

95. The Israeli genocide against the Palestinians in Gaza is an escalatory stage of a long-standing settler colonial process of erasure. For over seven decades this process has suffocated the Palestinian people as a group – demographically, culturally, economically and politically – seeking to displace it and to expropriate and control its land and resources. The ongoing Nakba must be stopped and remedied once and for all. This is an imperative owed to the victims of this highly preventable tragedy, and to future generations in that land." *Id.*

This means that in taking any decision concerning the criminal conduct of criminal governments and their international criminal responsibility, taking ethical decisions is not only necessary, but also vital for the survival of international criminal jurisdiction.

Each of these principles of international criminal justice needs embellishment or enhancement in the Security Council. This is based on the well-established fact that the Security Council sees itself as the most appropriate organ of the United Nations, and if this is not respected, then the question of justice simply becomes moot. This is actually not a joke, but the reality of how the system of international justice functions in the Office of the Security Council. With this in mind, we are analysing the essence of human values and groups, nations, or individual rights for existence. This indicates that reaching human rights principles is both necessary and a natural obligation.

Our demands and actions should not violate the rights of other nations, and we should not make rights in the system of international criminal justice into private institutions by dismembering the rights of other nations. The entire philosophy of the United Nations Charter, itself a demonstration of the power of multilateralism, aims to protect the rights of all people and nations in addition to preventing the violation of the rights of other nations. However, if the provisions of the Charter of the United Nations are true, then those who seem to be the main players in the establishment of the Charter should respect them. I am speaking here about the members of the Security Council that have nominated themselves to be the permanent members of the United Nations Security Council.

According to the provisions of Chapter VII of the Charter, these states are responsible for promoting justice, peace, security, and humanity. This can easily be read and seen even within other chapters of the Charter. Attempting to wrap around human rights with artificial norms would jeopardize our moral responsibility. In other words, accepting moral integrity and authenticity should be a priority for all governments, particularly those that claim to be guardians of peace and justice. Therefore, a reasonable effort towards achieving peace, justice, and rights must be made within the areas of international criminal responsibility and its evaluation. It is always necessary to keep the objectivity of principles of safety in mind and remember that no interests should be given priority over the rights of the victims.

The members of the Security Council, particularly the permanent members, must take their moral and ethical responsibilities into account. This is not a matter of choice, but rather an imperative duty of any member of the

United Nations.[70] This means that taking any decision concerning the criminal conduct of criminal governments and their international criminal responsibility, as well as taking ethical decisions is not only necessary, but also vital for the survival of international criminal jurisdiction. Each of these principles of international criminal justice or morality needs embellishment or enhancement in the Security Council.[71] This is based on the well-established fact that the Council recognises itself as the most appropriate organ of the United Nations, and if this is not respected, then the question of justice just becomes one of Volodymyr Zelensky's jokes (thereby indicating the absurdity of a significant and fundamental problem). This is actually not a joke, but rather the reality of how the system of international justice in the Office of the Security Council functions.

All of this means that we are analysing the essence of human values and groups, nations, or individual rights for existence. This indicates that reaching human rights principles is necessary and a natural obligation. It means our demands and actions should not violate the rights of other nations, and we should not occupy rights of others by claiming a right to dismember the rights of other nations. The entire philosophy of the United Nations Charter, a demonstration of the power of multilateralism, supposedly aims to protect the rights of all people and all nations and to prevent violations of the rights of other nations. However, if the provisions of the Charter of the United Nations are true, then the main actors in the establishment of the Charter should respect them.

---

[70] Examine *also* Farhad Malekian, *Imperative Philosophy of International Criminal Justice: Visible Power – Invisible Essence* (New York: Nova Science Publishers, 2022).

[71] Michael J. Perry, A Global Political Morality: Human Rights, Democracy, and Constitutionalism (Cambridge University Press, 2017); Farhad Malekian, *Tour de force of Moral Virtue in International Criminal Justice* (New York: Nova Science Publishers, 2022), p. 103. Consult also Farhad Malekian, *The Mirage of International Criminal Law, Kant Metaphysics of Mens Rea* (Cambridge Scholars Publishing, 2018).

Chapter 3

Confusing Barrels of Legal and Moral Judgements

1. Political Judgements Vacating Moral Truth

The preceding section in the previous chapter highlights the members of the Security Council who nominated themselves to be permanent members of the United Nations. In accordance with the provisions outlined in Chapter VII of the Charter, these members bear the responsibility for fostering justice, peace, security, and humanity. This responsibility is reinforced throughout various chapters of the UN framework. It is unrealistic to expect a cohesive approach to human rights while simultaneously establishing artificial norms that undermine our moral obligations within the international legal community. Thus, adherence to moral integrity and authenticity ought to be a guiding principle for all governments, especially those that claim to be custodians of peace and justice. Consequently, any substantial endeavour aimed at achieving peace, justice, and rights must be evaluated based on the moral accountability of every permanent member. Upholding moral and legal standards in relation to the principles enshrined in the United Nations Charter is indeed an essential requirement mandated by the Charter's provisions.

These provisions stipulate that any issues pertaining to violations of the international legal system must align with the political and legal arguments put forth in the Charter. This implies that the formulation and presentation of these provisions are subject not only to moral and legal scrutiny, but also to political assessments. It is the nature of these political considerations that determines whether the United Nations adequately serves its member states or not. Consequently, in all reasonable scenarios, the final decisions reached by the United Nations are often influenced by the political power dynamics among its permanent members. If these dynamics falter, decisions ultimately hinge on the veto right being exercised. This right has frequently been invoked in relation to particularly sensitive matters concerning human rights and international criminal justice. With the veto, legality and morality become irrelevant, and are instead dictated by the preferences of dominant political powers and therefore no longer grounded in genuine moral judgment.

I raise these specific issues with the aim of addressing the misleading statements made by the representatives of the permanent members of the Security Council and their disregard for any notion of international criminal accountability for the actions of the Zionist government over the course of several decades. In the theoretical framework of justice, it is imperative to trace arguments back to their origins, which reveal either the underlying causes or fundamental reasons behind the distortion or outright rejection of international criminal responsibility under coercive power.[72] The fundamental philosophy of justice raises several questions regarding the actions of states and governments, as well as their connection to moral and legal accountability. How can one fully accept the theories of amoral governance while believing that such theories should be upheld, thereby disregarding the principle of international criminal responsibility for states and governments? I direct my attention towards the Israeli government, which continues to evade international criminal accountability for the acts of genocide they have committed under the protective umbrella of the American government.

How is it that this permanent member of the Security Council, endowed with nuclear capabilities, poses a threat to global moral and legal standards? Through intentional acts of criminality, the United States sustains its alliances with various governments. This conduct is neither legally nor morally justifiable. Nevertheless, the influence wielded by military powers significantly dictates legal frameworks and their motivations. Consequently, we turn our focus to international human rights law. We must deliberate about how best to safeguard the rights of all individuals in our policy decisions, while also inadvertently providing support to criminal regimes. It is evident that despite the lack of enforceability inherent in legal provisions, the concept of international criminal responsibility for governments should not ignore deceptive practices within the Council. These deceptive behaviours, decisions, and actions have resulted in a significant loss of life and have led to some of history's most severe genocides facilitated under the authority of the Security Council.[73]

---

[72] See Farhad Malekian, *Imperative Philosophy of International Criminal Justice: Visible Power – Invisible Essence* (New York: Nova Science Publishers, 2022).

[73] In one of its earlier resolutions, the General Assembly of the United Nations properly condemned Israel, the United States, or the permanent member of the Security Council. "1. Condemns Israel's continued occupation of the Palestinian and other Arab territories, including Jerusalem, in violation of the Charter of the United Nations, the principles of international law and the relevant resolutions of the United Nations, and demands the immediate, unconditional and total withdrawal of Israel from all these occupied territories; 2. Reaffirms its conviction that the question of Palestine is the core of the conflict in the

---

Middle East and that no comprehensive, just and lasting peace in the region will be achieved without the full exercise by the Palestinian people of its inalienable national rights and the immediate, unconditional and total withdrawal of Israel from all the Palestinian and other occupied Arab territories; 3. Reaffirms further that a just and comprehensive settlement of the situation in the Middle East cannot be achieved without the participation on an equal footing of all the parties to the conflict, including the Palestine Liberation Organization, the representative of the Palestinian people; 4. Declares once more that peace in the Middle East is indivisible and must be based on a comprehensive, just and lasting solution of the Middle East problem, under the auspices of the United Nations, which ensures the complete and unconditional withdrawal of Israel from the Palestinian and other Arab territories occupied since 1967, including Jerusalem, and which enables the Palestinian people, under the leadership of the Palestine Liberation Organization, to exercise its inalienable rights, including the right to return and the right to self-determination, national independence and the establishment of its independent sovereign State in Palestine, in accordance with the resolutions of the United Nations relevant to the question of Palestine, in particular General Assembly resolutions ES-7/2 of 29 July 1980, 36/120 A to F of 10 December 1981, 37/86 A to D of 10 December 1982 and 37/86 E of 20 December 1982; 5. Rejects all agreements and arrangements in so far as they violate the recognized rights of the Palestinian people and contradict the principles of just and comprehensive solutions to the Middle East problem to ensure the establishment of a just peace in the area; 6. Deplores Israel's failure to comply with Security Council resolutions 476 (1980) of 30 June 1980 and 478 (1980) of 20 August 1980 and General Assembly resolutions 35/207 of 16 December 1980 and 36/226 A and B of 17 December 1981, determines that Israel's decision to annex Jerusalem and to declare it as its "capital," as well as the measures to alter its physical character, demographic composition, institutional structure and status, are null and void and demands that they be rescinded immediately, and calls upon all Member States, the specialized agencies and all other international organizations to abide by the present resolution and all other relevant resolutions, including Assembly resolutions 37/86 A to E; 7. Condemns Israel's aggression and practices against the Palestinian people in the occupied Palestinian territories and outside these territories, particularly Palestinians in Lebanon, including the expropriation and annexation of territory, the establishment of settlements, assassination attempts and other terrorist, aggressive and repressive measures, which are in violation of the Charter and the principles of international law and the relevant international conventions; 8. Strongly condemns the imposition by Israel of its laws, jurisdiction and administration on the occupied Syrian Golan Heights, its annexationist policies and practices, the establishment of settlements, the confiscation of lands, the diversion of water resources and the imposition of Israeli citizenship on Syrian nationals, and declares that all these measures are null and void and constitute a violation of the rules and principles of international law relevant to belligerent occupation, in particular the Geneva Convention relative to the Protection of Civilian Persons in Time of War, of 12 August 1949; 9. Considers that the agreements on strategic co-operation between the United States of America and Israel signed on 30 November 1981 would encourage Israel to pursue its aggressive and expansionist policies and practices in the Palestinian and other Arab territories occupied since 1967, including Jerusalem, would have adverse effects on efforts for the establishment of a comprehensive, just and lasting peace in the Middle East and would threaten the security of the region; 10. Calls upon all States to put an end to the flow to Israel of any military, economic and financial aid, as well as of human resources, aimed at encouraging it to pursue its aggressive policies against the Arab countries and the Palestinian people; 11. Requests the Secretary-General to report to the Security Council periodically on the development of the situation and to submit to the General Assembly at its thirty-eighth session." https://www.un.org/unispal/document/auto-insert-186308/.

When the veto power obstructs the rights of genocide victims, it undermines trust in the mechanisms of international criminal law. These actions indicate that a state is committing genocide while disregarding the principles of international criminal responsibility concerning the rights of victims. Furthermore, permanent members of the Security Council are not permitted to inflict genocide on the Palestinian population in the pursuit of expanding the territory of the Zionist government.[74] This raises a critical question: do we truly have no obligations arising from our permanent membership in the United Nations or the Security Council? Whenever the United States blocks the rights of victims within the Council it is a serious violation of international humanitarian law and addressing this issue not only fails to enhance the image of authoritarian powers, but it also undermines the very foundation of morality as a whole.

2. Political Rhetoric versus Responsibility

Moral philosophy is not covered by Chapter VII of the United Nations Charter. This Chapter has one specific objective, and that is to be fulfilled under the auspices of the powertionist governments. However, there are some special provisions in Chapter VII that give the impression that the Charter intends to protect the entire world.[75] The intentions in this chapter seem to

---

[74] Bertrand Russell points out the criminality of the British government by asserting that *"The tragedy of the people of Palestine is that their country was "given" by a foreign power to another people for the creation of a new state. The result was that many hundreds of thousands of innocent people were made permanently homeless. With every new conflict their numbers increased. How much longer is the world willing to endure this spectacle of wanton cruelty?"*

[75] Consult Articles 39 to 51of Chapter VII of the United Nations Charter. Article 47 reads that "1. There shall be established a Military Staff Committee to advise and assist the Security Council on all questions relating to the Security Council's military requirements for the maintenance of international peace and security, the employment and command of forces placed at its disposal, the regulation of armaments, and possible disarmament. 2. The Military Staff Committee shall consist of the Chiefs of Staff of the permanent members of the Security Council or their representatives. Any Member of the United Nations not permanently represented on the Committee shall be invited by the Committee to be associated with it when the efficient discharge of the Committee's responsibilities requires the participation of that Member in its work. 3. The Military Staff Committee shall be responsible under the Security Council for the strategic direction of any armed forces placed at the disposal of the Security Council. Questions relating to the command of such forces shall be worked out subsequently. 4. The Military Staff Committee, with the authorization of the Security Council and after consultation with appropriate regional agencies, may establish regional sub-committees."

intend to mislead and hide the facts and truth. We obviously point to the fact that no questions of the international criminal responsibility of governments and states are under the control of the Chapter—except for the interests of certain permanent members.

Even when the question of responsibility arises, there is no requirement for impartiality within the provisions, and speaking about impartiality in the Charter is nonsensical with reference to the important resolutions of the Security Council concerning human rights and the use of the veto right by the United States against the rights of the international community.[76] In particular, if any state tries to cherish its own dignity or that of others, the political position of the state comes under serious question and may be challenged by various political means. As I have emphasised in my earlier book on *Powertionism in International Criminal Justice*, Chapter VII presents and demonstrates a full exploration of the rights of others through the collective force of NATO. Thus, being released from the power of authoritarian governments is essentially an inevitable and indispensable necessity for the application of the system of international criminal responsibility. In other words, the moral and legal responsibility of governments cannot be accomplished as long as the theory of international criminal justice remains under the control of certain permanent members. We must try to create connections and winnow out contradictions in the provisions of Chapter VII.

Thus, the political rhetoric of the powertionist governments is used to control any questions relating to the norms of the barrel of international criminal responsibility that concern their own interests.[77] This means that every political party pays lip service to the idea of preventing other governments from acting against their interests. They make a lot of sense of their situation and have significant influence on the Charter, particularly in the Security Council. Consequently, upholding the dignity and full respect of the powertionist governments becomes the duty of all states of the United Nations if their governments want to survive.[78] Otherwise, the powertionist governments veto resolutions concerning international criminal responsibility.[79] The United States usually makes such an approach seem

---

[76] James E. Hickey, *Challenges to Security Council Monopoly Power over the Use of Force in Enforcement Actions: The Case of Regional Organisations, Ius Gentium* (2004), pp. 75.129.

[77] Farhad Malekian, *Powertionism in International Criminal Justice* (New York: Nova Science Publishers, 2022).

[78] *Id.*

[79] *Id.*

necessary for its moral and political ideas, which in turn prompts other permanent members veto the resolutions suggested by the delegation of the United States. The notion of morality, which is the most prominent source of value in the system of international criminal justice, has become a game concerning the notion of international criminal responsibility of governments.

As a result, the concept of morality as a whole is ignored, and only hidden political morality is entertained in all discussions and negotiations.[80] Consequently, the notion of responsibility is compatible with any assumption that the big and criminal political power considers appropriate. A clear example of this is how the world has been misled concerning the crimes of the Zionist government and the government's failure to be brought before any international criminal court for the commission of serious international crimes. This is why I have stated repeatedly that the whole theory of Chapter VII of human rights instruments and the notion of responsibility is the presentation of empty collective norms in the barrel.

I also argue that the character and extent of our duties concerning the prosecution and punishment of Zionist criminals is also a question of ethical norms and not just a silent concept of morality. Certain matters in the system of international criminal justice are not only judged by private motivations, but also by the very assumption of the united responsibility of nations to save populations from the unjustified and unlawful criminal conduct of their governments. This is the presentation of a huge barrel that can only be recognised with noise, words, and politics rather than rights and integrity. If someone were to ask me what the character of rights and integrity is, I may respond that our duty is to tell the truth and not present lies as the truth. This helps us to more clearly see what the duties of our entities, governments, or states are.

If we really wish to be moral and on the side of the truth and victims of abolished rights, then we should connect the notions of moral legality and legal morality to the principles of dignity and therefore abstain from harming the rights of victims in any way. We can then believe that we have done our best to help the victims achieve and approach their rights. Thus, we have to follow the order of legality and follow it with the notion of morality while respecting the proportions of wisdom of law and international criminal justice.[81] The victims of aggressive international crimes are not adequately

[80] Examine T. Gebrehana, *Duty to negotiate: An Element of International law* (1978).

[81] Examine Farhad Malekian, *Gravity of Wisdom in International Criminal Law* (New York: Nova Science Publishers, 2021).

treated by the legal jurisdiction and political philosophy behind the system of international criminal justice. Because of this, they are affected by this shortcoming. If the system of international criminal justice wishes to obey the commands of international criminal law and international human rights law with full respect for moral principles, it must then fully value their commands when violations are being committed. This is what the virtues of truth, justice, and true humanity really demand.[82] In other words, we need to promote respect for the law through the logic of the law, and not through the logic of guns.

3. Immorally Violating the Principle of Self-Abnegation

The system of international criminal responsibility is a system in which norms require reparation through the attribution of the notion of criminality to the relevant criminals. This is actually a formula that has deep roots and consequences for fusing two theoretically distinct issues—equality and respect. This means that if the notion of international criminal responsibility is mistreated, this indicates that the notion of equality has lost its value both under the system of international criminal justice and within the provisions of international human rights law.

This formula is not entirely meant to satisfy the victims, but rather to provide a clear illustration of the intentions of civil and criminal justice that have to be fulfilled and cannot be ignored. The modern philosophy of international criminal justice has tended to follow the moral philosophy of rights, and it seems to have abandoned the ideal of authoritarian power with reference to many human rights conventions.[83] In other words, the ethical and moral integrity of the rights of individuals has been given full respect. However, the actual practice and real tendency of the powertionist governments have been relatively different from the existing provisions of the system of international human rights law.[84]

The moral philosophy of the system of international criminal justice and the acceptance and attribution of international criminal responsibility to superiors, governments, and their states need the paradigm of self-abnegation in the system of justice. We thus must give more space and rights to the notion

---

[82] Farhad Malekian, *Tour de force of Moral Virtue in International Criminal Justice* (New York: Nova Science Publishers, 2022),

[83] Consult Farhad Malekian, *Documents on the Principles of International Human Rights* (Stockholm: Norstedts Juridik AB, 2007).

[84] *Id.*

of moral law. This is a philosophy that delivers judgment based on the wisdom of knowledge.[85] Therefore, with this basic philosophy, we respect the concept of maxims, principles, and rules that are applicable to every action carried out by all states and their governments equally. This indicates that the criminal actions of the Zionist government are ignored in the Security Council, and the Council, or the relevant members who support the criminal conduct, promote dishonesty.

A permanent member of the Security Council or a government can only support the moral good if they are motivated in accordance with their interests. Acts of predisposition do not show any particular sympathy for the established rights of victims. For example, in the Palestinian case, there is no space given to the idea of protecting the rights of victims and condemning the Israeli government. The United States government's immoral impulses can be seen with its use of its veto rights and its false statements regarding protecting and supporting the rights of victims. Here, I am not just speaking about Palestinian rights, but also about the rights of other nations that have habitually been targeted up by the attitudes of the government of the United States.

This indicates that the rejection of the idea of international criminal responsibility of the system of international criminal justice, which is strongly connected to the American government, by any subject is the foundation of the entire moral theory of the relevant government. According to the theory of the United Nations Security Council and its original members, there is no room for the idea of a morality of self-abnegation, only for a morality of self-love, self-confirmation, self-preservation, and self-selection among close allies, such as the Israeli government. The American and Israeli governments' ethics and morality are foreign to the theory of international criminal justice, violate the intentions of human rights provisions, and present them in a barrel of ambiguous, orchestrated sounds of inhumanity.

For this reason, all legal and philosophical arguments fail to offer a true view of the situation, even if principles of morality show that moral judgments can indeed be objectively true. This indicates that by resorting to veto rights, we take complete control of other immoral decisions regarding the existence of factual judgements that concern and describe the reality of the truth. The result is that when the decision on rights comes under the control of dirty political powertionist governments, the rights of victims lose their value and are lost to the aggressive criminal states and, in our case, to the Zionist Israeli

[85] Farhad Malekian, *Gravity of Wisdom in International Criminal Law* (New York: Nova Science Publishers, 2021).

government. This means that there is no way to rescue the principles of justice and the concept of international criminal responsibility of the Zionist Israeli government when the metaphysics of morality and justice have been destroyed by millions of soldiers. We can achieve the dignity and self-respect for the rights of all victims and the implementation of the notion of international criminal responsibility for the brutal actions of the Israeli government if we show our respect for humanity itself in all its forms, as modelled in the texts of different agreements. Despite this, the relevant governments, specifically the Israeli and American governments, fail to follow through on this.

4. Paralysing Ethical Reasons

The immoral decisions of certain governments both within and outside of the United Nations indicate that we implicitly or explicitly abolish the notion of international criminal responsibility of states, and as a result, the questions of international prosecution and the punishment of individuals, groups, organisations, governments, and states collapse. In reality, these amoral characters assert that the power of the system of guns lacks the essence of moral values. In the end, all concepts of value are interconnected and collectively supported by those following in the footsteps of the big powertionist governments. The Security Council of the United Nations eventually dismissed the theories of international criminal responsibility of states.

The question then is, where do the values of the system of international human rights law and international criminal justice go? Again, why are they powerless or paralysed when they should have enough power to establish the rights of the victims? These two questions reveal that our intentions concerning the creation of international criminal justice and international human rights are empty promises, and no one has the legal or moral force follow through on them. That is why we have created the veto right in the Security Council with the full intention of paralysing the system of international criminal justice whenever we deem it to be fit and reasonable. This indicates that the barrels of morality and legality are the dancing tools of hypocrisy in international criminal justice.[86]

[86] "Thus, the Palestinians have been designated as terrorists, despite the fact that Palestinians and Palestine have been the targets of brutal terrorist attacks carried out by the British, American, and Israeli governments for hundreds of years. These countries have waged wars against Palestinian independence and called it self-defence. This is how the system of

If we understand these forms of monopolisation of the system of justice—even just veto rights—then we can recognise how the metaphysical questions about the fundamental character in judgements of international human rights law are working for the implementation of the legal and moral values of the International Criminal Court.[87] This means that the General Assembly of the United Nations is only one of the players in the game of veto rights. It also means that the powertionist governments have full authority over the systems of international criminal justice and the International Criminal Court in The Hague.

If the system of international human rights were truly about human rights, as initially suggested by the United States government, it would first abolish the power of the Security Council and begin to value human beings in accordance with their natural rights. However, the primary example cited in this book, e.g., the situation in Gaza and the aggressive criminal activities of powertionist governments, demonstrates that the brutal values that are stated in the conventions and declarations of human rights are always nicely knit together but unfortunately have no power to establish the rights of the victims and prompt the prosecution and punishment of international criminals.

This concerns an act of kindness by human rights organisations that, in reality, are largely controlled and empowered by the powertionist governments of the United States, Israel, and the United Kingdom, which are the three countries mainly responsible for the suffering of mothers and children in Palestine. *All these decorative rights represent lies and natural morality can only save the world if gunpowder is transformed into love powder.*[88] *The fact is that the metaphysical opinion of the system of*

---

physical justice functions and how we modify the system of human rights to serve the interests of Western countries. In fact, the British criminal government created Israel in order to have control over their politics and lies. The Western world has been silent about the deaths of thousands of Palestinians, and when the Palestinians fight back in self-defence, they are condemned by the West. This is the real international Western physical justice and its hypocrisy against the victims." Farhad Malekian, Hypocrisy in International Criminal Justice (New York: Nova Science Publishers, 2025); Farhad Malekian, International Crime of Blackboard-Barbarism ((New York: Nova Science Publishers, 2025), pp. 120-121.

[87] See Farhad Malekian, *The Monopolization of International Criminal Law in the United Nations, A Jurisprudential Approach* (Stockholm: Almqvist Wiksell International, 1st ed., 1993, 2nd ed., 1995).

[88] Farhad Malekian, *Judgments of Love in Criminal Justice* (Switzerland: Springer: 2017, 2018); Farhad Malekian, 'The Heaven of Justice with Love,' *The Journal of the Henry Martyn Institute* (2017), pp. 5-29. Farhad Malekian, 'The Canon of Love against the Use of Force in Islamic and Public International Law: Part II: The Anatomy of Love Against Violations,' 15 *International Criminal Law Review*, 2015), pp. 861-895; Farhad Malekian, 'The Canon

international criminal justice yields essentially the same result as international human rights law, if the latter is given priority over the former. Doing this would help lead to the application of international criminal responsibility to states at the international level.

For some writers, lawyers, judges, and politicians, it may seem crazy and unjust to think that the values of the system of international human rights, in particular the international humanitarian law of armed conflicts, are just decorative and not enforceable.[89] In fact, there is nothing aside from the moral truth that can make a moral judgment true. This means that we cannot find value in the brutal acts of the Zionist government when the brutal provisions of the Security Council permit their enforcement. In other words, the barbaric crimes being committed against the population of Palestine are essentially empowered by the power of the Security Council, or Chapter VII of the United Nations Charter. Eventually, we lose the real values of human rights law and justice. We can no longer reach them, and we cannot invent them either.

5. Contingent Desires to Veto Judgements

It may seem meaningless to insist on the existence of principles based on the very high unity of our international human rights norms and their value for the international legal and political community as a whole. This is regardless of the fact that we have almost successfully disciplined the values of international human rights law. Moreover, we cannot believe that the values of the positive system of international criminal justice and the ICC's judgments should rest on the values of the veto right. We thus create darkness around our own fundamental moral and legal standards and customary disciplines. We may

---

of Love against the Use of Force in Islamic and Public International Law: Part I: The Chamber of Love within Legal Discipline,' 15 *International Criminal Law Review*, 2015), pp. 591-628; Mendus Susan, 'The Importance of Love in Rawls's Theory of Justice' 29 (1) *British Journal of Political Science* (1999), pp. 57-75; Muchnik Pablo, *Kant's Theory of Evil: An Essay on the Dangers of Self-love and the Aperiodicity of History* (Lexington Books, 2010).

[89] Examine Antonio Cassese, (ed.), *The New Humanitarian Law of Armed Conflict* (Naples: Editoriale Scientifica, 1979); Karima Bennoune, 'As-Salamu 'Alykum? Humanitarian Law in Islamic Jurisprudence,' 15 *Michigan Journal of International Law*, (1994), pp. 605-643; Kesolofetse Lefenya, 'Use of Explosive Weapons in Densely Populated Areas: Implications for International Humanitarian Law,' *African Yearbook on International Humanitarian Law* (2014), pp. 68–86; Thomas G. Weiss, *Military-Civilian Interactions: Humanitarian Crises and the Responsibility to Protect* (2nd ed., Rowman & Littlefield Publishers Inc, Lanham (MD), 2005).

therefore find more evidence in the otherwise mysterious extinguishing of the rights of nations such as Palestine.

The fact is that the veto right extinguishes the notion of international criminal responsibility of states and governments, as seen with the criminality of Israel. The veto right could also potentially destroy the dignity and dimensions of traditional nations. We must not forget the two fundamental principles of the system of international law, international jurisdiction, and national legislation—equality and responsibility. As we have seen, both of these principles can easily be abolished and replaced with the aggressive principles of paternalism and their authority over all principles of morality.[90]

Consequently, according to the norms of morality, we are required to take the principal ideas of international criminal justice seriously as along with its intentions concerning the notion of international criminal responsibility in all forms, including governments and their states. This is the only way to strengthen the rights of victims and prevent professional criminals from committing further crimes. Of course, its feasibility depends again on the decision of the criminally powertionist government of America. Any further condition that is suggested ought to still be treated under the codex of the provisions of Chapter VII and the veto right of the permanent members.

The reality is that any natural or legal disposition of the concept of international criminal responsibility is linked to the veto right, and, as a result, there is no sympathy for the aggressive and criminal rights of the victims. On the contrary, there exists a large and profound disconnect between the cause of our ethical morality and the lies presented during negotiations in the Security Council. Representatives of the United States, Israel, and the United Kingdom speak without honesty, and their arguments serve to defend the criminal conduct of the apartheid and Nazi regime that is the Israeli government. The same is true of the views of the German and Swedish governments. Consequently, any moral beliefs about criminal conduct carried out in Gaza and the West Bank and any defence of those beliefs are grounds alone for suspicion that these beliefs are not essentially true and even humiliate the rights of human civilisation as a whole.

Therefore, the notion of the international criminal responsibility of governments and their states faces the difficult task of confronting imperialist powers and authorities to write the law and control it. Nevertheless, one must admit that in the course of dissecting the ideas of jurisdiction and the notion

---

[90] Farhad Malekian, *Conundrums of Paternalism in International Criminal Justice* (New York: Nova Science Publishers, 2024).

of international criminal responsibility, the ultimate nature of criminal conduct, and the widespread commission of genocide with full intent, the truth about all criminal activities cannot be wiped out through the use of veto rights under any circumstances. The use of veto rights to block the rights of a nation therefore supports the criminals and does nothing to prevent further heinous crimes by various governments including those of Israel, the UK, the United States, Germany, Canada, Australia, the Netherlands, Sweden, Denmark, Finland, and a number of other Western countries.

Criminal defiance can always demonstrate that it is strong, but at the end of the day, it reveals its malicious nature and moral character. This has been seen during the Vietnam War, the Gulf War, Libyan War, the Syrian War, and the Afghan War, to name but a few examples.[91] Consequently, we do not need to present any conclusions concerning the nature of crimes carried out as a result of lies that were revealed at a later point. Any other statements about the nature of crimes being committed and hidden behind the term 'veto' are often taken to have a blatant and unembellished sceptical consequence for the rights of victims. Thus, as Mao Zedong stated, political power "grows out of the barrel of a gun."[92]

The reason for this is that political powers create their own truths. As was the case with the attacks of September 11th the majority of people believed the big lies and accepted them as the truth.[93] Revealing the truth in such circumstances can lead to undesired consequences. The satisfaction of the

---

[91] See the earlier statement of Professor Jeffrey Sachs to President Trump: Please Get U.S. out of Syria, "We've Done Enough Damage" (13th April, 2018); Available online at https://www.realclearpolitics.com/video/2018/04/13/jeffrey_sachs_to_president_trump_please_get_us_out_of_syria_weve_done_enough_damage.html. The current collaboration between the pro-Israeli and pro-Turkish governments of the United States serves as another example of their involvement in the region. In reality, these oppressive regimes have nearly devastated Syria. They assert that they are combating the former dictator of Syria and while simultaneously seeking to expand own territories. Israel's focus primary interests lie in securing oil resources expanding furthering territories.

[92] Quoted in Benjamin Ginsberg, *The Dark Side of Politics: Essays on the Unpleasant Realities of Political Life* (2023), p. 2.

[93] Thierry Meyssan, 11 September 2001: L'effroyable imposture (2002); Chossudovsky M., *War and Globalisation: The Truth Behind September 11* (Global Outlook, 2002) ; David MacGregor, 'September 11 as 'Machiavellian State Terrorism,' in Paul Zarembka, *The Hidden History of 9-11-2001* (New York: Seven Stories Press, 2008); Zarembka Paul, *The Hidden History of 9-11-2001* (New York: Seven Stories Press, 2008); Arthur Naiman, *9/11: The Simple Facts - Why the Official Story can't Possibly be True* (US: Soft Skull Press, 2011); John Farmer, *The Ground Truth: The Story Behind America's Defence on 9/11* (New York: Riverhead Books, 2009); Don Paul and Jim Hoffman, *Waking Up from Our Nightmare, the 9/11/01 Crimes in New York City* (New York: I/R Press, 2004); Paul Zarembka, *The Hidden History of 9-11-2001* (New York: Seven Stories Press, 2008).

system of international criminal justice may never be achieved for the victims, but certainly the situation demonstrates the significant desire concerning the supposedly more realistic nature of the crimes produced and presented by the political and philosophical traditions of Western governments.[94]

6. Correct or Erroneous Interpretations

Obviously, we may reasonably answer all the arguments made concerning the rejection of the concept of international criminal responsibility of states and their governments and believe that our answers are not only logical, but also moral. This is how the criminal regime of the Israeli government responds to accusations concerning its international criminal activities in the United Nations General Assembly and the Security Council. The Israeli government views their criminal activities as moral and frames their victims as the perpetrators of international crimes that thus possess international criminal responsibility. This is because they have the full protection of the criminal government of the United States and its representatives, which in turn is dependent economic and political power of Zionist groups.

It is not without reason that the international criminal justice system witnesses the commission of international crimes by the Israeli government against the population of occupied lands in the name of eradicating resistance groups from their own territory. The ongoing expansion of this long chain of criminal activities has therefore paralysed the future development of the rights of the victims, and as a result, the best explanation of why the system of international criminal justice does not function is the strong sound of the barrel of inhumanity, which provides a sufficient justification for the opinions supporting the criminal regimes of criminal governments.

Consequently, we are confronted with lies and misinterpretations being presented as the truth and used to justify the suffering of the victims. Whatever answer we provide about all these misinterpretations and whatever idea of moral forces with causal powers we present time and again, the facts do not

---

[94] Robert F. Kennedy, Why the Arabs don't want us in Syria: They don't hate 'our freedoms.' They hate that we've betrayed our ideals in their own countries — for oil in http://www.politico.eu/book/why-the-arabs-dont-want-us-in-syria-mideast-conflict-oil-intervention/; Washington's Secret Agendas – Truth is being Disguised to Suit, available online at http://www.oneworldofnations.com/2014/09/washingtons-secret-agendas-truth-is.html; 'Former Liberian dictator Charles Taylor had US spy agency ties' available online at http://www.bostonglobe.com/metro/2012/01/17/mass-escapee-turned-liberian-dictator-had-spy-agency-ties/DGBhSfjxPVrtoo4WT95bBI/story.html.

change, and the truth of the immoral criminal activities does not project the sound of the barrel, which is controlled by the political criminal regimes of the British, American, and other governments of the world against innocent children. If we are incorrect, then the entire theory of international criminal responsibility is a delusion—which it is in reality. But perhaps I am wrong and am making erroneous interpretations and poor deductions, or do you think that moral facts can cause governments and their representatives to form true moral opinions?

When we carefully examine the views of governments and thoroughly investigate their criminal conduct, we may conclude that there is no correlation between what I have proposed and the nature of the moral opinion of governments.[95] *I have just disproven two assumptions that may be wrong in the opinions of the readers, but that does not really matter. The assumptions are that the governments in the Security Council are not only following the legal assertions of the law, but also moral ones. Additionally, it has been repeatedly proven that these governments are violating the legal and moral presumptions of the law. As a result, the impact of political hypotheses is so great and influential that the real face of the truth hides itself and lies grow. This means that we already reject any theory of international criminal responsibility of governments and their states.*

7. The Moral Truth that Agitate Criminals

It is possible that my views lack sound reasoning, given that the legal and political reasoning of powertionist governments seem to be accurate, legal, and moral judgments. This implies that power politics draw the line between the correct and incorrect reports of the legal and moral truth. Most governments follow the lines of thought presented by the big political parties, and although they are aware of the footsteps of criminals—they pretend to not

[95] Consult Farhad Malekian, *Powertionism in International Criminal Justice* (New York: Nova Science Publishers, 2022), pp. 92-93; Farhad Malekian, *Classical Morality in International Peremptory Criminal Law* (Newcastle upon Tyne: Cambridge Scholars Publishing, 2018, republished 2021); Martti Koskenniem, *The Politics of International Law* (Hart, 2011); Martti Koskenniemi, *The Gentle Civilizer of Nations: the Rise and Fall of International Law*, 1870-1960 (Cambridge University Press 2002); Martti Koskenniemi, Mónica García-Salmones Rovira, and Paolo Amorosa, International Law and Religion: Historical and Contemporary Perspectives (2017); Read also views of Friedrich Nietzsche, *Beyond Good and Evil* (2014); Friedrich Nietzsche, *On the Genealogy of Morality: A Polemic* (19998); Clark, *Maudemarie Nietzsche on Truth and Philosophy* (1991).

be aware of the criminal policies of those governments in order to protect their own interests. Otherwise, they would not be so worried or anxious to protect the falsely presented hypotheses of the powertionist governments. *My arguments regarding illegal and immoral acts of governments are not protective of my own rights to any extent, but rather signal their destruction, since the more you write about the criminal plans of the big powers, the more status and supporters you lose.*[96]

There are rules, principles, and provisions in the system of international criminal justice that concern what counts as an adequate reason for upholding the international criminal responsibility of individuals, governments, and states. As understood in the system of international criminal justice, the notion of criminal responsibility is the consequence of a breach of a serious norm of international criminal law that should not have been violated and should have instead been protected in the practice of the relevant state or government. One could argue that the best basic explanation of why we speak about the violations of certain norms as criminal violations and create the concept of international criminal responsibility is that the respect of those norms is fundamentally imperative for the security of humanity.[97] However, we might be tempted to suggest a different and more reasonable answer to the identical question of the system of international criminal justice. This can be down to different propositions. Nonetheless, the basic facts of the case do not change, and any violation of a serious criminal nature gives rise to the concept of international criminal responsibility.

Some may believe that my arguments are contentious or hostile based on their personal views. However, others may not only believe that they are harmless and worthwhile values, but also that they seek to protect the victims of armed conflicts. This indicates that the arguments are welcome. We should remember that it is the sensitivity of the moral truth that concerns the nature of criminal activities and the decisions of the big powers. The truthfulness of evidence points out the wrong, worthy, or unworthy evaluations that have been made. Naturally, when the population of the world recognised the moral truth of the big political powers, no further explanation was needed regarding evidence of their criminality. Their condemnation is complete unless the contrary is proven. It is a risky strategy for me to defend facts instead of

---

[96] *Id., Powertionism in International Criminal Justice.*

[97] Consult Farhad Malekian, *Imperative Philosophy of International Criminal Justice: Visible Power – Invisible Essence* (New York: Nova Science Publishers, 2022).

defending the criminal decisions of the big powers to cover up their criminal conduct. However, doing so would immorally exhaust my own conscience.

Moral facts cannot take away criminal responsibility and in fact does the opposite. The foundation of morality lies in righteousness and wisdom.[98] Again, there is no reason to believe that the myth of injustices under the power of the Security Council can be abolished by writing and expressing the truth. We have not even had a shadow of a correct decision in the Council to create hope concerning disarming the terrorist governments. This demonstrates that immorality is more powerful than any notion of ethical morality. Relatively few writers put their understanding of the facts into writing, since it can jeopardise their personal interests. This means that they present all matters in a diplomatic way in order to protect their positions. As a result, the evil mentalities of the powertionist governments occupy and block the true principles of wisdom and their application in the system of international criminal justice.[99] We might then realise or at least speculate about moral or legal emotions that have been absent from international criminal courts, thereby resulting in the complete abolition of the notion of the international criminal responsibility of states.

---

[98] Farhad Malekian, *Gravity of Wisdom in International Criminal Law* (New York: Nova Science Publishers, 2021).

[99] *Id.*

Chapter 4

Barrel of Immoral Criminal Responsibility

1. Constructivist Interpretations

Without any hesitation, the international criminal responsibility of governments and states is a fact, however it is difficult to attribute to and impose on criminal governments and states. The system of international criminal justice has certain masters who dominate a significant number of imperialist powers using their military strength. As a result, the moral and legal responsibility for violations of the system of international criminal law is dependent on self-preservation. Therefore, in one way or another, the moral philosophy of international human rights law is the theory of revival between the notion of morality and the attitudes of self-preservation. This is because the notion of truthful morality speaks about the prevention of any kind of self-preservation, particularly when the rights of the victims have intentionally been diminished by the perpetrators of international crimes.

In exploring a more precious depiction of the nature of international human rights law and its effects on the concept of international criminal responsibility of states and governments, we need to be conscious concerning what we are doing to humanity and should ignore how we wish humanity to be interpreted based on our governmental interests. The victims should take precedence over all other matters when international crimes have been committed. The reason for this is that we have a natural and legal responsibility for our wrongs, particularly concerning the mass murder of the Palestinian population. The notion of responsibility in this case does not really concern the moral aspects of the given matter, but rather relates to how we ignore the very facts of the truth and replace it with lies. That is why the notion of international criminal responsibility of governments not only has the potential to be dealt with under the procedures of an international criminal court, but also under the procedures of national courts in order to ensure that criminals receive impunity for their heinous crimes against humanity.

Our suggestion unites the collective notion of the responsibility of all governments to demand the implementation and attribution of the concept of accountability of superior orders and their governments to the system of international criminal justice structured in the International Criminal Court.

Nonetheless, we have not yet been able to implement any of the requirements of criminal justice when it comes to big criminals. This indicates that I am also speaking about the constructivist method of approaching the system of international criminal responsibility along with how the system has been violated and broken by powertionist governments. This theory of constructivism is Kantian and was expanded upon by Rawls.[100] We should look at the question of accountability of governments and states from the point of view of the categorical imperative.[101] This indicates the legal and moral duty of the Security Council and the General Assembly to deal with the questions of massive violations of the system of international criminal law and the commission of international crimes more seriously and urgently. Constructivist theory is, in the words of Rawls, another term for the presentation of the theory of the categorical imperative and its fundamental value concerning the presentation of right and wrong.[102] This not only concerns moral judgments, but also appropriate international legal judgments.

One of the main intentions of the system of international human rights law is to advance justice to the point that it does not revive the various concepts of self-preservation, self-tactics, self-regulation, and self-enforcement of the system of international criminal justice by powertionist governments. Therefore, under the system of international human rights, we are forced to discover violations of the law by adopting the proper rules of law that are not influenced by the aggressive decisions and conduct of governments. Based on this, we should construct our moral and legal judgments by requesting and

---

[100] Consult the book on A Theory of Justice. For Kant theories consult Immanuel Kant, 'Religion within the Limits of Reason Alone,' in *Religion and Rational Theology*, ed. and transl. *Allen Wood and George di Giovanni* (Cambridge University Press, 1996); Immanuel Kant, 'Religion within the Limits of Reason Alone', in Religion and Rational Theology, ed. and transl. *Allen Wood and George di* Giovanni (Cambridge University Press, 1996); Kant Immanuel, *Answering the Question: What is Enlightenment?* (1784); Immanuel Kant, *Critique of Judgment* (1790); Immanuel Kant, *Critique of Pure Reason* (1781); Immanuel Kant, *Groundwork of the Metaphysic of Morals* (1785); Kant Immanuel, *Metaphysical Foundations of Natural Science* (1786); Immanuel Kant, *Opus Postumum* (1995); Kant Immanuel, *Perpetual Peace, and Other Essays on Politics, History, and Morals* (1784); Kant Immanuel, *Perpetual Peace: A Philosophical Sketch* (1795); Immanuel Kant, *Practical Philosophy* (editor: Mary J. Gregor, 1999); Immanuel Kant, *Prolegomena to Any Future Metaphysics* (1783); Kant Immanuel, *Religion within the Bounds of Bare Reason* (1793); Immanuel Kant, *The Critique of Practical Reason* (1788); Immanuel Kant, *The Metaphysics of Morals* (1797); Immanuel Kant, *The Only Possible Argument in Support of a Demonstration of the Existence of God* (1763); Immanuel Kant, *The Science of Right* (1790).

[101] Examine Farhad Malekian, *Imperative Philosophy of International Criminal Justice: Visible Power – Invisible Essence* (New York: Nova Science Publishers, 2022).

[102] *Id.*

inquiring into what international criminal legal principles are and what they aim to achieve. Is their achievement in the interest of the public or in the interest of the superpower's hidden political policies?

There is a particular legal duty and obligation upon all states, i.e., an internationally recognised customary norm, which is a maxim that must be followed by all governments and their states as well as all national and international organisations that deal with the principles of international criminal justice. Thus, fixing the principles of justice through the rudimentary construction of our personal political wills should not violate the notion of international criminal responsibility when we have committed serious international crimes. The aim is to maximise international criminal justice and its objectivity, and prevent it from facing certain situations wherein certain powertionist governments are empowered under the provisions of Chapter VII of the United Nations to orchestrate their musical political symphony with the false sound of a barrel claiming to promote human rights practices.

2. Extinguishing the Value of Egalitarianism

One could argue that the system of international criminal justice is complete and does not need any more modifications or additional provisional measures. However, there is one serious problem with such a statement—it destabilises the system of international criminal justice and prompts a serious examination of certain basic moral and political principles that have been falsely interpreted and therefore cannot be considered true. Thus, in recognising the concept of international criminal responsibility of governments and their states, understanding and proving their foremost aims is imperative and a necessary requirement for the identification of the idea of egalitarianism.[103]

The main intention behind all these movements is to prevent the misuse and misunderstanding of the system of international criminal justice and prevent any conduct that threatens the notion of international criminal responsibility of governments that commit crimes under the guise of supporting humanity. We are referring here to the immoral conduct that has been carried out by the Israeli government over the course of hundreds of years of occupation in the name of establishing humanity for the supporters of Zionist ideology and rights. The nature of ideologies and rights is constructed

[103] Consult also Farhad Malekian, *Imperative Philosophy of International Criminal Justice: Visible Power – Invisible Essence* (New York: Nova Science Publishers, 2022).

and promoted through the serious violation of the system of international criminal justice. This translates into treating everyone under the rule of Zionist criminal acts and the annihilation the Palestinian population. More concretely, it requires the activation of the most serious form of genocide imaginable against the basic constitution of the system of international criminal justice. The position involves eroding the value of egalitarianism or fairness in the practical implementation of the system of human rights and justice.

When a state resorts to committing serious violations of the system of international criminal justice and claiming it was necessary, that is in and of itself a violation of the primary requirements for the interpretation and application of the law. It also creates more superficial circumstances around the system of international criminal justice. States then claim that their actions were necessary and unavoidable. Killing and forcing millions out of their homelands cannot and should not be defended under any circumstances or positioned as necessary. When a state, its government, or various agencies of the state, engage in actions that are intended to extinguish the existence of a population, it cannot be interpreted as the implementation of the system of international human rights or an act of self-defence. In such situations, we use the barrel of human rights conventions in order to pursue our interests and can no longer claim that the system of international human rights represents fairness.

Within the system of international criminal justice, the respect for certain fundamental and intuitive humanitarian principles is so essential and vital for its existence that it cannot be defended by various political lies and corruption. [104] As a matter of fact, the general role of the concept of moral justice is to connect fundamental, intuitive, and humanitarian principles in order to create a fair system of international criminal justice.[105]The notion of accountability means that those who transgress the agreed principles of humanity should universally receive prosecution and punishment.

My suggestions are based on the core principles of international criminal justice, which deliver equality and international criminal responsibility for all States Parties. This indicates that the original position of justice rests on the expected moral truth. While there may be many more principles and discussions concerning the question of international criminal law and its principles, we should approach all matters from a position of equality and

---

[104] Examine Antonio Cassese, (ed.), *The New Humanitarian Law of Armed Conflict* (Naples: Editoriale Scientifica, 1979).

[105] *Id.*

accountability when we witness the serious violations of the criminal justice system occurring in Gaza and the West Bank.

The system of international criminal justice cannot change its closure of justice or its gavel of justice with reference to the fact that criminals are very powerful and may pose a threat to the prosecutor and the pre-trial Chamber of the Court if those who have grossly violated the system of international criminal justice and continue their violations are arrested. The notion of positive construction of Justice as Fairness does not refer to its words, but rather its practical actions. What is the purpose of having beautiful terms and vocabulary in the system of international criminal justice and international human rights when they are not relevant? When should such terms be shown to have their basic and substantive purposes?

How can we claim to fully respect international criminal justice principles if the principles have a double morality and do not apply to their norms in situations involving genocide, crimes against humanity, and torture? We cannot defend powertionist governments that enforce their system of international criminal justice by saying that they have their own private interests. Doing so would cause the basic provisions of international criminal justice, which must to be respected by all governments and their states, to lose trust and the integrity of the value of enforceability. The absence of egalitarian values leads to certain states taking precedence over others within the system of international politics, and eventually to violations of the primary norms of human rights.

3. Illegitimate Claim of Necessity

We should be very careful not to confuse the international public about different terms of international criminal justice in order to monopolise the system of international criminal responsibility of states.[106] This has been done repeatedly by powerful states whose policies and economies are dependent on the Zionist criminal government of Israel. One of the serious problems with the practical mechanism of the system of international criminal justice is that it is not controlled by the judges of international criminal courts and is instead

[106] Consult Farhad Malekian, *The Monopolization of International Criminal Law in the United Nations, A Jurisprudential Approach* (Stockholm: Almqvist Wiksell International, 1st ed., 1993, 2nd ed., 1995).

controlled by the power of the armed forces.[107] This indicates that in differentiating between the notions of governments, we should legally achieve the same result and not give priority to one state's international legal personality over another's. This is how the system of international criminal justice, in particular the criminal responsibility of states, is ignored. Therefore, we may examine many principles, issues, and pieces of evidence relating to international criminal responsibility in order to understand the circumstances and conditions under which powerful governments ignore their own crimes and give greater value to their actions to preclude or reveal the wrongfulness of an act by their own government or state.

In the recognition of an international crime and the application of the concept of international criminal responsibility to the offending state, we should not protect the criminal conduct of the said state. Obviously, resorting to self-defence is an established legal right of any state, albeit with the caveat that resorting to the right of self-defence must be done correctly and proportionally. The immediate and basic objective of self-defence is to protect a state from the aggression or criminal conduct of another state. However, this does not mean that the state in question is free to interpret any counteraction by any group, nation, or government as an attack on this freedom and justification for the state to attack the other.

Acts of resistance by groups in pursuit of self-determination or freedom from occupation should not be considered criminal and do not create a right to self-defence.[108] Any defence of this nature constitutes a breach of the rights of the occupying population and calls upon the international criminal responsibility of the occupied power and its government. Therefore, acts of resistance cannot be identified as acts of aggression and should not jeopardise the activities of the resisting population. It is essential for the state that has committed violations and occupied another state's territories through force, aggression, and political manipulation to reflect upon its own unlawful actions, which have provoked protests from the victims of international crimes.

---

[107] Farhad Malekian, *Conscience of Judges in International Criminal Law, the Heart of Judgements* (New York: Nova Science Publishers, 2021); Farhad Malekian, *Conscience of Lawyers in International Criminal Law, the Burden of Doppelgängers* (New York: Nova Science Publishers, 2021); Farhad Malekian, *Conscience of Prosecutors in International Criminal Law, the Heart of the Matter* (New York: Nova Science Publishers, 2021).

[108] Moreover, Miko Peled clarifies that "what is clear beyond doubt is that they will not defeat the Palestinians. Call it HAMAS or something else. It doesn't matter what you call it. It doesn't matter what movement the Palestinians belong to. The Palestinians will not be defeated." Examine *also* https://mikopeled.com/.

In other words, a state should not initiate war against the population of occupied territories and consider any protests against their actions as acts of war and terror. The points that will be made later will show how the system of international criminal justice is used by the big political parties of the world to accuse victims, impute the concept of international criminal responsibility on the victims, and make them accountable for their own international criminal violations. This is typical of most horrible interpretations and uses of the provisions of the system of international criminal justice by states to serve their own interests. We shall confine our arguments here to the observation that there is no comparison between the interpretation of self-defence presented by the powertionist governments and states of necessity, which grant all states of the world certain rights to protect their interests.

In other words, an international customary rule allows a state to breach an international obligation if there is a grave and imminent peril. This is referred to as a state of necessity. Our focus is on the state's legal justification for breaching an international obligation as the sole means of defending these vital interests. This means that the acts of powertionist governments cannot be defended under the plea of the state of necessity in order to justify their aggressive international criminal violations against resistance groups in regions that are suffering as a result of the criminal conduct of the powertionist government.

After careful thought concerning human rights values, the population of Palestine is definitely pursuing a policy of self-defence or self-protection and confronting a peril that is threatening their existence. We are referring here to the danger caused by the criminal activities and criminal conspiracy of a number of Western governments against the Palestinians. Populations in similar positions are permitted to take action against immoral interpretations of the concept of international criminal responsibility by certain states against its existence and the extermination of its ethnic, cultural, religious, and traditional sovereignty. Wrongful criminal acts that are brutal and perpetrated by a state, such as the Zionist state of Israel and its associate governments of Western states, through different perspectives of juridical interpretations, cannot in any way be considered acts of defence against the resisting population of Palestine.

Such acts violate the basic constitution of the system of international criminal justice and the immoral attribution of the notion of criminal responsibility to those who are defending their rights that have been occupied for almost over one hundred years by the British, American, and Israeli governments. Those criminal acts can no longer be defended as a breach of states' international obligations under international criminal justice jurisdiction. On the other hand, as we have previously asserted, when a state justifies its aggressive criminal conduct as being in line with international criminal obligations and international criminal justice and links it to the resistance movements in the occupied country, it is simultaneously implying that the system of international morality, the concept of international human rights, and the system of international criminal justice do not exist. Acts of such states are in violation of the system of international criminal responsibility and by no means covered by the theory of defence. Thus, a state is less likely to claim that it has been the victim of an armed attack by resistance movements in occupied lands.

4. Constructivist International Criminal Responsibility

The barrel of the immoral criminal responsibility is intended to collect and present rightful conduct as wrongful conduct, and consequently paint the defence of victims as harmful and criminal. The history of international civilisation has seen this on occasion and has been named by criminals as self-defence. This places victims in a position where they do not have any rights, neither in the system of customary international law nor within international human rights as a whole. The situation of the victims may consequently be interpreted as falling within an overlapping space between the prior agreements between the powertionist governments and the principles supported by their military, which are, in essence, the clear presentation of discrimination, apartheid, and slavery. As a result, the victims are condemned for taking parts of the true basic reasons, which are truly their rights regarding broader ethical and sovereign legal rights, including moral evidence.

This is how the notion of international criminal responsibility of states and their governments is erased and fails to be implemented in the ICC or similar courts/tribunals. Every government must accept the basic structure of the framework of the system of international criminal justice, which includes the common principles in the presentation of an equal system of international criminal justice. These basic principles of the structure of the corridors of criminal jurisdiction must be given sufficient care and space in terms of implementation. However, the reality is rather different and controversial, and as a result, the original models of the same principles of justice undermine its essence and do not accept the ambition to be united together in the peace and dignity of human beings and protect each other's rights.

Indeed, the condemnation of victims is inconsistent even with the most extreme varieties of the notion of morality because it does not recognise that the system of international criminal justice or the notion of international criminal responsibility of governments should not be employed in immoral forms of interpretation. However, it is. Due to this, the method of identifying the system of international criminal responsibility is inconsistent with the attribution of the basic practice of understanding the system of international criminal justice and identifying the real criminals. This therefore causes widespread scepticism about the moral truth in the body of international human rights law, and calls into question whether the United Nations Charter has any trace of moral truth within the content of its provisions at all. The idea of approximating certain principles, decisions, or the content of the resolutions of the Security Council to moral truth has been very controversial. This in turn has led to the presentation of false truths because of the development of lies amongst the ethical intentions of justice.

The fact is that the notion of a constructivist doctrine of international criminal justice in the International Law Commission is based on the principles of justice as the truth concerning the "*internationally wrongful conduct of a state.*" This addresses the original position of international criminal responsibility. The aim is simply to attribute the concept of responsibility to the correct subject—not the victims. This concept is viewed as a workable approximation to the legal and moral facts that exist in the system of international law and its virtue, which in turn seeks to identify the correct subject for the attribution of the notion of international criminal responsibility.[109] Consequently, the notion of constructivism in the system of international criminal justice challenges a theory about the character of international criminal responsibility and the basic reasons why we have assumed that it can be attributed to the wrongful acts of states or governments and that victims can get their violated rights restored by international criminal courts.

When the system of international law in the United Nations and particularly in the Security Council closes its eyes to the facts and realities of the barbaric violations of the rights of the victims, then hunting the criminals becomes a utopian dream and masters of lies run around the International Criminal Courtrooms.[110] Modifying the rights of victims and the barrel of lies

---

[109] Farhad Malekian, *Tour de force of Moral Virtue in International Criminal Justice* (New York: Nova Science Publishers, 2022).

[110] Examine Farhad Malekian, *The Mirage of International Criminal Law, Kant Metaphysics of Mens Rea* (Cambridge Scholars Publishing, 2018).

will ultimately cause silence to fall on the entire international community, and the rights of victims will become the rights of the offenders. Can this downgrade, relegation, and banishment of the rights of victims function under the monopolised system of the Security Council?[111] We must repeatedly ask ourselves: how can these common principles of the system of the international responsibility of states and governments function when the leading authorities making decisions are the real terrorists who are committing the most serious criminal acts against various nations of the world? This is obviously not the intention of the system of international criminal justice as decided and codified through the integration of various international agreements and treaties.

The fact is that we have changed the real features and functions of the system of international criminal responsibility and made it immoral under the monopolised system of the United Nations Charter. Moreover, the entire system of the United Nations is controlled by the system of paternalism, which elevates the governments that believe themselves to be the true judges of all courts.[112] This includes existing courts as well as ad hoc or temporary tribunals. As this political idea and monopolisation of the system of international law in the United Nations develop, the right to demand justice and the right to bring big international criminals under prosecution and punishment becomes less of an interest. The gravity of the crimes becomes less interesting and we intentionally extinguish the notion of international criminal responsibility of superior orders and their governments and states. As a result, the International Criminal Court sounds like just an empty barrel, without any interest in the prosecution, accountability, or punishment of accused subjects of criminality.

5. The Barrel of Criminal Accountability in Genocide

The difficulty of recognising the problems faced by the victims along with their perpetual suffering becomes even more serious when the United Nations Security Council demonstrates that it has become the full private entity of

---

[111] Consult Farhad Malekian, *The Monopolization of International Criminal Law in the United Nations, A Jurisprudential Approach* (Stockholm: Almqvist Wiksell International, 1st ed., 1993, 2nd ed., 1995).

[112] Farhad Malekian, *Conundrums of Paternalism in International Criminal Justice* (New York: Nova Science Publishers, 2024). See also Farhad Malekian, I*mperative Philosophy of International Criminal Justice: Visible Power – Invisible Essence* (New York: Nova Science Publishers, 2022); Farhad Malekian, *Tour de force of Moral Virtue in International Criminal Justice* (New York: Nova Science Publishers, 2022).

criminal governments, such as the Zionist government, the American government and the British government. The result is that the hope of identifying conceptions and standards that provide the best proof for the notion of international criminal responsibility is controlled by criminal terrorist governments and, in our case, by Zionist economic power. This in turn means that the Israeli government controls the economy and can monopolise any form of civil or criminal justice.

This is a significant facet of the attribution of the unfeasibility of the concept of international criminal responsibility and ignoring crimes against humanity, war crimes, genocide, torture, rape, aggression, or apartheid. *The point here is not that any interpretive account of the system of international law must be free from economic consequences, but rather that the notion of the economic monopolisation of international law, international human rights law, and international criminal justice is the evillest form of control of the system of criminal justice.*[113] *It ultimately creates a barrel full of evil eels dancing for the humiliation of the integrity of human civilisation. Consequently, true moral justice dies and the evil mentality of criminals and those who present the lies as truth becomes accustomed to the practices of international organisations. This practice ultimately found its way into the ICC and ICJ.*

Of course, this situation must be analysed against the background of moral theory, which is essential for understanding and conceiving the norms of justice. One could take a constructivist approach to creating a kind of scepticism in the colour of lies and present it in the colour of truth. This indicates that we face a form of utipolitianism that not only has a strong desire to monopolise the power of international law, but also has strong, deep roots in the system of international criminal justice, including as it concerns the definition, modification, and application of the concepts of the crime of aggression or genocide. Although the international crime of genocide is one of the most serious crimes within the system of international criminal justice, the serious and barbaric genocide being committed by the Israeli Zionist government has been removed from the history of the resolutions of the Security Council and has been treated as a resort to self-defence by the criminal government of Israel and other criminal Western governments. The political position of the Israeli government also confirms the statements of the

[113] Consult Farhad Malekian, *The Monopolization of International Criminal Law in the United Nations, A Jurisprudential Approach* (Stockholm: Almqvist Wiksell International, 1st ed., 1993, 2nd ed., 1995).

United States political representatives, and such statements have also been supported in the Security Council by the American diplomatic representatives violating the system of international criminal justice. Accepting the commission of severe genocide in the history of civilization is the way we implement international human rights law.

The development of the idea of genocide is associated with Nazi practices. According to Article 2 of the United Nations Convention on the Prevention and Punishment of the Crime of Genocide.[114] The term "genocide" is defined as:

> any of the following acts committed with intent to destroy, in whole or in part, a national, ethnical, racial, or religious group, as such: killing members of the group; causing serious bodily or mental harm to members of the group; deliberately inflicting on the group conditions of life calculated to bring about its physical destruction in whole or in part; imposing measures intended to prevent births within the group; [and] forcibly transferring children of the group to another group.

This definition has even been used in the procedures of the International Criminal Court and ad hoc tribunals such as the International Criminal Tribunals for the Former Yugoslavia (ICTY) and for Rwanda (ICTR).[115] According to these tribunals, criminal responsibility for genocide extends to those who "planned, instigated, ordered, committed, or otherwise aided and abetted in the planning, preparation, or execution" of one or more of the aforementioned genocidal acts.[116]

The activities of the Zionist criminal government in Israel not only fit these descriptions of the international crime of genocide, they have also been confirmed in the statements of the office of the prosecutor of the ICC and the International Court of Justice. Moreover, according to Article 25(3) (e) of the Rome Statute of the International Criminal Court, a person who "directly and publicly incites others to commit genocide" has violated international law.

---

[114] Convention on the Prevention and Punishment of the Crime of Genocide, 9 December 1948. Visited in https://ihl-databases.icrc.org/pt/ihl-treaties/genocide-conv-1948.

[115] Statute of the International Tribunal for the Former Yugoslavia, 1993; Statute of the International Tribunal for Rwanda, 1994; see also John E Ackerman and Eugène O'Sullivan, *Practice and Procedure of the International Criminal Tribunal for the Former Yugoslavia with selected material from the International Criminal Tribunal for Rwanda* (2000); Schabas W. A., Justice, Democracy and Impunity in Post Genocide Rwanda: Searching for Solutions to Impossible Problems, 7 *Criminal Law Forum* (1996).

[116] *Id.*

This indicates that the Court and the states that arrest criminals must apply the concept of international criminal responsibility. However, this has not happened since the ICC is a vassal Court of the big political parties such as the United States, the United Kingdom, France, Australia, Canada, New Zealand, Germany, Austria, Hungary, the Czech Republic, and even Egypt.

6. Multifarious Justification Dependency

The fact is that the power of the Security Council has strongly reduced the notion of the international criminal responsibility of individuals, governments, organisations, and states, which indicates that the extermination of the Palestinian population is being carried out with the full gravity of the criminality of a terrorist state. We must emphasise the fact that rejecting Zionism and condemning Israeli war crimes is not anti-Semitic. This is because we are focusing on the structure of the system of international criminal justice and a subject of the law that can be identified as bearing international criminal responsibility for having committed the most serious international crimes over the course of several decades.

In the system of international criminal justice, there is no explicit requirement that genocide actually be committed. This indicates that one who "orders, solicits, or induces the commission of such a crime" can be found guilty of genocide. In this context, war crimes and crimes against humanity carry criminal responsibility for the perpetrator(s) if the criminal conduct "in fact occurs or is attempted." In other words, inciting war crimes and crimes against humanity is a crime that can only be punishable when the crimes are carried out or attempted, however incitement to genocide is a crime that can be punished even if it is not attempted or carried out. The trial judgements of the International Criminal Tribunal for Rwanda with reference to the drafters of the Genocide Convention confirmed that convictions on the basis of incitement do not require the actual execution of genocidal acts.

All this indicates that the crime of genocide that is being committed by the Zionist Israeli government triggers the international criminal responsibility of the perpetrators and their accountability before the jurisdiction of an international criminal court. There is even evidence that the Israeli Zionist government officially encourages its population, military personnel, and settlers in the West Bank to commit genocide through various means. Thus, the state has made a strong, vivid, and direct call for the commission of genocide through the statements and conduct of its leaders. The level of the effectiveness of such statements is judged by the context and audience it was intended for. Despite being unclear to outsiders, the incitement can still be considered a directive as long as the intended audience immediately comprehends the message to commit genocide or feels they have permission to commit genocide.

As a result, any acceptable theory of international criminal justice must be drawn from a plausible interpretation of the traditions of international criminal jurisdiction or draw our attention to the basic philosophy of the International War Crimes Tribunal in Nuremberg. The tribunal followed the notion of criminal responsibility for those who committed crimes against humanity and war crimes against *innocent Jews.* It would be entirely impossible for the tribunal not to find the accused criminals guilty and release them. However, in the case of crimes against the Palestinian population, the Security Council and the judges of the Pre-Trial Chamber appear to have a different policy: there are virtually no convictions, even after arrest warrants have been issued for the perpetrators. This proves that utipolitianist governments have completely different views and try to wash the bloody faces and hands of the perpetrators and themselves with reference to religious promises, which is in itself a serious insult to the theological philosophy of any belief system.

The problem is that we do not regret our actions and decisions, since we have enough to worry about concerning our relationship with the big political powers of the Security Council to also be worried about the victims' rights and lives. Our governments want to stay in power and not be criticised by their citizens and the Security Council. The theory of international criminal responsibility thus has a limited validity concerning our policies, politics, and records, even though we know that we will be criticised by those who discover the truth. That will be just the pleasant sound of a barrel for our government and not the sound of loss, since, as long as we are following the footsteps of the big political parties, we will always be on good platforms of interest, even though we are aware that the platform was built with the blood of the victims of war crimes, crimes against humanity, aggression, rape, and genocide. We will still pretend that our hands and politics are clean of the blood of the victims. It demonstrates that the integrity of international criminal justice has been violated.[117]

---

[117] Farhad Malekian, *Trading Virginity of International Criminal Justice* (Nova Sciences Publishers, 2020); Farhad Malekian, *The Mirage of International Criminal Law, Kant Metaphysics of Mens Rea* (Cambridge Scholars Publishing, 2018), pp. 61-2. Farhad Malekian, *Powertionism in International Criminal Justice* (New York: Nova Science

Of course, enforcing international criminal responsibility for the subjects of international criminal justice is a very difficult goal. This is in part because the issues at stake concerning the attribution of the notion of international criminal responsibility require a significant force of law to be given to the International Criminal Court at The Hague, which in practice means that the great powers must be in full support of the implementation of such a requirement. This is precisely what is missing from justice today, and it is principally complex and puzzling. The difficulty of this situation is in part due to the fact that egoistic self-preservation so often stands in the way of the system of international criminal justice, and, consequently, the existence of any notion of criminal responsibility becomes a struggle against injustices itself. We should try to recognise the true extent of the problem of international criminal justice both when it is being implemented and when the big powers are distracting us from the true challenges.[118]

7. Egoistic Traps of Hypocritical Rulers

The system of international criminal justice has witnessed many serious violations that have amounted to the commission of genocide. This includes violations during the Vietnam War, during the reign of the Khmer Rouge, during the Yugoslav wars, the Rwandan genocide, the Gulf War, and the East Timor genocide. The powertionist governments of the world have been the true perpetrators behind all of the crimes committed against victims with the full purpose of their extermination. However, the systems of international criminal justice and human rights have been unable to prevent these crimes and call upon the international criminal responsibilities of the perpetrators of international crimes.

Two of the most heinous of the aforementioned examples are the genocide in Vietnam and the genocide in Iraq, both of which were under the power and control of the powertionist government of the United States. Both examples

---

Publishers, 2022); Farhad Malekian, *Imperative Philosophy of International Criminal Justice: Visible Power – Invisible Essence* (New York: Nova Science Publishers, 2022); Farhad Malekian, *Tour de force of Moral Virtue in International Criminal Justice* (New York: Nova Science Publishers, 2022).

118 G. Schwarzenberger, 'The Problem of an International Criminal Law,' 5 *Current Legal Problems* (1950); G. Schwarzenberger, *International Jus Cogens?,* 43 *Tax. L. Rev* (1965), p. 476; D. Shelton, 'Normative Hierarchy of International Law' 80 *American Journal of International Law* (1986), 1; see also Egon Schwelb, *Crimes Against Humanity, British Yearbook of International Law* (1946) 178.

include the murder of millions of people who had nothing to do with American domestic policies. The provisions of the system of international criminal law were brutally violated by the American government due to its international economic, political, and military interests. The commission of genocide, war crimes, and crimes against humanity in Vietnam were originally based on the United States's desire to fight against Communist ideologies.

In some sense, there is no way of moving away from the fact that the wrong conclusions that were drawn by the United States government in conjunction with the British government made the situation unthinkable to the extent that the Vietnamese were regarded as uncivilised people who could not understand the criminal theories of the Western powers. Similarly, the United States government was involved in waging wars against the Iraqi regime in the name of protecting civilians from the atrocities committed by Saddam Hussein's regime. However, the true motivation behind these wars was to gain access to oil. This is also why millions of people were killed during the war between Iran and Iraq, which was also initiated by the United States government and its intelligence agency, the CIA. This is how the dictatorship of a regime and serious internal problems are taken advantage of by powerful governments to escape from their international criminal responsibility. These governments use international criminal justice as a barrel of intentions and solving the problems between nations.

Incorrectly describing what the system of international criminal justice wants is always the political tool of power politics, and it is true that we cannot justify a legal or moral judgement in this way and believe that our description is going to work for the victims. The explanations of the system of international criminal justice simply follow from the content of its basic principles of whether international criminal justice is meant to function properly and in accordance with its requirements. What is claimed by the powers in the Security Council therefore has nothing to do with reality, and consequently we are in some way trapped within the realms of lies and mistreatment of the victims of genocide and war crimes.[119] As a result, it is impossible to escape from the notion of international criminal responsibility unless we follow the wills of strong governments.

A clear example of this is the position of the Western powers and their assistance in the decimation of the Palestinian population. The fact is that all

[119] Even examine Fein Bruce, *'Hillary Clinton's 5 lies about Syria, Terror Threat'*, The Washington Times (25 October, 2016). See also Farhad Malekian, *Trading Virginity of International Criminal Justice* (New York: Nova Science Publishers, 2020).

these governments deny the existence of the international criminal responsibility of the subjects of international criminal justice when it comes to themselves and their allies. For example, saying that we cannot bring the Israeli government into the corridors of international criminal justice implies that we escape from the realm of descriptive and normative functions of international criminal law because we are unable to face the truth. This means that we actually have no answer to the question of the international criminal responsibility of the perpetrators of war crimes. It also indicates that moral judgements do not exist and can simply be ignored and trapped by our private political interests. The price of all this is the murder and genocide of a population struggling for the establishment of its legal and political rights against a Nazi government.

On the contrary, our argument shows exactly how the system of international human rights can be used to extinguish the rights of victims. Thus, it is very difficult to answer if any particular international legal and moral judgements exist in our decisions since we deliver our judgements, not based on the foundations of the system of international criminal law, but rather based on the choice and policies of certain powertionist governments. Thus, we distance ourselves from the reality of the crimes being committed against the victims and fulfil the requests of certain powers in the Security Council to serve our private egoistic norms. Such actions cause the virtue of the system of international criminal justice to disappear from the humanitarian nature and get closer to the evil morality of the big, hypocritical, powerful states.[120]

8. The Ugliness Against Criminal Responsibilities

The miserable, untrue sounds of the barrel of international human rights law and international criminal justice are not just the issues of international criminal responsibility, but also the very question of international environmental law. How can the members of the criminal organisation of NATO speak about the necessity of protecting the international environment and bring up the issue in UN meetings all while assisting in the commission of genocide against the population of Palestine in their own occupied lands? This is the face of the double morality and mixed nature of the system of

[120] Examine Farhad Malekian, *Tour de force of Moral Virtue in International Criminal Justice* (New York: Nova Science Publishers, 2022).

international hypocrisy of those who publicly claim to support humanity and the human environment while destroying both with their weapons.

All this reflects the true face of the Israeli Zionist government and the American justification to steal the traditional position of Palestine through various political, military, and economic games. The fact is that the American government has historically proven that it enjoys committing barbaric international crimes, carrying out sexual crimes against thousands of prisoners, and violating international humanitarian law all over the world, including in Palestine. All these actions have the deep economic and political intentions of powerful hypocrites. Additionally, the criminal government of the United States of America speaks about the hierocracy of the freedom of the seas but not about the freedom of the population of Gaza from the brutal and barbaric crimes of the Zionist government.

We do not ignore the questions relating to the freedom of navigation because we believe that it is the right of the big, powerful states to navigate any areas as they please, and yet they should be saved because they are delivering weapons of mass destruction to be used to kill Palestinians and occupy their territory. How can we ignore innocent children's right to life while speaking about the right to navigate the seas to deliver weapons to be used in the genocide of the same children? As a matter of fact, the present situation and the criminal activities of the chief instigator of NATO are much more concerning than these philosophical contemplations about the system of international criminal justice and deliberating the notion of international criminal responsibility for all these criminal acts under the system of international criminal justice.

What is the real reason why the powertionist governments ignore the concept of international criminal responsibility for themselves and not for others? The important question is what causes the policy of the Security Council—we speak about the wrongs of other nations or states like Iraq, Libya, or Syria and not about the criminal acts committed by our own allies. How the barrel of the system of the Security Council sound can highly informed about the criminal activities of other states but remain mute concerning our own crimes? Snakes in Security Council use lateral undulation to slither over rough ground and across battlefields. Similarly, why does a barrel of NATO power ignore the decades of tears of Palestinian children all while prioritising its own evil criminal wishes?[121] *The system of international*

---

[121] Farhad Malekian, *International Criminal Vacations: Tears of Justice* (New York: Nova Science Publishers, 2024).

human rights was not created to bargain about rights.[122] *If there are questions of rights, all rights are equal when the true presentation of rights has been introduced.*[123] *We cannot say that the centuries of rights of a nation should be eliminated by the British and American imperialist criminal governments since they forcibly expelled millions of Palestinians during the Nakba.*

The question is: how often have events similar to the Nakba taken place and led to deaths? The Nakba was the ethnic cleansing of the Palestinians, which was organised, forced, and armed by the British and American governments with the full intention of aggressive, violent displacement and dispossession of the land, property, and belongings of the Palestinian population to create a hypothetical land for the criminal Zionist Jews. These criminal activities were carefully orchestrated to wipe out the entire population of Palestine. They therefore succeeded in massacring the population of territories that had been living there for centuries with the support of the newly established Zionist government of Israel. The Nakba was committed by the guns and criminal conspiracies of the colonial powers, causing the destruction of Palestinian society and the suppression of their cultural identity, political rights, and national existence.

Consequently, the term "Nakba" is used to describe the events of the 1948 imperialist Western War against Palestine and the displacement of an innocent population of a sovereign land that had no hand in the crimes committed by the German Nazi government against the innocent Jewish population in Germany and Europe. The displacement of Palestinians by Israeli Zionist groups was violently carried out against a population that was not at war with any other nation. During the Nakba, the rights of the Palestinian population were taken away through the immeasurable use of unlawful, aggressive force. The Nakba demonstrates that the Palestinian population has an undeniable right to fight against the Israeli government for the establishment of its extinguished rights. It covers the right of Palestinian society to recover the rights that had been originally pirated at the behest the British criminal imperialist government. The right is undisputable or unquestionable in accordance with the provisions of the system of international criminal justice and international human rights law, which also include *international peremptory jus cogens* norms.[124]

---

[122] *Id.*

[123] *Id.*

[124] "Therefore, *jus cogens* norms, along with *erga omnes* norms, are obligatory and no impunity should be granted to those who violate them. That is one of the most serious problems facing the systems of human rights and criminal justice and has led to the problem of

selectivity as well as dependency on the decisions of the powertionist governments of the world—especially of the United States, which compels other nations to follow its lead." "When we use the notion of selectivity regarding the accused, we adopt a particular form of powertionism that is not recommended by authentic criminal justice procedures and is condemned by all means." Farhad Malekian, *Powertionism in International Criminal Justice* (New York: Nova Science Publishers, 2022), p. 130 and 240; see aslo Cassese A., 'For an Enhanced Role of Jus cogens' in Cassese, A (ed.), *Realizing Utopia*, (2012); Cassese A., *International Criminal Law* (Oxford: Oxford University Press, 2nd, ed., 2008) ; Cassese A., (ed.), *The New Humanitarian Law of Armed Conflict* (Naples: Editoriale Scientifica, 1979) ; Cassese A., 'First Annual Report of the ICTY,' *Yearbook of International Law Commission*, (1994); Cassese A., On the Current Trends Towards Criminal Prosecution and Punishment of Breaches of International Humanitarian Law, 9 *European Journal of Internaitonal Law* 2 (1998); Cassese A., Albin Eser, Giorgio Gaja and Robert E. Conor, *Justice at Nuremberg* (1980).

Chapter 5

Barrel of the Prosecutor of International Criminal Court

1. Suing the Accused with Quiet Norms

The control of the moral barrel of international criminal justice is in the hands of the Security Council of the United Nations and other sub-organisations alone. As I have mentioned in other parts of this work, the entire system of international criminal courts is under the complete control of certain members of the Security Council, and has been since the establishment of the Court. The Court actually functions under the power of superior orders, which means that the most powerful states have complete control over the actions of the Court. This also indicates that the big powers, such as the UK, the USA, and France, can all exercise control over the choices made by the judges and the prosecutors of the ICC. Therefore, as I have indicated in another work, the Court has a vassal character and its external power is under the control of others.[125] However, this is not a fair description of the position of the Court since the internal decisions of the Court, particularly those concerning matters relating to the big powers, must be made in consultation with powertionist governments. This is despite the fact that the system of the International Criminal Court in The Hague claims to be an unbiased, impartial criminal jurisdiction. The issue lies in the fact that every system of laws has a significant number of additional doors, windows, and cracks.

We have already seen that the system of international criminal justice does not function, and when it does, it does so only under the orders of the controlling governments that played significant roles in its creation such as the British criminal colonial authorities with a mechanism of control over the community of nations. However, we can presume that a moral statement correctly matches reality, and the system of international criminal justice will function with a truthful moral barrel and not a barrel of colonial authorities. Moral reasoning in the system of the ICC refers to how the judges and the prosecutors of the Court ought to act morally. Included within this are the

---

[125] Farhad Malekian, *Utipolitianist International Criminal Justice* (New York: Nova Science Publishers, 2025).

requirements of truthful conscience in the identification, interpretation, and understanding of rules of law within the provisions of the Statute of the ICC. This indicates that the ICC does not act with one-eyed justice and does not ignore the system of international criminal responsibility, which is applicable to the criminal acts of individuals, groups, entities, and governments.

Nevertheless, regardless of how we define the theories of the system of the ICC, the fact is that the ICC has no power to enforce the concept of international criminal responsibility on certain states. This is due to several possibilities: a) A state and its government may not be parties to the provisions of the ICC, b) Locating and arresting the authority of a state may be impossible due to the military power of the state in question, c) A state may seriously threaten the prosecutor or judges of the Court, d) Promises may have been made to the prosecutor of the Court with the intention of corrupting the jurisdiction of the Court, e) A state party to the court may be allied with the criminals.[126] *This all indicates that while the barrel of justice may sound strong, in reality the prosecutor is suing the representatives of criminals while touching the barrel of the ICC. This in turn suggests that there is a failure to apply the relevant provisions.*

Promoting faith in justice must always be the chief goal of any jurisdiction. However, in the case of the jurisdiction of the international criminal court, there must be strong faith in the military power of the powertionist governments that clarifies the position of the ICC regarding the accountability of those who have violated the system of international criminal law. We cannot imagine how any political or military power can control the entire system of international criminal responsibility if we do not submit our understandings to the realities of the truth. Thus, we then suggest that the truth for the application of a fair system of international criminal jurisdiction requires authentic evidence. True evidence cannot be modified if the system of international criminal justice is prepared to accept the reality of the presented evidence. This is where the bar of political power must lose its position and the system of international criminal responsibility must be applied definitively.

---

[126] Examine the American representative John Bolton declaration against the ICC https://www.aljazeera.com/news/2018/09/full-text-john-bolton-speech-federalist-society-180910172828633.html (visited 18 September 2019); USA hotar Internationella brottmålsdomstolen med sanktioner - om krigsförbrytelser i Afghanistan utreds', available online at https://svenska.yle.fi/artikel/2019/03/15/usa-hotar-internationella-brottmals domstolen-med-sanktioner-om-krigsforbrytelser (visited 4, November 2019).

For example, there is no wise explanation for the Palestinian genocide and the violence in the West Bank and Gaza and the truth is reflected in the ongoing and historical murder of children, women, the elderly, and the vulnerable. This is how the basic philosophy of the system of international criminal justice must be interpreted in order to overcome the lies and hierarchy of the authoritarian powers of the international criminal court. We can certainly ask whether we must be acting as servants of power politics, or if we should follow what the imperative moral truth demands at all times.[127] We cannot always refer to the argument of promoting our interests when doing so harms human civilisation.

Strictly speaking, we should not affirm actions that are unfair and contradict the intentions of the rules and principles of international criminal justice that create the right to fight against injustices and protect the rights of the victims of war crimes, crimes against humanity, torture, sexual crimes, and genocide. Even those who discard a specific metaphysical form of international criminal responsibility can nonetheless face what moral responsibility would require for the states that position themselves as ambassadors of peace, justice, and humanity within the structure of international criminal justice. In such a position, moral justification in international criminal law may affect and influence the political philosophy of such individuals and guide them towards becoming responsible politicians. However, I am sure powertionist governments do not work with the moral philosophy of understanding the rights of victims but instead with the destruction of their rights. There is a knife in the heart of justice.

2. The Barrel of Arresting Criminals

The prosecutor of the ICC has actually initiated the procedures necessary for the arrest of criminals in the Gaza area, however he did so too late. Moreover, these efforts have remained unsuccessful and the Pre-Trial Chamber I of the ICC continues to remain quiet about this case. As a result, we are unable to make any sense of the case that has been submitted to the Court concerning the arrest of criminals. Interestingly, the case submitted by the prosecutor is very conservative and controversial because it does not use the word genocide, which is the most essential element of the crimes being committed by the

[127] Read *also* Farhad Malekian, *Imperative Philosophy of International Criminal Justice: Visible Power – Invisible Essence* (New York: Nova Science Publishers, 2022).

Israeli government against the Palestinian population. Regardless of what is being used to justify the moral and legal beliefs of the prosecutor of the ICC and his office, and whether or not those beliefs are the presentation of the entire truth and have not been manipulated by the political powers, we can prove the truth of what has been happening during the war in Gaza war thanks to all of the evidence and documentation of the war as well as the massacre of civilians with the weapons of the Western powers.

Perhaps the best explanation of this process of international criminal justice and the barrel of arresting the Israeli criminals lauded by the prosecutor is that it is a show being put on by the ICC rather than a confirmation of the crimes on the part of the ICC. This is because the prosecutor of the ICC is well aware of the fact that the Israeli criminals will never be arrested due the hidden power of the British and American governments, both of which were behind Karim Kahn's appointment as the official prosecutor of the ICC. Thus, there are certain motivations behind the issuance of the arrest warrant in this case and it seems to function more as a productive cargo of justice than an actual good. If the International Court of Justice and the International Criminal Court do not issue arrest warrants, then both courts would remain in their current state as decorative elements of justice.

The judges of both courts are clearly responsible for the commission of international crimes, particularly genocide, if they fail to issue arrest warrants for the dangerous criminals of our time. Should the arrest warrants not have been issued by the judges of the International Criminal Court, they ought to be held accountable under universal jurisdiction for infringing upon the principles of conscience and faith in justice through their involvement in acts of genocide. As this case has shown, there is no real justice in the corridors of the ICC. Moreover, it is a very unfortunate fact that after a year of genocide and waiting several months for an arrest warrant to be issued, the three judges of the ICC have done nothing, and it even appears that they are afraid of the consequences of the case and are only pretending to be good judges with the arrest warrant issued in their office.

Additionally, the request by Karim Khan demonstrates that he is just playing a game in the corridors of the International Criminal Court and his office. He is indubitably controlled by his British and American masters and guided by their dirty colonial criminal policies. This shows that the International Criminal Court and its judges and prosecutors are just following orders. Given this, how can we claim that the provisions of the system of international criminal justice are authentic?

A summary of the previous works of the ICC demonstrates that the court took more of an interest in crimes committed in Africa against the orders of the European masters and that the juridical legislation of the Court does not function when it comes to the aggressive terrorist criminals of Western powers, including Israel. Thus, speaking about the theory of the accountability of superior orders or leaders of governments is meaningless within the court. This is particularly evident as it concerns the theory of international criminal responsibility of states and their governments and its failure to function in practice. The powerful government has designed the existence and persuasions of self-consciousness to ruin the victims in an international civilised society.[128] We can see how the weapons industry is destroying the entire international society. In sum, a peculiar force of military strength nominates judges and prosecutors of the ICC and plays the evil barrel of justice without any trace of the norm of justice.

3. Miscarriage of Applicable Justice

None of the judges of the ICJ or ICC have sought to explain why international justice, and particularly international criminal justice, is wrong and lacks the power of the essence of the substantial values of the rules of law and practical values. We form the assumption that the peculiar military forces of the powerful governments force moral conviction to modify its intentions, and in the end, the victims are forced to suffer in their struggle for the consolidation of their own abolished rights and preventing terrorist governments from taking their country and properties. It is apparent that the hypothesis that powertionist governments employ protective measures to defend and shield the victims is indeed incorrect. As a result, no one is safe from the aggressive criminal acts of the big powers that are even influenced by the judges and prosecutors of international criminal courts. As a result, my arguments concerning the enforcement of the concept of international criminal responsibility fall flat.

---

[128] Farhad Malekian, *Classical Morality in International Peremptory Criminal Law* (Newcastle upon Tyne: Cambridge Scholars Publishing, 2018, republished 2021); Martti Koskenniem, *The Politics of International Law* (Hart, 2011); Martti Koskenniemi, *The Gentle Civilizer of Nations: the Rise and Fall of International Law*, 1870-1960 (Cambridge University Press 2002); Farhad Malekian, *Paralysing International Criminal Justice* (New York: Nova Science Publishers, 2021), p. 214; Farhad Malekian, *Gravity of Wisdom in International Criminal Law* (New York: Nova Science Publishers, 2021).

The fact is that the system of international criminal justice is being bribed, blackmailed, and threatened by the big powers. Moreover, the judges of the International Criminal Court should leave their positions if they are not strong enough to fight for moral and legal justice, moral truth and legal truth, as well as the entire system of international criminal responsibility. They should resign and allow those who are strong enough to take big decisions against the big criminals to take their place. However, all judges are afraid of the intelligence agencies working for the big powers and of being murdered at their hands. *I should conclude that the propaganda of the powerful governments concerning international human rights does not help us form true moral beliefs. Nothing suggests that military force, economic force, or political force in any way correspond to the moral truth, nor are they comparable to it or evidence thereof. If this were the case, then we would be making the wrong judgements and going in the wrong direction. Only by thinking correctly and being aware of what is right and wrong will we be able to speak about moral issues and moral truth.*

The system of international criminal justice and its principles can only work if we promote a form of international criminal justice that is free from political ties and in which criminals have no power as a result of military and/or political force. Obviously, I realise that it is very difficult and practically impossible to establish such a system, and the fact remains that the serious problems are always in the corridors of international criminal justice. This means that it is difficult to find true justice, and justice will always be affected by the strong interfering in legal, economic, and moral conflicts.

However, the lawyers of the big political powers and those who love money think the opposite of me and express that the system of the enforcement of the ICC is not only just, but also equal. Therefore, we are forced to look for something distinctive about the notions of the moral truth and legal truth that are tainted by the evil notions of immorality and illegality from the outset. Therefore, when we ponder substantive moral issues with the full intention of monopolising the system of international criminal justice, the correct and authentic issues of moral philosophy no longer function and are seriously violated by our policies of monopolisation.[129]

[129] Consult Farhad Malekian, *The Monopolization of International Criminal Law in the United Nations, A Jurisprudential Approach* (Stockholm: Almqvist Wiksell International, 1st ed., 1993, 2nd ed., 1995).

4. Trailing the ICC's Necessary Requirements

The framework of the system of international criminal justice gives the impression that it is excellent and firmly intends to bring criminals under prosecution and punish them for the violations of the most serious norms of international criminal justice. The Statute of the International Criminal Court creates the illusion that its provisions are really true and will be implemented. However, once we find ourselves back where we started with our examination of the Court's basic provisions and its legal authority, we are confronted with the harsh realisation that the decorative provisions of the statute not only fail to respect the principle of equality, but they also promote a colonial version of inequality among the various subjects of international law.

It is clear that the provisions of the statute have been formulated to only prosecute and punish those in inferior positions who lack the ability to produce weapons. We thus have to suppose that if the system of international criminal justice is violated (as it continually is) by former colonialist powers, then the ICC can prosecute the weaker or the victims again and bring the new form of colonialism jurisdiction into reality. As a result, victims face prosecution and punishment. My question is obviously irrelevant to those who truly understand that the system of international criminal justice is powerless.

It is very surprising to witness how British lawyers and judges are continually selected to work in these international courts or tribunals and serious punishments against others while their masters or government are themselves killing millions without consequence at the same time. Despite this, their lawyers are chosen to prosecute and punish the individuals of other states that have been subjected to their ongoing slave trade. The extent to which the philosophy of international criminal justice works is indeed a very serious question. Through which medium the functions of the conscience of such British lawyers works is one of the main questions in the barrel of justice. Another significant question is how the moral barrel of justice can or the conscience of British lawyers, such as Niece or Geoffrey Robertson, be silent about the crimes of Winston Churchill, Franklin D. Roosevelt, Margaret Thatcher, Tony Blair, George Bush, Barack Obama, Joe Biden, and many others?

Writing influential books about crimes against humanity or judging such cases is pointless if our actions do not align with our words and we only target certain criminals. This is the most dangerous policy concerning the development of impunity and the destruction of the basic principles of international criminal justice as a whole. A lawyer cannot work with full moral, legal, or even conscious truth if they know that their masters are violating the main intentions of the system of international criminal justice. Do we only judge with one-eyed justice? This may not matter to certain American, British or Iranian\Canadian lawyers who work, decide, interpret, and demand the reasoning of their leading masters.

If the American lawyer Michael P. Scharf cannot see that the American government has not been subjected to the processes of justice, prosecution, and punishment despite having committed serious international crimes, how can such a lawyer work for the same government concerning the punishment of Saddam Hussein? The aforementioned individual mentioned worked with the CIA for different reasons. My questions may, however, be seen as irrelevant since the most significant thing for international criminal lawyers is to speak about the provisions and principles of international criminal law and how they are applied in The Hague. *The question then is, what is the true quality of our conscience and the basic structure of our faith in the moral and legal truth?*[130] What is the primary objective of studying law?

It is obvious that the statute of the International Criminal Court has been monopolised along with all relevant legislation that deals with criminal justice and criminal responsibility.[131] An international court cannot be authentic when its jurisdiction only applies to certain nations. *More importantly, how can the Court uphold the principles of international criminal justice when the big powers are not parties to the Court and yet control what the Court does? This is the comical situation that the systems of international criminal justice and international criminal responsibility are facing. In other words, the most dangerous, terroristic governments and states are the ones who are manufacturing the weapons and have nuclear power are the masters of the law and determine when and where the Court should act. This is really an ironic situation that the system of international criminal courts is facing and reflects the existence of one-eyed justice. Therefore, instead of dealing with a true notion of criminal responsibility, we are left with criminal irresponsibility.*

---

[130] Read the wise discussion of Spooner Lysander, *Natural Law; or the Science of Justice: A Treatise on Natural Law, Natural Justice, Natural Rights, Natural Liberty, and Natural Society; showing that all Legislation whatsoever is an Absurdity, a Usurpation, and a Crime.* Part First. [1882], available at http://oll.libertyfund.org/titles/spooner-natural-law-or-the-science-of-justice-1882 (Accessed 2023).

[131] Abtahi Hirad and Gideon Boas (eds.), *The Dynamics of International Criminal Justice - Essays in Honour of Sir Richard May* (2005); examine also Brian Barry, 'Justice as Reciprocity' in Eugene Kamenka and Alice Erh-Soon Tay (eds.), *Justice* (1979).

5. Intentional Complications of Just Words

In order to know which of the beliefs and principles of the system of international criminal justice are authentic, we do not need to study its provisions and analyse it to determine who has provided an accurate interpretation of the system of international criminal justice. I hope it is now clear that we need not be clear and eloquent in our philosophy of justice and the words and complications that judges, lawyers, or prosecutors of the Court express and deliver. This is neither relevant nor important. It is actually a necessary requirement in the system of international criminal justice to speak convolutedly with complicated phrases, terms, and idioms that create the impression that we deeply understand the body of international criminal justice and are of clear mind.

Such interpretations exist to mislead witnesses, the accused, and the victims. However, if genocide is being committed by the Zionist government, it is genocide; if genocide is committed by the American governments, it is genocide; and if British governments have killed millions, then international criminal justice has been violated and there is no need for further interpretation of the matter nor for making confusing conclusions. Simply put, one cannot massacre a nation with the intention of wiping them out or annihilating them—this is plain genocide, no further proof required. *The Holocaust or genocide against the Jews during the Second World War did not even require the establishment of an international criminal tribunal since the crimes committed against the innocent Jews were so obvious and destructive that they could even be seen by the dogs and cats in the streets of Germany. The crimes against the Palestinians and Lebanese can be seen by all as well.*

Theoretically, it is normally a misperception of what can count as an argument for the basic understanding of the truth of a moral conviction. This means that we cannot work with the judgements and conclusions of British, American, or French lawyers who have been selected to protect and defend the interests of their superiors by condemning others while saying nothing about the actions of their own masters. It is certainly improper that such lawyers express that they are working for justice just based on their position. The argument against those lawyers is not their knowledge, but very simply their conscience. We may be left with improper interpretations of the system of international criminal justice that led to individuals, groups, governments, entities, and states not facing international criminal responsibility.

When we search for justice, and particularly the legal and moral truth, we do not search and yearn for lies. Rather, we want to reveal the truth and witness true conscience. However, the system of international criminal justice has taken to prioritising the arguments of those who are not parties to the International Criminal Court but rather those who have the gavel of justice under their control. How can the system of international criminal justice be true, and how does the prosecutor of the ICC, Karim Khan, not feel shame about his position? How can the position of prosecutors, judges, or even defence lawyers be correct when the prosecutor already knows that the moral barrel of justice had a secret hand in their appointment? Does the prosecutor have a clear conscience?

The arrest warrant for Russian President Vladimir Putin was immediately publicised. Pre-Trial Chamber I tried to make it known to the public that they might contribute to the prevention of further commission of crimes while the alleged atrocities were still being committed. However, in reality, all this criminal conduct was instigated, supported, aided, and assisted in the proxy war between Ukraine and Russia by the American, British, French, Canadian, and German governments, among others. Karim Khan feels that the population of the world is blind and unwise, however he should realise that the opposite is true. Thus, all those who speak about justice and its significant function in establishing the rights of victims should be aware that the essence of justice is not blind. Instead, the essence is the moral truth of people.

Some legal thinkers and academics believe, and continue to trust, that the system of international criminal justice presents the positivist aspects of the system of international law, and therefore its rules cannot be monopolised.[132] This line of thinking can be found in the opinions of Scandinavian writers, who typically do not argue about the moral aspects of the law. Specifically, Swedish lawyers are generally positivists, and although they work with some aspects of human rights, they cannot recognise that the systems of international criminal justice and human rights law have been monopolised by the big, powerful nations. However, for these writers, positive international law means helping enforce the will of governments that are opposed to the Russian government, such as those of the United States, Britain, and France. All three are representations of actual terrorist states. The unfortunate fact is that most of these lawyers are strong supporters of NATO, and therefore, they cannot see that the system of international criminal justice has been monopolised.[133] In other words, they fully trust the work of the ICC and its

[132] Consult Farhad Malekian, *The Monopolization of International Criminal Law in the United Nations, A Jurisprudential Approach* (Stockholm: Almqvist Wiksell International, 1st ed., 1993, 2nd ed., 1995).

[133] *Id.*

impartiality, even though the ICC only functions when it comes to certain states and governments. This should be clear to every writer in the world, but unfortunately this is not the case in Scandinavia. Like politicians, most Swedish lawyers have a great deal of respect for American policies and follow their government's lead.[134]

We could take their actions and decisions to mean that they have perceived the truth of the criminal conduct of the powertionist governments to some degree. However, since their governments and they themselves depend on the support of the United States, they remain silent and do not express any opinion about their actions. With this silent and positivist policy, they also follow in the footsteps of the International Criminal Court and fully respect its decisions. For example, the Swedish academics reached a consensus about the arrest warrant of Russian President Putin. The Trial Chamber of the International Criminal Court confirmed the statements of the prosecutor of the ICC in a timely fashion, and the Chambers' statement was immediately published.

6. Barrel of Justice in Pre-Trial Chamber I

On 17 March 2023, Pre-Trial Chamber I of the International Criminal Court issued arrest warrants for Vladimir Vladimirovich Putin and Maria Alekseyevna Lvova-Belova. The ICC believed that Vladimir Putin "is allegedly responsible for the war crime of unlawful deportation of population

[134] The most significant and egregious aspect of apartheid was endorsed by certain Swedish legal practitioners who professed to champion human rights, notably Professor Jacob Sundberg. Additionally, the Norwegian-Swedish academic Atle Grahal Madson, while discussing refugee and asylum legislation, occasionally collaborated with military operations associated with the Pentagon in the United States. His adherents and subsequent followers ascended to positions as professors specializing in human rights, refugees, or asylum law at the Wallenberg Institute of Human Rights. Researchers who emulated their path without engaging in critical debate were able to attain their degrees. The institute was supported by the government of Zionism, which has been implicated in criminal apartheid practices in South Africa. Sundberg's sister publicly opposed her brother and asserted that he was no longer a member of their family. Nevertheless, decades later, the Swedish Advocates Organization—comprising acquaintances of Sundberg and even his father, who was also an academic during that period—sanitised crimes committed against the South African populace by bestowing commendations for human rights upon him and his sisters after extensive negotiations with his sister to secure her favourable approval. This exemplifies how Swedish lawyers facilitate support for human rights, international criminal law, and international criminal justice. The phrase "the Swedish barrel sounds like tooto toto" serves as a cautionary signal.

(children) and that of unlawful transfer of population (children) from occupied areas of Ukraine to the Russian Federation (under articles 8(2)(a)(vii) and 8(2)(b)(viii) of the Rome Statute)." The Court further added:

> There are reasonable grounds to believe that Mr. Putin bears individual criminal responsibility for the aforementioned crimes, (i) for having committed the acts directly, jointly with others and/or through others (article 25(3)(a) of the Rome Statute), and (ii) for his failure to exercise control properly over civilian and military subordinates who committed the acts, or allowed for their commission, and who were under his effective authority and control, pursuant to superior responsibility (article 28(b) of the Rome Statute).

The Pre-Trial Chamber I of the International Criminal Court (ICC) also issued a statement clarifying that Ms. Maria Alekseyevna Lvova-Belova, Commissioner for Children's Rights in the Office of the President of the Russian Federation, is responsible for the same crimes and that "there are reasonable grounds to believe that Ms. Lvova-Belova bears individual criminal responsibility for the aforementioned crimes for having committed the acts directly, jointly with others, and/or through others (Article 25(3)(a) of the Rome Statute)."

As we can see, the moral barrel of justice is very noisy when it comes to the crimes that are being committed during the US's proxy war between Ukraine and Russia. Any claim that the war is not a proxy war that is being waged deliberately by the United States government is illegitimate. The reality regarding the motives of governments that conceal the true nature and impact of their deadly weapons due to punitive or delusional decisions has certainly been concealed. However, since the proxy war is being supported by the powertionist governments, they immediately reacted to the ICC and Trial Chamber I. The fact is, all of the ICC judges are aware that they cannot and should not go against the United States government or its allies under any circumstance. If they believe this conclusion is wrong, then they are rejecting their own existence. This is particularly evident in the case of the Israeli Zionist government, which is the political partner of the American government, and thus any actions taken against Israel are seen as affronts to the US government.

Evidently, the moral *barrel* of international criminal justice was silenced by various American politicians. In fact, a considerable number of politicians in the US government openly threatened the judges of the ICC if they took any further decisions against the Israeli criminal government.[135] The question is how can the Pre-Trial Chamber I of the ICC take action against Russian politicians while deliberately prolonging its decision regarding Israeli politicians? What is really behind all these questions of international criminal justice and international human rights that disappear when it comes to the criminal, aggressive, and brutal acts of the powertionist governments? Obviously, the ethical and moral issues are dead as it concerns the rights of victims and the genocide being committed against them. If the system of international criminal responsibility was respected by the Court and state parties this would not be the case. I must insist that we cannot form a reliable belief about any judgement of the International Criminal Court if its judgements are informed by one eye-justice.

Moreover, this is a purely logical truth that should be accepted by the Court and its judges, and since it is not, the Court works selectively, and it officially and legally establishes discrimination between the subjects of the Court.[136] Unless the invisible force and political powers behind the system of international criminal justice are modified, the Court judgements should be viewed as theoretically and philosophically invalid. This is because we are unable to bring certain criminals under the jurisdiction of the Court due to their military backing. *If the justice of the Court and its principles are applicable due to the strength of guns, then we have not established an equal international criminal court but rather a court that makes judgements based on the power of weapons. The situation is thus very simple: the victims of international crimes such as genocide face a paradox in the system of international criminal responsibility. And if this is true, then we have no capacity to deal with morally true and legally true, and are instead left with gun-true and powertionist-true. My statement is obviously ironic and painful for those who sit on their knees in the ICC to save their positions and wallets as well as for those who prefer imprisonment but do not give up the truth, even though the moral barrel of justice is always used against them.*

---

[135] Situation in the State of Palestine: ICC Pre-Trial Chamber I reject the State of Israel's challenges to jurisdiction and issues warrants of arrest for Benjamin Netanyahu and Yoav Gallant, https://www.icc-cpi.int/news/situation-state-palestine-icc-pre-trial-chamber-i-rejects-state-israels-challenges.

[136] Examine Farhad Malekian, 'Emasculating the Philosophy of International Criminal Justice in the Iraqi Special Tribunal,' *Cornell International Law Journal*, 58/5 (2005), pp.675-725; Robert Cryer, *Prosecuting International Crimes, Selectivity and the International Criminal Law Regime* (Cambridge University Press, Cambridge, 2005).

7. Incapacity of Pre-Trial Chamber I

The fact is that the system of international criminal justice was codified to re-establish rights—not to cause causalities. This is the first principle of the system of international criminal justice. However, a considerable number of writers may distrust the various arguments in the book and believe that the system of international criminal justice is objective. Among such individuals are the majority of Swedish authors who have received their positions based on their connections with who rides who. That is why the most well-known Swedish lawyer clearly stated that "the Swedish lawyer functions, in the first instance, on friendship or family relations." This is not an unusual statement. Therefore, we believe, and it has been proven, that the system of the International Criminal Court functions based on personal and governmental connections and alliances. This demonstrates how the theory of international criminal responsibility for states and their governments operates in national or international courts.

It seems too quick a refutation of what a considerable number of lawyers believe and do. However, none of the arguments presented here seek to isolate facts from their sources. The reality must be acknowledged, even if it is painful for certain parties. All statements about the truth of moral judgements must be made, even if they are not believed. The fact is that the judgements of the Court have been selective since its establishment and have changed depending on how the powertionist governments of the world have supported a given case. As a result, many cases have been rejected due to powerful states being involved in the commission of international crimes, such as genocide, crimes against humanity, war crimes, and aggression.[137]

Expressing the contrary would be nonsensical. The selection of the cases by the court or its prosecutor's office creates serious doubt about its judgements, which in turn causes us to lose faith in the case and the court's judgement. Similarly, it is not a question of the cases that have been judged by the Court, but the very notion of selectivity that paralyses the Court when it comes to the very serious crimes that have been committed by strong governments without consequence. There are many good and necessary reasons to protect the judgements of the ICC. However, the question then is what we count as a sufficient reason to trust the judgements that have been

[137] Also see Hans Blix, *Sovereignty, Aggression and Neutrality* (1970); M. Gillett, 'The Anatomy of an International Crime: Aggression at the International Criminal Court', 3 *International Criminal Law Review* (2013) 829–864; N. Weisbord, 'Conceptualizing Aggression', 20 *Duke Journal of Comparative & International Law* (2009) 1–68.

delivered by the ICC because terrorist governments such as the American and British allowed them to be delivered. This affirms that the crimes of the terrorist governments are ignored, and only the passage of time slowly and gradually cleans up the horrendous crimes that have been committed by those greedy for oil.[138]

The situation above is reflected in the delay of Pre-Trial Chamber I concerning the savage genocide being committed by the Israeli government against the Palestinian population in Gaza and the West Bank.[139] It took over half a year for the Pre-Trial Chamber I to issue warrants of arrest for Israeli criminals. The amount of physical evidence that exists in this case is so overwhelming that a trial is not even necessary. The orchestrators of this genocide should thus be punished along with those that supported their crimes, including criminals from the United States, the United Kingdom, Australia, Germany, Canada, France, and even Sweden. All these states have not only violated the body of international criminal conventions, but also the very essence of international customary law, which should be respected by all governments and states in the world. There is so much evidence concerning the criminality of certain leaders of those countries it feels unnecessary to discuss here.

8. Criminal Rules without the Power of Enforcement

There are numerous provisions in the system of international criminal justice that call for the international criminal responsibility of its subject, with the sole intention of holding those who have violated these provisions and committed

[138] Examine the facts in the article written by Robert F. Kennedy, Why the Arabs don't want us in Syria: They don't hate 'our freedoms.' They hate that we've betrayed our ideals in their own countries — for oil (2016). Available online at website https://www.politico.eu/article/why-the-arabs-dont-want-us-in-syria-mideast-conflict-oil-intervention/; See also Robert Roth, 'What's Really Happening in Syria: Who Started the War, Who Can You Trust to Tell the Truth?', available online at https://www.globalresearch.ca/whats-really-happening-in-syria-who-started-the-war-who-can-you-trust-to-tell-the-truth/5570297; James W Carden, How Libyan 'Regime Change' Lies Echo in Syria. Available online at https://consortiumnews.com/2016/09/25/how-libyan-regime-change-lies-echo-in-syria/.

[139] See also the corrupted dissenting opinion of Judge Péter Kovács from Hungary in Pre-Trial Chamber I (2021). The judge follows the American, Israeli, British, and Hungarian footsteps in the way in which he satisfies his legal and political masters. ICC Pre-Trial Chamber I issued its decision on the Prosecutor's request related to territorial jurisdiction over Palestine, https://www.icc-cpi.int/news/icc-pre-trial-chamber-i-issues-its-decision-prosecutors-request-related-territorial.

international crimes accountable. The framework of such a responsibility is consequently conclusive. This is not a question of the possibility of coincidence; rather, the notion of international criminal responsibility is an established element of international criminal justice that should never be denied—neither by the Court nor by the subjects of the Court. The notion of international criminal responsibility is imperative, and thus the Court is obliged to protect and apply it. Of course, the Court has really only enforced the international criminal responsibility of individuals from Africa and not that of other governments, states, or big criminals.

How conscientious prosecutors or judges of the International Criminal Court react to serious violations has been exclusively restricted to the criminal responsibility of individuals or superiors alone. The current situation concerning the alleged criminal actions of the Israeli government, as reported to the Office of the Prosecutor of the International Criminal Court (ICC), and the subsequent delays experienced for several months within Pre-Trial Chamber I of the Court, serve as a significant illustration of one of the most reprehensible instances of criminal behaviour committed by individuals, organizations, governments, and states, all under the influence of American administrations. Despite this, the case was unfortunately been ignored by the Court for prolong period of time. The concept of criminal responsibility has not only not been enforced, it has been completed hindered concerning individual criminal responsibility. The Court has not initiated any case against criminal individuals, organisations, governments, or states that have been committing crimes in Gaza. This means that we have not only surrounded ourselves with criminals in an important case concerning the concept of international criminal responsibility of governments and states, but we have also prevented the initiation of any criminal proceedings against the superiors of the Israeli government or those of the states that have been supplying deadly weapons to the Israeli criminal government.

Even if the superiors of the Israeli government are ever brought under the jurisdiction of the ICC, only individuals may be held criminally responsible and not the governments involved. Moreover, the fact is that such a court will never be established as long as the United States government continues to commit crimes behind both open and closed doors in the Security Council. As a result, the savagery of the Israeli-American government will never be punished or investigated in court because of the power of guns and the power of NATO in the United Nations. The same can be said about the savagery of the British, German, and other governments. This is not really a case of discrimination in choosing who should punish or who should not punish.

Rather, it is a question of the power of the strong dictatorship and paternalistic order of the authoritarian governments that have the driving role of the norms under position. This indicates that the enforcement of the concept of international criminal responsibility is essentially paralysed.

A careful examination of the ongoing atrocities against the Palestinians and their traditional sovereignty is clear evidence of the fact that taking the contrary view to that of the powertionist government is not welcomed. Moreover, the International Criminal Court in The Hague is both unable to prevent crimes such as the deaths of over 25,000 children as well as to condemn the terrorist governments. It therefore ignores the notion of international criminal responsibility and gives greater value to the lives of all judges of the ICC, its prosecutor, and those who are supposed to assist him. Unfortunately, there are no longer any general convictions in the system of international criminal courts because of the crimes that have been ignored by the Court. However, it is true that there has never been respect for the judgements of the International Criminal Court because of the selectivity of the cases brought under its jurisdiction. This means that many Western criminal leaders have not only been applauded at home, but they have also received Nobel Prizes or awards from the British Queen. This is how the system of international criminal responsibility of individuals, superior orders, and heads of states, organisations, groups, military personnel, governments, and their states is interpreted under the system of international criminal courts.[140]

The enforcement of the provisions of national and international jurisdictions is the most significant part of the problems facing criminal justice. If there is not enough support for the enforcement of the provisions of the statue of the ICC, there is then no criminal court aside from the provisions of a statue of lady justice. By examining the specificity and significance of international issues, we will see how greed drives powertionist governments to discriminate against and condemn the victims while saving their own individuals from facing their criminal responsibility. The greed of powertionists engages us in these complex interpretations of international criminal justice in order to present another reflection, expecting to find its own interests and most recognised targets of political, military, and economic gains. Consequently, the very solid judgement about affirmative achievement in moral and legal truth and their omission, leaves victims in a state of moral

[140] Examine Prince Williams, Barack Obama Is A War Criminal [September 29, 2021]. Visit https://harvardpolitics.com/obama-war-criminal/.

disagreement. As a result, justice loses its harmony with the evil sounds of the barrel of powertionist governments.

9. Barrel of Impure Justice

What do we really wish to see from the office of the Prosecutor and in the reactions of the judges of the International Criminal Court in The Hague? Surely, we expect that the system of international criminal responsibility that was originally created by Vespasian Pella, Garcia Amador, and Roberto Ago be empowered and applied to the active criminals in Western governments who have caused the deaths of millions of innocent victims globally, including in Gaza and the West Bank. The situation of the Palestinians has had a devastating impact on the lives of the original sovereign people of the land. This sovereignty was taken from the nation of Palestine by Israeli forces using British and American weapons during the Nakba. However, the system of international criminal responsibility created by the aforementioned individuals and affirmed by the International Law Commission has received no particular attention in the decisions of the prosecutor nor in the actions of the Pre-Trial Chamber I of the Court.

Obviously, the International Criminal Court has involved itself in the commission of crimes, and this can be seen in the silencing of the barrel of Pre-Trial Chamber I. Since the arrest warrants of professional criminals have been issued, we are still facing very serious corruption in the system of international criminal justice courts, which claims to be the most powerful, authentic, and independent Court. This situation reminds me of the system of international criminal justice that was written about in in the book *Masters of War: Latin America and U.S. Aggression, from the Cuban Revolution through the Clinton Years*. Even if the Court were to issue an arrest warrant today, it would be too late. The Court is responsible for the deaths of innocent people. Due to delays in their decisions, the judges have undoubtedly been complicit in the genocide of the Palestinian people.

The fact that the barrel of the international criminal court is contributing to corruption is not new. This was also seen with the case of the prosecutor from Argentina, namely Luis Moreno Ocampo, where he spurned justice and got too close to American political diplomacy. He believed that "[his] salary wasn't enough during my time in office [at the ICC]." The chief prosecutor was paid 150,000 euros a year, tax-free between 2003 and 2012.[141] Corruption is unfortunately one of the most serious illnesses plaguing the majority of criminal or civil jurisdictions globally. Zionist movements have the economy of the world under their control, and thus criminal conduct occurs. The same applies to other groups as well. That is why the big criminals are released and pardoned behind the closed doors of many national and international courts in many cases. This has also been seen with the present regime of Iran, where the big criminals have been released and pardoned in order to keep the stolen gold and money in their private accounts in foreign countries.[142]

It is therefore not be surprising to see how the system of international criminal justice is being ignored in the rooms of the Pre-Trial Chamber I of the Court. The theory of given conscience and faith is simply a game that has occupied the basic task of the Court with expressing that it is respected and executed with good will and good faith. Thus, speaking about the duties and tasks of the Assembly of State Parties is not only controversial, but also meaningless since many of the parties are close allies of the big criminals of the world. In addition, the British government is a member of the criminal organisation NATO, which directs and leads almost all governmental crimes. The relevant organisation has no reason to think that it is correct in its decisions. Such a right embraces the whole system of international criminal justice and generates controversy concerning the position of the system of international criminal justice and the Court in general.

Thus, not only is the moral truth necessary in the evaluation of the system of international criminal justice, it is also fundamental for underscoring the fact that international criminal justice should not be sold by prosecutor or judges. On the contrary, the entire system of international criminal justice must not only be protected against bribery and corruption, it must also be given the chance to keep the framework of justice unharmed and therefore stable. We should always doubt the ability of the judges or the prosecutors of the Court to maintain the standards of their given conscience and not violate the system of the true presentation of truths. The body of international criminal responsibility cannot function when guided by dishonoured hands and corrupted minds. The theory of judgement of the International Criminal Court in The Hague is not the affirmation of the wills of the criminals but the contrary. If this cannot be achieved through the judges passing appropriate

---

[141] https://www.legal-tools.org/doc/56cfa8/pdf/.

[142] At the same time, we should not forget the fact that the Iranian government genuinely supports the rights of the oppressed population of Palestine.

judgements with faithful and clean minds, then we are not only working with a vassal Court of Justice, but with an organisation that is much more dangerous than criminals. The faith of people across the globe is compromised by the piracy of justice, which is based on common knowledge and politicians know it.

It would therefore not be incorrect to conclude that the contemporary system of international criminal justice has the nature and character of the international crime of piracy, with the difference that piracy normally occurs at sea. This form of piracy instead occurs in the corridors of the International Criminal Court in The Hague. The pirates of international criminal justice continue to believe that they are just and have the system of good justice under control, all while they are actual pirates and fail to protest the ongoing serious, brutal international crimes being conducted and guarded by the criminal governments of the world. *That is why, when Alexander the Great captured a famous pirate, he asked him, why are you committing piracy? The pirate responded, why do you use your power against civilisations? I am the King. What is the difference? You are a pirate on land, and I am a pirate at sea. I am a robber king at sea, and you are a robber king on land. The business is the same for both of us. The question then arises: what is the difference between those who commit atrocities against the Palestinian population and those at the International Criminal Court or faculties of law who remain silent? Their resounding silence reflects their lack of conscience.*[143]

[143] For analysis of the history of international criminal court examine Vespasian V. Pella, *Plan d'un Code Répressif Mondial,* 6 *Rewe International de Droit Pénal* 1948 (1955); United Nations War Crimes Commission, History of the United Nations War Commission and the Development of the Laws of War. 445-450 (1949); Vespasian V. Pella, Towards an International Criminal Court, 44 *American Journal of International Law* 57 (1950); Sowilet A, *The Problem of the Creation of a Permanent International Criminal Court* (Nendeln, Liechtenstein : Kraus reprint, 1951); Yeun-Li Liang, 'The Establishment of an International Criminal Jurisdiction: The First Phase,' 46 *American Journal of International Law* (1952); Quincy Wright, Proposal for an International Criminal Court, 46 *American Journal of International Law* 60 (1952); Bienvenido C. Ambion, '*Organization of a Court of International Criminal Jurisdiction,'* 29 *Philippine Law Journa*l 545 (1954); Fannie Klein & Daniel Wilkes, 'United Nations Draft Statute for an International Criminal Court: An American Evaluation,' in *International Criminal Law* 526 (Gerhard O. W. Mueller & Edward M. Wise, eds, 1965); Stone Julius and Robert Woetzel, *Toward a Feasible International Criminal Court* (1970). William A. Schabas, The International Criminal Court: A Commentary on the Rome Statute (Oxford University Press, 2016); Farhad Malekian, *Jurisprudence of International Criminal Justice* (Introduction by Professor Benjamin B. Ferencz, the former Prosecutor of the Nuremberg Tribunal (Cambridge: Cambridge Scholars Publishing, 2014); Carsten Stahn, *The Law and Practice of the International Criminal Court* (Oxford University Press, 2015).

Chapter 6

Criminal Responsibility Pursuant to the Barrel of the ICC

1. Position of Criminal Norms against Victims

The truth is that the systems of international criminal justice and international human rights law, the constitutions of international criminal courts/tribunals, and the theory of international humanitarian law of armed conflicts represent various knives in the barrels of justice, and it is rare to achieve a form of criminal justice that can help to establish the rights of the victims.[144] The location and position of these barrels are similar to a Japanese bag during the application of capital punishment against the accused and condemned. The bag contained numerous knives that concerned the execution of the criminal and dealt with different bodily organs of the criminal. The relatives of the accused eventually try to bribe the executioner, the hangman, headsman, or provost to take out the heart knife such that the accused would suffer less. However, the barrel or the bag of the International Criminal Court in The Hague is used contrary to its legal functions by the prosecutors and judges of the Court. Therefore, there will be more victims until the Zionist government and its allies accomplish their goals. The victims will suffer more until they are forced out of their properties, homes, lands, and historical ancient sovereignty.

The question is if the judges or the prosecutor of the ICC who witness the atrocities in Palestine and fail to take action have any reason to think they are irresponsible for not fulfilling their international moral and legal duties? They have intentionally abstained from their legal and personal duties and abandoned the criminal bag of the ICC containing norms against criminals and

---

[144] Examine Antonio Cassese, (ed.), *The New Humanitarian Law of Armed Conflict* (Naples: Editoriale Scientifica, 1979); Karima Bennoune, 'As-Salamu 'Alykum? Humanitarian Law in Islamic Jurisprudence,' 15 *Michigan Journal of International Law*, (1994), pp. 605-643; Kesolofetse Lefenya, 'Use of Explosive Weapons in Densely Populated Areas: Implications for International Humanitarian Law,' *African Yearbook on International Humanitarian Law* (2014), pp. 68–86; Thomas G. Weiss, *Military-Civilian Interactions: Humanitarian Crises and the Responsibility to Protect* (2nd ed., Rowman & Littlefield Publishers Inc, Lanham (MD), 2005).

norms against the victims. This is how the system of international criminal justice is currently working against the victims—by ignoring the international criminal responsibility of individuals, groups, organisations, governments, and states. In this context, any abstentions translate to one less vote against the crimes of the Israeli Zionist government and thus permit them to continue to carry out brutal injustices and promote unwise and criminal policies.

In general, nothing permits abstention in the International Criminal Court except for the private interests of the judges or prosecutors of the Court behind closed doors. We are referring here to political exchanges between those who claim to represent international justice and those who are the masters of wars, conspiracies, and committing genocide against the sovereignty of the victims of international crimes. A dissenting opinion in a judgement also serves a similar function to abstention or veto in the case of Palestine, as we saw with the decision of a Hungarian judge in 2021.[145] A dissenting opinion by a judge normally expresses disagreement with the majority opinion of the Court, or in our case, the Trial Chamber of the International Criminal Court.

There is no principle to describe how right the judges or the prosecutor of the ICC are. The reason is simply that they are exercising their own basic personal understanding of a case, even though they are working directly with the evidence. Hundred years-worth of crimes against Palestinians and the occupation of their sovereignty by the guns of the powertionist governments were not enough for Hungarian Judge Péter Kovács to recognise the commission of crimes by the Zionist Israeli government. Thus, the international crimes being committed somehow do not involve judges or prosecutors since they have their own interpretations that are protected by those who gave them their positions in the Court. *Overall, this is a Court that functions based on a one-eyed justice. We mean that whatever our understanding is and however I speak—whether its right or wrong—it makes no sense, since no plausible theory can convince the big criminals of the truth due to their legal and political beliefs. In other words, the moral truth does not function and has no effective influence when the prosecutor or a judge of the court has already decided to turn a blind eye to the extreme suffering of children.*

That is why I have insisted throughout this short work that justice under the Statute of the International Criminal Court is like a moral barrel that sounds great, but the norms in the barrel have no legal effect as long as the

[145] Examine the footnote. Concerning the views of Judge Péter Kovács, who has been without any hesitation supported the Israeli Zionist government.

Court remains monopolised by powertionist governments.[146] *The barrel is full of rusty norms of justice that do not function.* The question is therefore, on what grounds the judges of the Pre-Trial Chamber believe that the reasons for judgements of the International Court of Justice in The Hague and the statements of so many lawyers of different parties against the powertionist politics are incorrect. Obviously, their opinions cannot be less trustworthy than those who protect the criminal policies of big criminals in some way. The difference is that the documentation of the history of criminal activities of powertionist governments has proven futile, and these governments follow the politics of guns while the victims are struggling for the establishment of their banished rights imposed by the British, American, and Israeli criminals.

This indicates that we should not be afraid to say that the system of international criminal responsibility within the structure of the system of international criminal justice has been completely controlled and ignored by the prosecutor of the ICC who has in turn failed to take timely action. He understands that the Pre-Trial Chambers' decisions are only symbolic. *This proves that all these responsible individuals who claim to be the prosecutors, judges, or those who serve as the ICC Prosecutor's Special Adviser on international crimes know very well that issuing an arrest warrant for the prosecution of big criminals is one part of the political game. Thus, speaking about legal truth or moral truth is just a political game in the chest of the barrel of justice. Any sting in that concession of the system of international criminal justice is thanks to the Court's enslavement to the immorality of power politics.* The fact is that if the judges or prosecutor of the ICC were really cognisant of the notion of moral truth, they would have long since resigned in protest for the sake of justice. Moreover, the moral truth stands on its own merits.

2. Theoretical Argumentation of Barrels

I have been contemplating the crucial differences between various explanations of international criminal justice and facing the fact that moral responsibility is also a moral question that relates to the essence of our *somebodiness*. This in turn is connected to our personal, cultural, ethnic, and

[146] Examine Farhad Malekian, *The Monopolization of International Criminal Law in the United Nations, A Jurisprudential Approach* (Stockholm: Almqvist Wiksell International, 1st ed., 1993, 2nd ed., 1995).

national origin, among other matters. The theory of *somebodiness* refers here to the integral and immutable rights of individuals based on the provisions of natural law and international human rights law and how judges or prosecutors of the ICC will protect their common duties in seeking justice for the victims.[147]

We should also remember that the system of international criminal justice and the legal power of the International Criminal Court in The Hague cannot automatically apply international norms. Instead, they have to be empowered. However, this cannot be done by the victims or its supporters, as long as the prosecutor has not felt that they have received clear permission from their masters, i.e. authoritarian states. These states thus control all of the decisions and judgements of international criminal courts. None of these situations should influence the moral responsibility of a prosecutor or judge of the International Criminal Court.

The theory of moral responsibility calls upon individuals to act in accordance with the theories of international human rights law and the natural rights of man.[148] Due to the existence of the principle of *somebodiness*, we therefore cannot plausibly denounce the basic integral rights of a person out of a desire to protect our position under the system of international criminal justice. This situation reflects the present situation of victims and their right to *somebodiness* that has been taken away by the powertionist criminal governments, thereby positioning them in a state of *nobodiness*. Moral arguments and legal provisions are therefore necessary for the deep understanding of our reasonable rights. If the system of international criminal justice in The Hague cannot distinguish between the truth and false arguments, then the position of justice is indeed in danger.

Nothing can re-establish the rights of victims if integrity, judges, and prosecutors of the International Criminal Court are not working to promote the truth if they continue to attack the personal integrity of nations and put them in the position of *nobodiness*. This is how the system of justice works and treats the victims as an express of justice and its policy to reach out to the rights of victims. How can the rights of victims be established and the

---

[147] Examine Farhad Malekian, *International Criminal Law, the Law of Somebodiness, the Law of Nobodiness* (New York: Nova Science Publishers, 2021); Farhad Malekian, *International Criminal Law: The Legal and Critical Analysis of International Crimes* (2 vols. 1991).

[148] Examine Theodor Meron, 'On Hierarchy of International Human Rights' 80 *American Journal of International Law* (1986); Theodor Meron, *The Humanization of International Law* (Netherlands: The Hague Academy, 2006); Farhad Malekian, *Paralysing International Criminal Justice* (New York: Nova Science Publishers, 2021);

criminals of the powerful states be arrested and brought into courtrooms when the judges of the court are not actively pursuing them? Is it an accident that they wasted time and took no decisions in Chamber I concerning the arrest warrants during several months or is it the position of the victims in the state of *nobodiness* in the system of international criminal justice that has been decisive in the works of the Chamber? Is it a coincidence that the arrest warrant for the Russian president went through very rapidly, or are the proxy interests of the American government what made it feasible?

This is why the barrels of international criminal justice are stored in the office of the prosecutor of the ICC, with the hope that the contents of the barrels will not be pirated and will instead be saved. But the fact is that certain governments have put the barrels of justice in the central office of violations, bribers, pirates, and robbers of justice that can only be accessed by certain judges and prosecutors of the ICC. To say that we trust the system of international criminal justice and its officers in the offices and courtrooms of the ICC is just a way of misleading the population of the world concerning the true nature of the system of international criminal justice. Many of the philosophers of the systems of international criminal justice and international human rights, seek to keep justice moving in the right direction. However, this is not the reality and the basic intention and policy of international criminal justice has continued to weaken in the office of those lawyers or professors who claim to be human rights advocates but are really just advocating for their own interests.

The fact is that the main reason that international criminals receive impunity is due to our own secluded policy of interests. The provisions of international criminal responsibility in the barrels of justice in the International Criminal Court could not be pirated if the prosecutor of the ICC and the judges of the Court knew that those outside of the Court would not let it happen. However, when the theories of international criminal justice are modified and misinterpreted with the intention of misleading the international community, Karim Khan will probably relax in his international office since he will not see himself as being responsible for the incorrect interpretations presented by the leaders of powertionist governments.[149] Then he will give the green light to the judges of Pre-Trial Chamber I, as he has done, who pull the strings of

---

[149] Farhad Malekian, *Conscience of Judges in International Criminal Law, the Heart of Judgements* (New York: Nova Science Publishers, 2021); Farhad Malekian, *Conscience of Lawyers in International Criminal Law, the Burden of Doppelgängers* (New York: Nova Science Publishers, 2021); Farhad Malekian, *Conscience of Prosecutors in International Criminal Law, the Heart of the Matter* (New York: Nova Science Publishers, 2021).

justice as much as possible since the treasures of the barrels are already a part of the occupation of the big powers. Thus, do not be worried about the hypothesis of international criminal responsibility since it is no longer in our possession—although it never was when it came to crimes committed by powertionist governments.

3. Differentiation of the Norms of Barrels

Obviously, it is true that international human rights and international criminal justice do not function in the office of the relevant Chamber of the Court. The notion that humans are all equal is definitely false. Through the use of justice's language, it guides humans into a barrel of injustice. By reiterating that the rights of Palestinians are respected and their *somebodiness* is equal to the *somebodiness* of the Western population, we are obviously speaking with the wrong perspective voice.[150] The only possible conclusion is that the provisions of human rights and international criminal justice are in a barrel of *nobodiness* that is called Palestine, Gaza or the West Bank.

Additionally, the same provisions of human rights and international criminal justice with which the Western politicians treat their communities are called the barrel of *somebodiness*. What do we hold to be true about this theoretical argumentation? I say theoretical since we are permitted to argue about this matter speaking only in theories and not in practical realities. This is because the prolonged hundreds of years of brutal war has proven that Palestinians and their sovereignty are in the state of non-existence, and the Palestinians who have survived have endured tortuous and inhumane conditions. This means that the relevant nation not only does not have the right to exist, but speaking about the concept of international criminal responsibility of the brutal Israeli Zionist government is indeed a utopian dream.[151]

If we set aside the determination of the legal and natural strength of moral truth, we would not have any arguments to convince the theory behind the silent position of the judges of Chamber I of the International Criminal Court. This indicates that invisible ties exist between what is considered criminal

---

[150] Examine Farhad Malekian, *International Criminal Law, the Law of Somebodiness, the Law of Nobodiness* (New York: Nova Science Publishers, 2021); Farhad Malekian, *International Criminal Law: The Legal and Critical Analysis of International Crimes* (2 vols. 1991).

[151] Farhad Malekian, *The Mirage of International Criminal Law, Kant Metaphysics of Mens Rea* (Cambridge Scholars Publishing, 2018).

responsibility and what is known as the impunity of big criminals for their international crimes. Certainly, we are facing a dilemma of justice and jurisdiction in the corridors of the ICC and even in the United Nations as a whole.

Believing that the Court and the Security Council act correctly is equivalent to believing that we are fools who do not understand the reality of the truth and the criminal decisions behind the Court's jurisdiction, particularly in the Office of the Prosecutor, Karim Khan. That is why the prosecutor of the ICC has several Barrels of Justice stored in his office for different positions and different powers and nations. These barrels can be summarised as follows:

a. The barrel which bears the Palestinian flag due to their rights being ignored;
b. The barrel which is used to hold the financial support from the Zionist government;
c. The barrel in which the United States' interests are stored and formed;
d. The barrel which is home to the first master of the prosecutor, i.e., the British criminal colonial government;
e. When powertionist governments are in danger, this last barrel is used to make a ruckus. This is the so-called barrel of NATO membership.
f. The barrel which can hide the interests of the judges of the International Criminal Court;
g. The barrel which exists for those who acts as advisors to the prosecutors in different states;
h. The barrel which is exclusively used to save the prosecutor's home, bank accounts, and family.
i. Then there is the barrel of x. This is a barrel for when the prosecutor succeeds in cheating the international community and but claims that they were not adequately compensated. This prosecutor is also promised jobs in the United States, including at several universities.

4. Barrels of Justice Containing Decriminalisation

Our intention here is not to attack the prosecutor of the ICC. Obviously, the reader understands this. However, the fact is that he has surpassed the legal limits with the propaganda of his office that he is looking for criminals.[152] At the same time, the international legal and political community is fully aware of the fact that the Zionist terrorist government in Palestine is annihilating the ancient nation of Palestine that has centuries of history living and working the land that is under attack. Thus, it does not matter if the international community and its lawyers speak about the international criminal responsibility of governments and their states and it does not help. If we talk about the prohibition on the commission of crimes against humanity, war crimes, genocide, torture, apartheid, and rape, it still does not prevent brutal criminals from committing crimes.

In other words, implementation is different from the list of legal words. Terms of the law do not own the souls of legal personalities of the International Criminal Court, as long as they have not proven their power of accountability and punishment under the procedures of the Court. It is very embarrassing to witness international criminal violations being committed by the most powerful nations of the world against the weakest nations of the world without any response on the part of the International Criminal Court in The Hague. The question then is, what is wrong with the system of international criminal justice that causes it to still be impeded after eight decades of establishing international war crimes tribunals?

There is not much more to say except that the system of international criminal justice depends on, and functions based on, the needs of the big powers. For example, even though several million people were killed during the Second World War and the International War Crimes Tribunal in Nuremberg was established by the big powers, it lost its most significant legislative power when it came to the rights of the weak nation of Palestinians. There is no doubt that a new system of international criminal justice has been established, but there is neither any doubt nor any misgivings that it was based on the legacy of the Nuremberg Tribunal, the law of which remains an integral part of customary international criminal law to this day.

In reality, this indicates the power of the old colonial states over the international legal personality of customary international criminal law. This should not be denied by any realistic international lawyers or judges of

[152] Examine Robert Cryer, 'The Doctrinal Foundations of International Criminalisation,' in M. Cherif Bassiouni, ed., *International Criminal Law*, Vol. 1, (2008), pp. 107-128. See also Robert Cryer, *Prosecuting International Crimes, Selectivity and the International Criminal Law Regime* (Cambridge University Press, Cambridge, 2005).

international criminal courts or tribunals.[153] The question then is: Where are their consciences and courage guiding them to fight against the dictatorship of certain Western governments that are swallowing the Palestinian land and nation? Certainly, they are aiding, assisting, helping, cooperating, supporting, and associating in the commission of international crimes against weak nations. Their purpose is clear, i.e., they wish to fulfil their own political, economic, and military interests.

The crimes that they are committing can be seen by any object that moves on earth. Even immovable subjects are also facing these sorts of responsibilities in the conduct of criminals. You might well have different beliefs and explanations concerning international crimes and violations. However, if you as a lawyer cannot see how deeply children are suffering due to the criminal acts of these barbaric offenders, then there must be something wrong, not only with your knowledge of international criminal law and justice, but also with your knowledge of criminal responsibility. This knowledge is the essential reason for the existence of criminal justice across the world and demands the basis for the attribution of criminal responsibility to the offenders. This means that international criminal justice can be affected by a lack of knowledge concerning criminal responsibility.

The great admiration for the system of international criminal justice is essentially based on the concept of international criminal responsibility, which includes every provision of the system of international criminal law. If the system did not approach the questions of international criminal responsibility, then the system would be paralysed by its own curriculum vitae of criminal jurisdiction. In this case, the entire system would only be a decoration of norms without any significance for the final intention. Understanding the notion of international criminal responsibility, particularly of the system of international criminal justice, is one of the necessary requirements for lawyers.[154]

---

[153] Examine Farhad Malekian, *Conscience of Judges in International Criminal Law, the Heart of Judgements* (New York: Nova Science Publishers, 2021).

[154] Cassese A., *International Criminal Law* (Oxford: Oxford University Press, 2nd, ed., 2008) ; Cassese A., 'For an Enhanced Role of Jus cogens' in Cassese, A (ed.), *Realizing Utopia*, (2012) ; Cassese A., (ed.), *The New Humanitarian Law of Armed Conflict* (Naples: Editoriale Scientifica, 1979) ; Cassese A., 'First Annual Report of the ICTY,' *Yearbook of International Law Commission*, (1994); Cassese A., On the Current Trends Towards Criminal Prosecution and Punishment of Breaches of International Humanitarian Law, 9 *European Journal of Internaitonal Law* 2 (1998); Cassese A., Albin Eser, Giorgio Gaja and Robert E. Conor, *Justice at Nuremberg* (1980).

This understanding is particularly imperative concerning international criminal norms.[155] In other words, the barrel of international criminal justice must have an ample number of norms concerning criminal responsibility. Otherwise, how can it be possible that the barrel contains full international criminal norms without any semblance of criminal responsibility? In any case, my belief is that the system of international criminal justice and its ability to deliver international criminal responsibility are abstract concepts—despite their known existence. It is we, as politicians, governments, states, and sold lawyers, that change their basic function based on our private *interests.*

5. Omitting the Notion of Criminal Convictions

We should not exaggerate the misleading terms and provisions of the system of the International Criminal Court. The ICC has, without doubt, a considerable number of provisions that are good and intend to prevent the impunity of international criminals. However, the fact is that these good provisions are not trustworthy. The beauty of a Christmas tree does not guarantee it a long life. It may only be by accident that we trust reasons for the good presentation of the system of international criminal justice that are really effective and do not pretend to be true. That is why the victims will only truly believe in the system once justice is served authentically and properly. Similarly, if we hang the norms of international human rights on the Christmas tree, it will look beautiful, but will it function or survive? The theory of effectiveness cannot function with a system that lacks roots, and the roots are essentially in the barrel, and it is up to the owner to decide when to water the roots and when not to.

If the victims of the hundreds of years of *genocide against their sovereignty and population lose their temper and resort to self-defence, then failing to convict terrorist governments and their leaders for their crimes falls on the ICC. This is based on its weak position and dependency on the confirmation of its policies by the big criminals in the Security Council and NATO. Our simple question regarding the system of international criminal justice is: how many times has the ICC failed to enforce the international criminal responsibility of the British, French, Israeli, and American*

[155] Farhad Malekian, *Imperative Philosophy of International Criminal Justice: Visible Power – Invisible Essence* (New York: Nova Science Publishers, 2022).

governments? This indicates that the victims have no legal, moral, or universal rights to reach their traditional rights.

In this situation, whether our moral convictions concerning the system of international criminal justice can be true and effective, instead of just pretending to be, is itself a lofty moral demand. The fact is that the system of international criminal justice in the Court does not function based on moral issues, but rather on connections. This is how the barrels of the ICC function and how Karim Khan delivers his views and issues arrest warrants. This means that the provisions of the system of international criminal justice are reasonably well calculated to be identified or not in the Court based on Khan's decisions. This precludes any notion of moral truth if deemed necessary, since the ICC is the prisoner of the powertionist governments, and its prosecutor and judges are the prisoners of the criminal terrorist governments, which in turn are misleading the system of justice and monopolising its power of enforcement against the rights of the victims in the name of human rights.[156] What is the solution to this problem? There is no way out of the barrel of international criminal justice for the victims who are trapped and forced to hear horrible noises, din, and dings.

This is why we believe that the system of international criminal justice that has been under the Court's jurisdiction since its foundation focuses on imposing the power of the authoritarian states over the victims in the name of violating the system of international criminal justice. This political tactic has contributed to why the concept of international criminal responsibility has been ignored in practice and why it continues to be presented as the positive aid of authoritarian governments to re-establish the rights of the victims. The Gulf War was just a play that was orchestrated in the name of establishing justice to cover up the occupation of the rights of a nation to its resources.[157] A similar situation also occurred in Libya.

Further examples of such situations include those in Syria and Iran. Although these countries have had domestic problems, this does not mean that the American or British governments attempted to establish democracy. The arguments made by NATO along with the American and British governments reflected the games they were playing as part of their political plans. How could these terrorist governments then establish democracy, justice, and human rights laws? This is indeed a very serious question that concerns the

---

[156] For further discussion about human rights examine Javaid Rehman, *International Human Rights Law* (Longman Pub Group, 2nd ed., 2010),

[157] Farhad Malekian, *Condemning the Use of Force in the Gulf Crisis* (Almqvist & Wiksell International, 1st ed., 1992).

moral and legal truth. The extent to which we should assume that their arguments are true is indeed meaningless and disrespectful to the values of a nation and the rights of victims.

It would be pointless to ask what probabilities and likelihoods can achieve moral conviction in this juggle of international criminal justice, where all matters of substantial importance for human rights and moral support of the victims are corrupted. *The legal, political, and even moral supposition that all moral thoughts are equally likely to be true is itself wrong and creates discrepancies concerning the truth. Consequently, with the moral truth, we refer to a moral opinion that cannot be rejected due to its clarity. When we see the sun, we cannot claim that it is the moon, or vice versa. This is because the sun is the superstar and the centre of the solar system—at least according to our current knowledge. The existence of the moral truth does not need to be proven because its truth speaks for itself.*

Therefore, good moral reasoning does not always show the validity of our argumentation for the existence of international criminal responsibility for those who commit crimes against humanity, war crimes, genocide, aggression, or apartheid, but any thought that is clearly visible without any arguments. The moral faith can only be the proof of its strangeness. The value of any argument concerning the international criminal responsibility of those who commit crimes against the fundamental principles of international criminal justice and human rights lies in the plausibility of the given circumstances of the case. This is the value of the genuine evidence of facts which clearly show that the barrel of international criminal justice is deliberately avoiding attributing the concept of international criminal responsibility to criminals.

6. Disappearance of the Barrel of Criminal Judgements

At various points throughout the history of national criminal justice and international criminal justice, we have examined case law and evaluated the judgements delivered by the judges of the Court. As a result, case law is a very significant source of international criminal justice and provides more juridical evidence for the concept of international criminal responsibility.[158] This

[158] Article 25 of the Statutes of the International Criminal Court reads that "Individual criminal responsibility: 1. The Court shall have jurisdiction over natural persons pursuant to this Statute. 2. A person who commits a crime within the jurisdiction of the Court shall be individually responsible and liable for punishment in accordance with this Statute. 3. In accordance with this Statute, a person shall be criminally responsible and liable for

concept of criminal responsibility is "irrelevance of official capacity"[159] which also includes criminal responsibility of commanders and other superiors.[160] This is why the judges of the *ad hoc* international criminal tribunals and the International Court in The Hague refer to the judgements of the other court when necessary. The intention in doing this is to strengthen justice and provide additional evidence for the notion of international criminal responsibility. All these matters are not only connected with legal theories, but also with moral theories. Due to this, there are no significant objections when the accused is convicted and punished. As a matter of fact, punishment is an integral part of criminal procedures and represents the final theory of criminal responsibility.

---

punishment for a crime within the jurisdiction of the Court if that person: (a) Commits such a crime, whether as an individual, jointly with another or through another person, regardless of whether that other person is criminally responsible; (b) Orders, solicits or induces the commission of such a crime which in fact occurs or is attempted; (c) For the purpose of facilitating the commission of such a crime, aids, abets or otherwise assists in its commission or its attempted commission, including providing the means for its commission; (d) In any other way contributes to the commission or attempted commission of such a crime by a group of persons acting with a common purpose. Such contribution shall be intentional and shall either: (e) In respect of the crime of genocide, directly and publicly incites others to commit genocide; (f) Attempts to commit such a crime by taking action that commences its execution by means of a substantial step, but the crime does not occur because of circumstances independent of the person's intentions. However, a person who abandons the effort to commit the crime or otherwise prevents the completion of the crime shall not be liable for punishment under this Statute for the attempt to commit that crime if that person completely and voluntarily gave up the criminal purpose. 4. No provision in this Statute relating to individual criminal responsibility shall affect the responsibility of States under international law."

[159] Article 27 of the ICC reads that "Irrelevance of official capacity: 1. This Statute shall apply equally to all persons without any distinction based on official capacity. In particular, official capacity as a Head of State or Government, a member of a Government or parliament, an elected representative or a government official shall in no case exempt a person from criminal responsibility under this Statute, nor shall it, in and of itself, constitute a ground for reduction of sentence. 2. Immunities or special procedural rules which may attach to the official capacity of a person, whether under national or international law, shall not bar the Court from exercising its jurisdiction over such a person."

[160] Article 28 of the Statute of ICC concerning responsibility of commanders and other superiors reads that "In addition to other grounds of criminal responsibility under this Statute for crimes within the jurisdiction of the Court: (a) A military commander or person effectively acting as a military commander shall be criminally responsible for crimes within the jurisdiction of the Court committed by forces under his or her effective command and control, or effective authority and control as the case may be, as a result of his or her failure to exercise control properly over such forces, where: (b) With respect to superior and subordinate relationships not described in paragraph (a), a superior shall be criminally responsible for crimes within the jurisdiction of the Court committed by subordinates under his or her effective authority and control, as a result of his or her failure to exercise control properly over such subordinates, where. All these Articles 25 to 28 should also be read in conjunction with Article 29 providing "Non-applicability of statute of limitations: The crimes within the jurisdiction of the Court shall not be subject to any statute of limitations."

After the punishment is carried out, the theory of international criminal responsibility has been fulfilled, and the intentions of criminal responsibility have been achieved.

My intention is to say that the Court's system of international criminal justice under the power of judges and the Court does not establish criminal jurisdiction. Consequently, the court avoided issuing arrest warrants and prosecuting criminals for over six months in the case of Israel. The arrest warrant issued against the Israeli leaders is considered by the big criminal governments to not be valid. This includes the United States, United Kingdom, Australia, Canada, and Germany. Their objections aid in hindering the intentions of criminal justice and promotes the impunity of criminals. Even though issuing an arrest warrant may seem to be dangerous for the prosecution and judges of the Court, they can simply resign in protest. We should not forget the fact that, as a matter of principle, the judges are not chosen to have a position on the Court. That was not at all the intention of the establishment of the Court. However, their duties include applying international criminal responsibility equally to all those who have committed international crimes—both the powerful and powerless. If they are unable to fulfil this duty for any reason, they should resign. This helps us confront the true function of the system of international criminal justice and reveal the fundamental monopolisation of international criminal justice.[161]

It would be more realistic and simpler to show how the moral barrel of international criminal justice works and how it finds its criminals or releases them from punishment. I am not trying to cheat various estimations of the system of jurisdiction and judgements of the judges of the International Criminal Court—they are free to decide what they deem as appropriate. However, they should not forget the fact that the system of international criminal courts is not a private institution that should not challenge the true face of justice with clear evidence of the commission of serious international crimes to any extent. *Certainly, the judges of the ICC and its prosecutors are bound not only by the rules of the Court and appropriate morality, but also by the strength of good moral reasoning for their decisions, actions, and judgments. Obviously, when the judges of the court or the prosecutor avoid fulfilling their tasks and duties, then the procedures of justice are damaged and the jurisdiction and judgements of the court remain paralysed during the*

---

[161] See Farhad Malekian, *The Monopolization of International Criminal Law in the United Nations, A Jurisprudential Approach* (Stockholm: Almqvist Wiksell International, 1st ed., 1993, 2nd ed., 1995).

next hearings. Allowing any fear, personal interests, or any other peril to interfere with the procedures of justice is equivalent to collaborating with the criminals and denying the established rights of the victims.[162]

The decisions and actions of the corrupt prosecutor and judges of the Court are equivalent to the disappearance of the barrel of criminal justice and silencing its voice at the behest of the perpetrators of international crimes. This means that the barrel of justice, which speaks about the international criminal responsibility of criminals, does not work, and the theory of international criminal responsibility is only a shadow of that what does not really exist and cannot be enforced. The process involves selecting one item at a time from a jar that contains some valid, however mostly false, sounds from orchestral musical records. We must then ask: What are the odds of actually establishing international criminal justice? Even if we could separate all those falsified sounds in the moral barrel of international criminal responsibility, the facts remain the same, and the theory of non-applicability of criminal responsibility and punishment persists without any positive or moral changes. We must then assume the truth of some convictions concerning the concept of international criminal responsibility of governments and their states, but the reality is that governments and states are controlled by those who have committed the most brutal international crimes.

7. Absence of Trustworthy Barrels

The fact is that any judgement, even a possible international criminal judgement against professional criminals, cannot be effective without the permission of the superior leaders of the Security Council. This in turn leads to the disappearance of criminal judgements in various ways. The system of international criminal responsibility and its application under the power of the Court needs much more legal force as that is the only way to ensure justice. However, this is neither practical nor sufficient. Drafting and ratifying any more conventions to strengthen the enforceability of the provisions of the Court would be equivalent to throwing another convention into the sea of justice and then finding someone to save its provisions. This does not work to any extent, since the sea is not protected from the activities of the enemies of international criminal justice and international criminal responsibility. This is not an opinion or statement against the international criminal justice but rather

---

[162] Ronald Dworkin, *Justice for Hedgehogs* (Harvard University Press, 2011), p. 422.

the private barrel of the radio of the ICC in its Chambers and in the minds of its judges.

Criminals do not express any positive consent to the content of international criminal justice because it contradicts their aggressive and terrorist decisions. It is an equally grave mistake to give any concrete norm of international criminal justice to them. Although we do not say that international criminal justice is not under their control, giving in to their decisions would be equivalent to committing suicide without any more need for proper justice, a trustworthy prosecutor, and faithful judges.[163] It means that the present position of justice has an elastic mechanism that bends it in different directions based on the needs of the great powers of the world. We cannot arrive at an integrated set of international criminal principles that are automatically enforceable on all criminals, strong or weak. That is absolutely impossible.

Unfortunately, the popularity of the systems of international criminal justice and international human rights has been based on the sound of their barrels. This is how the systems of justice have been empowered and fused for the sake of victims. However, this is not the reality, and it is evident that all powertionist governments try to claim that any movement by any government against their will constitutes an act of terrorism. It is for this reason that the majority of sanctions are imposed upon governments that do not follow that the lead of authoritarian governments. Due to this, sanctions function as an illegal international criminal court controlled by the powertionist governments that are levying criminal accusations. This indicates that the real international criminal court is the Security Council, certain members of which function as powerful paternalist states with a single aim: to frame the victims as the criminals and force them to accept their decisions or be met with sanctions.[164]

This system of sanctions is similar to a Nazis government that has no ears to hear the voices of the innocent and punishes victims for things they did not do. There are no other expectations of such forms of justice that function using one-eyed justice and only protect the interests of those in power. The unlimited power in the Security Council and the strong militaries of the powertionist

---

[163] Examine Farhad Malekian, *Conscience of Judges in International Criminal Law, the Heart of Judgements* (New York: Nova Science Publishers, 2021); Farhad Malekian, *Conscience of Lawyers in International Criminal Law, the Burden of Doppelgängers* (New York: Nova Science Publishers, 2021); Farhad Malekian, *Conscience of Prosecutors in International Criminal Law, the Heart of the Matter* (New York: Nova Science Publishers, 2021).

[164] Farhad Malekian, *International Criminal Vacations: Tears of Justice* (New York: Nova Science Publishers, 2024);

governments are why the moral barrel of international criminal responsibility does not function and is like a statue that looks beautiful but does not serve any real function for the victims. Moral philosophers have tried to interrogate the double moralities of governments, albeit without success. Some have also tried to show that more specific criminalisation can help address the shortcomings of the system of international criminal justice and empower the theory of international criminal responsibility of governments and their states. However, the result of this was the current genocide of the Palestinian population.

The fact that the theories of moral and legal reasoning refuse to accept reality is related to the concrete monopolisation of the law and the notion of international criminal responsibility. Obviously, any response to the true function of the barrel of justice in the office of the prosecutor is itself clear evidence of collaboration between criminals and the Statute of the ICC. This can be easily denied by the prosecutor of the ICC or Pre-Trial Chamber at any time and concerning any case. Moreover, we should not forget the fact that when individuals working for the superpowers have been prosecuted in the past, it has been in their own courts where judgements were largely decided behind closed doors in advance and the accused went free. This is the consequence of the omission of the notion of criminal conviction function and reflects how the barrel of criminal responsibility sounds.

8. Imperative Connotation of Criminal Responsibility

The theory behind international criminal law and international human rights is the consequence of imperative regulations.[165] No authority in the world is permitted to violate the rules of international law and human rights that connected to our natural rights and therefore should not be ignored. Thus, the

[165] Examine Pardo Pilar Villanueva Sainz, 'Is International Criminal Law a Living Discipline?,' 3:4 The International Journal of Human Rights (1999), pp. 92-100; Farhad Malekian, *Tour de force of Moral Virtue in International Criminal Justice* (New York: Nova Science Publishers, 2022); Farhad Malekian, *Imperative Philosophy of International Criminal Justice: Visible Power – Invisible Essence* (New York: Nova Science Publishers, 2022); Farhad Malekian, *Powertionism in International Criminal Justice* (New York: Nova Science Publishers, 2022); M. Cherif Bassiouni, 'A Comprehensive Strategic Approach on International Cooperation for the Prevention, Control and Suppression of International and Transnational Criminality, Including the Establishment of an International Criminal Court,' 15 Nova Law Review 353 (1991).

imperative character of both systems is a matter of necessity and not choice.[166] We have developed and conceived a system of international criminal justice with no power of enforcement. This imperative character of international criminal law and human rights explains the phenomena that lie in the substance of both legal systems for the good of man and that direct governments to the platforms of truth. There are those who challenge the system of international criminal law for the purpose of altering it to suit their needs. This is particularly common among those who believe that the imperative function of both systems should be controlled by certain members of the Security Council and by NATO in certain situations.[167]

The imperative function of international criminal law and international human rights law has not often been challenged by any government. However, the term "imperative" has been interpreted and given value with reference to the conclusions of powertionist governments. Certain basic forms of both systems are acceptable to all nations, depending on their national and international policies.[168] The imperative function of both systems has been indirectly rejected by governments that control the colonial system of the United Nations and cannot survive without monopolisation of the rights of other nations.[169] Based on the given arguments, we must conclude that the systems of international criminal law and human rights were created by the support of super governments that had and still have various nefarious intentions concerning their enforcement, including empowering militarily strong nations and their policies. This means that the substance of recognition is subjective and biased in both legal systems.

The philosophical and legal theories explained in the arguments concerning the imperative functions of both legal systems are therefore in a permanent battle with one another, with the difference being that those who support the imperative function of international law in all states are always in a much lower position than those who defend the power of the interpretations of the powertionist governments. Thus, an argument that seeks to explain the real function of the system of international human rights is certainly correct, but lacks the power of application or implementation.[170] Therefore, the

---

[166] Examine Farhad Malekian, *Imperative Philosophy of International Criminal Justice: Visible Power – Invisible Essence* (New York: Nova Science Publishers, 2022); Farhad Malekian, *Powertionism in International Criminal Justice* (New York: Nova Science Publishers, 2022).

[167] *Id.*

[168] *Id.*

[169] *Id.*

[170] *Id.*

advocates of truth for the imposition of the notion of international criminal responsibility are always met with the internationally wrongful acts of powertionist governments. This has become a routine, and demanding the imperative function of international criminal responsibility has no place within the arguments, even in the office of the ICC.[171]

Therefore, to say that there is an imperative connection between responsibility and the barrel is not an exaggeration. This is because international criminal responsibility refers to the official requirement that is made under the system of the International Criminal Court with the intention that violators of international criminal law face prosecution and punishment, and consequently that the impunity of criminals is prevented. This is why there is a connection between the provisions of international criminal justice and the internationally criminal wrongful acts of criminals. This is what the barrel of justice is expected to do to establish the rights of victims. Regrettably, the requirements of criminal justice are automatically paralysed by the very strong impulses of certain members of the Security Council. This strategy used by the system of international criminal justice to reconcile the rights of victims has undeniably caused a division between the essence of imperative norms and their assumed intentions. Thus, the barrel of the international criminal responsibility of individuals, governments, and states no longer functions.

9. Imperative Duty to Prevent Lawlessness

If the validity of the international criminal justice system is assessed based on its practical function, the convictions regarding its legitimacy appear to be nothing more than a manipulation of the beliefs held by those who still trust in the cognitive capacity of international criminal justice.[172] Similar to the perception of the understanding of norms of international human rights, the International Criminal Court has an imperative duty to prevent any abuse of the spirit of law that violates the rights of innocent victims. However, the system continues to do nothing about the on-going brutal international crimes being committed against the Palestinian population. This means that the imperative function of international criminal justice has lost its power and is

[171] *Id.*

[172] Consult Farhad Malekian, *The Mirage of International Criminal Law, Kant Metaphysics of Mens Rea* (Cambridge Scholars Publishing, 2018); Farhad Malekian, *Tour de force of Moral Virtue in International Criminal Justice* (New York: Nova Science Publishers, 2022), p. 103.

basically presenting the rules and roles of lawlessness. We cannot therefore present the more common perceptions of the system of international criminal justice, wherein the theory of international human rights is the theory of bloodshed and slaughtering victims.

This is how international criminal justice functions within the system of corrupted offices of the prosecutor and dishonourable judges of the Court. A court does not need to be declared corrupt and receive money from criminals to be designated as compromised. It is sufficient to have personnel who do not perform their duties related to the systems of criminal justice and righteousness.[173] *If the theory of righteousness is not respected by the judges of the Court, how can we expect and believe that other national, regional, or international social personnel will carry out their duties appropriately? These are not my sophisticated explanations for international criminal justice and the re-establishment of the rights of victims, rather forms of justice that speak for themselves.*

Thus, it is not at all significant if the barrels in the office of the prosecutor of the ICC are jam-packed and filled with the wine or blood of victims. However, it is important to recognise that the barrel has no connection with the invisible force of criminals. If the essence of righteousness in justice is respected, then the strength of imperativeness is achieved.[174] This is the point where we can demand the implementation of the provisions of international criminal justice and accountability of criminals. The fulfilment of the provisions of international criminal responsibility is therefore incredibly urgent as it concerns the victims of genocide in Gaza and the West Bank. For how much longer do we need to document the system of private international criminal justice courts before they will take action and prevent the barbaric commission of international crimes? The volume of crimes is so high and so intensive that it amounts to the commission of the *international crime of blackboard-barbarism*.[175] This is a crime that includes the nature or character

---

[173] See generally Farhad Malekian, Concreting Righteousness in International Criminal Justice (New York, Nova Sciences Publishers, 2024); Farhad Malekian, *International Criminal Vacations: Tears of Justice* (New York: Nova Science Publishers, 2024).Farhad Malekian, *Powertionism in International Criminal Justice* (New York: Nova Science Publishers, 2022);

[174] Farhad Malekian, *International Criminal Vacations: Tears of Justice* (New York: Nova Science Publishers, 2024).

[175] Farhad Malekian, *International Crime of Blackboard-Barbarism* ((New York: Nova Science Publishers, 2025).

of all international crimes and that is carried out with the intention of annihilating the victims.[176] It means that:

> Blackboard-barbarism can be defined as a *crime committed by certain government authorities, the commission of which violates the basic principles of international human rights and international criminal justice. In other words, certain government authorities fight against certain groups with a bloodthirsty mentality. The barbaric mentality of a government refers to actions or reactions that give priority to one nation over another. These governments are relentless in committing all kinds of brutal crimes in order simply to prove they are above all other nations on earth. Spilling the blood of children and their mothers is one of the brutal acts carried out during the commission of blackboard-barbarism. The situation is much uglier and leads to more bloodshed when authorities with barbaric mentalities and no sense of humanity demolish buildings where civilians live. All these brutal attacks not only attest to the existence of a barbaric mentality in the nature of man, but also to its use as an enabler of economic and political greed.*
>
> We could strive to develop a clearer definition of *international blackboard-barbarism*. The reason for this is simple: the crime is so broad and brutal that words fail to sufficiently describe the brutality of the crime. Blackboard-barbarism is a collective notion of all international crimes within the same framework. *Consequently, the elements of the crime are so broad and numerous that a limited, succinct definition of the crime is not possible. Blackboard-barbarism makes all government authorities responsible for their superior orders to commit international crimes at the same level. They can motivate their crimes by using a fanciful model to defend their legitimacy. They design a model of imaginary occupation and then bring it into reality through the commission of blackboard-barbarism.*
>
> For authorities who commit blackboard banning, their actions seem reasonable in the hypothetical discussions of their meetings in parliament and behind closed doors. Their crimes therefore take shape during sessions of parliament, which implies *mens rea*. Then, they bring their plans of committing the savage international crime into the phase of *actus reus*. This refers to the concrete actions taken by their criminal military organisation. This is the process of determining the state of the offence. These arguments therefore suggest that the international crime of blackboard-barbarism refers to encouraging the annihilation of a nation

[176] *Id.*

that is occupied by the immoral, unlawful, illegal, and unjustified conduct of political Zionists through the violations of integrities. This means that they give different titles to the population in order to dehumanize them.

The population is accused of being cockroaches, human animals, or subhuman, among other things. Therefore, the population faces intimidation or terrorization as a result of the use of weapons guns and the threat of destruction. This is then followed by the actual destruction of an ancient nation's history, culture, and international social existence. When a political criminal government uses these strategies, which are not much less malicious than those of the Nazis, it shows the evil personality and wicked character of their nature. These states knowingly violate the nature of international human rights law and international criminal justice in a variety of ways. The international crime of *blackboard-barbarism* creates derelict nations, cultivates homeless nations, develops increased suffering for starving individuals, encourages slavery systems, and finally, massacres a nation in the name of God and with the clear intention of claiming to be the chosen government of God.[177]

10. Rejecting the Perception of Accountability

The system of international criminal responsibility deals with a certain complex criminal jurisdiction that is very difficult to deal with. That is why we rely on the opinions of the prosecutor and judges of international criminal courts to help us understand the system of international criminal justice. This indicates that we trust and believe that international criminal justice and its provisions that have been violated by certain cruel criminals will properly function and prompt the perpetrators of international crimes to acknowledge their criminal responsibility and that of others. With more extreme cases that may require a deeper examination of evidence, we refer to both previous and present analyses. This is what has been done with reference to the jurisdiction of the ICC. This means that for deeper consideration and proper examination of criminal accountability, we resort to the jurisdiction of a permanent, temporary, or ad hoc court to deal with possible criminal cases.

It is the awareness of the violations of international criminal principles that drives the situation and leads the Court to investigate certain cases. We

[177] Farhad Malekian, *International Crime of Blackboard-Barbarism* ((New York: Nova Science Publishers, 2025), pp.25-26.

must then ask: how can a number of given situations not persuade the prosecutor of the court to take action? What is the reason for his cautious approach to situations? The office of the International Criminal Court may sensibly reach the conclusion that it has detected possible violations, and therefore, it may take some time to release its decisions. However, when the decision of the prosecutor does not come in a timely fashion and the number of victims of brutal international crimes increases, then the situation begs the question of what is really wrong with the moral barrel of justice and why it is avoiding making a decision concerning a number of cases such as Biden, Obama, Clinton and Bush.[178]

Nonetheless, I agree that at the end of the day and after examining all statements of the ICC, we come to understand that the Court is unable to make any decisions and is confronted with the quandary of whether it should remain silent or instead react to the monopolisation of the Court. Providing justice and re-establishing the rights of the victims then becomes a question of faith in the personality of the prosecutor and every judge of the court, and whether they are strong enough to expose the hidden truth both within and outside their offices. They may therefore submit themselves to the orders of the powerful criminal governments or speak against the criminals despite having already given their consent to be silent about the case. They thus reject any semblance of accountability by those who are the guardians of international criminal justice in the Court of the UN members.

Some may still argue that the court and its prosecutor and judges are working to convince the criminals that their actions violate international

---

[178] The American governments are more susceptible to violating the international criminal justice system and denying its legal or moral jurisdiction over their criminal activities. According to Obama's memorandum, all US military forces dispatched to Mali will not be subject to prosecution in The Hague. "By the authority vested in me as President by the Constitution and the laws of the United States of America, and consistent with section 2005 of the American Service members' Protection Act of 2002 (22 U.S.C. 7424), concerning the participation of members of the Armed Forces of the United States in certain United Nations peacekeeping and peace enforcement operations, I hereby certify that members of the U.S. Armed Forces participating in the United Nations Multidimensional Integrated Stabilization Mission in Mali are without risk of criminal prosecution or other assertion of jurisdiction by the International Criminal Court (ICC) because the Republic of Mali has entered into an agreement in accordance with Article 98 of the Rome Statute preventing the ICC from proceeding against members of the Armed Forces of the United States present in that country." Mark Kersten, Unfortunate but Unsurprising? Obama Undermines the ICC, posted in 2014 *Justice in Conflict*, https://justiceinconflict.org/2014/02/04/unfortunate-but-unsurprising-obama-undermines-the-icc/. Consult *also* Mark Kersten, examine also Genocide doesn't "just happen" – Israel, Gaza and Genocide as a Process, not an Event (Posted on January 19, 2024), Justice in Conflict, https://justiceinconflict.org/2024/01/19/genocide-doesnt-just-happen-israel-gaza-and-genocide-as-a-process-not-an-event/.

criminal justice and work against the truth. This is only possible if we close our eyes and believe that the system of international criminal justice and the provisions of international human rights work consistently. The fact is that when international crimes are committed, it is naïve to assume that the criminals will regret their actions or stop because the moral and legal truth function based on the united essence of man, which is not up for trade, interpretation, or exchange. When moral truth becomes the subject of ongoing violations, the struggle to explain the righteousness of our actions weakens and poisons the truth.

While we may not succeed in proving what is going on behind the closed doors of the International Criminal Court, that does not reduce our legal ability nor the presentation of the moral truth. It may seem to some that my interpretations target the powertionist governments that are helping to support the legislation, economy, and weapons industry to benefit Zionist criminal government and enable their massacre of the innocent population of Palestine. However, it is of no concern to me as to how they interpret my conclusions. The facts remain the same, and any other conclusions potentially violate the basic principles of justice and international human rights law. It is faith in justice that endures and recognises said justice—not the lack of a said faith being used as justification for our consensual relationship with the body of international criminal justice. If we submit ourselves and our consciences to the criminal conduct of the powertionist criminal governments, then we have already tried the criminal justice system and fallen to our knees, resulting in the killing of innocents. This indicates the fact that we are supporting the evil barrel of barbarity and corruption under the system of power of the International Criminal Court.

Chapter 7

Invading Barrels of Moral Justifications

1. Invading Egalitarian Principles of Internationality

The theory of international criminal justice is strongly connected with the notion of international legal personality, which in turn speaks about the independent character of subjects of international public law with the ability to negotiate and ratify international treaties.[179] Personality deals therefore with the independent character of a subject that has been recognised to have the full capacity to deal with different matters and ongoing international issues. The system of international personality is therefore a system that presents the full qualifications of a subject to deal with all matters of interest and prevents the interference of other subjects in its domestic and international decisions. This means that states parties to the Statute of the International Criminal Court voluntarily created and accepted the binding rules of the Statute of the ICC with the intention of granting it an independent international character. Therefore, the ICC has the ability to prevent any interference by any state in its legal and political decisions. This independence of the ICC should not threatened or attacked by any international legal entities that can interfere in the fulfilment of its prescribed duties, such as states or organisations.

In other words, the international legal personality of the ICC is the result of many political and military matters that have threatened the existence of peace and the possible implementation of international human rights. This notion aims to effectively prevent this danger. Any threat or use of force against the international legal personality of the ICC is equivalent to violating the international legal personality of the ICC, which can in turn be submitted to the International Court of Justice or to the United Nations.[180] However, the

---

[179] Examine T. Gebrehana, Duty to negotiate: An Element of International law (1978).

[180] As I have mentioned in my other book "if the use of force is prohibited by all means, it cannot be permitted by any means. If the application of capital punishment is abolished, it cannot be justified in any situation, as is the case in Article 6 of the Covenant. If the norms of legality are correctly divided into primary and secondary rules, then we cannot deprive them of their high human values. Likewise, if Islamic law is a permanent brotherhood, then it cannot be removed from this significant principle. If the communist idea is to share greater common interests of humanity, then it cannot be isolated from other theories. The norm of love is built on the strength of justice and our ability to understand that if every

rapidly increasing complexities of political powers and divisions of the world tries to weaken the connection between the International Criminal Court and state members, and if this evil theory of powertionist governments does not work, invading the international legal personality becomes much more crucial for the paternalist governments that control the ICC and its power.

Thus, authoritarian governments have adopted the political strategy of shifting legal authority from the International Criminal Court (ICC), thereby diminishing its legal principles. Since the independence of the ICC is not based on military power, safeguarding the integrity of its international legal personality has become exceedingly challenging.[181] Consequently, we might say that this situation detracts from its intended purpose. This implies that the rights and obligations of the ICC are primarily the concern of states that possess military power, leading to the invalidation of the concept of international criminal responsibility in practice, which itself constitutes a significant aspect of the Court's duties and obligations.[182] In other words, the judgments, decisions, and sanctions issued by the Court—critical components of its legitimacy—become null and void, thereby lacking any practical force.

This situation is very dangerous, and there have been grave violations of the rights of victims, taking into account that the International Court of Justice (ICJ), which was established in 1949 under the auspices of the United Nations can no longer function, even though it also has an independent international legal personality. Firstly, the ICJ in The Hague is not an international criminal court. Secondly, its decisions are non-binding in certain situations. The power of guns in the possession of the big powers obliterates any notion of accountability for the big powertionist terrorist governments and their crimes under the jurisdiction of an international criminal court. By invading the international legal personality of the ICC, we also act against all international

---

human being has the inherent right to life, freedom of speech and marriage, this is a collective inheritance, and therefore no human being should be isolated from this right by any means. Particularly, the above rights are an integral part of peremptory norms of international law." Farhad Malekian, *Judgments of Love in Criminal Justice* (Switzerland: Springer: 2017, 2018), p. 125.

[181] Farhad Malekian, 'Emasculating the Philosophy of International Criminal Justice in the Iraqi Special Tribunal,' *Cornell International Law Journal*, 58/5 (2005), pp. 675-725; Farhad Malekian, 'Comparative Substantive International Criminal Justice,' in Ronald Slye (ed.), *The Nuremberg Principles in Non-western Societies: A Reflection on their Universality, Legitimacy and Application* (2017), pp. 10-44. Consult also Farhad Malekian, 'The Laws Governing Crimes against Women Constituting *Obligatio Erga Omnes*' in David Wingeate Pike, *Crimes Against Women* (2011).

[182] *Id.*, Emasculating the Philosophy of International Criminal Justice in the Iraqi Special Tribunal.

conventions dealing with international criminal law and international humanitarian law in armed conflicts.

The policy of the big powers is extremely dangerous to the procedures of the international criminal court as it concerns holding individuals internationally responsible for committing international crimes with the incorrect sound of the moral barrel.[183] This is particularly important given that the ICC's mandate is to prosecute individuals using international criminal provisions and to prevent impunity following the commission of crimes such as genocide, war crimes, and crimes against humanity.[184] The ultimate consequence of invading the freedom of international legal personality of the ICC by various means ends up dampening the sound of the barrel of international criminal justice, which although sometimes superficially useful, it is more often destructive concerning the norms of authentic international criminal justice. It distributes the rights of the terrorist governments that claim to respect the rights of victims and fight for the re-establishment of their vanished rights.

When barrels of international criminal justice are controlled by powertionist governments, the control of moral justice disappears, and moral and legal truth fall under the control of criminals. This is why the barrels of the prosecutor of the ICC and the judges of the Chamber I of the ICC do not work and these individuals continue to be complicit in the commission of international crimes. In the book on Utipolitianist International Criminal Court, I discussed how certain powertionism governments control the power of the system of international criminal courts of any form. Therefore, the incentive for the Security Council to carry out monopolisation becomes clear

---

[183] For instance see Days after United States Vetoes Security Council Resolution Calling for Immediate Gaza Ceasefire, Special Coordinator Warns against Undoing Decades of Work towards Peace, https://press.un.org/en/2024/sc15911.doc.htm.

[184] Additionally, numerous international legal documents affirm the right to equality, justice, and peace for all individuals, groups, or nations. Conventional or official international documents include the Charter of the United Nations, 1945; Universal Declaration of Human Rights, 1948; The Four Geneva Conventions of 12 August 1949; The 1977 Protocols Additional to the Geneva Conventions of 12 August 1949; International Covenant on Civil and Political Rights, 1966; International Covenant on Economic, Social and Cultural Rights, 1966; International Convention on the Elimination of All Forms of Racial Discrimination, 1965; Convention on the Elimination of All Forms of Discrimination against Women, 1979; Declaration on the Elimination of All Forms of Intolerance and of Discrimination based on Religion or Belief, 1981; Convention on the Rights of the Child, 1989; Statute of the International Tribunal for the Former Yugoslavia, 1993; Statute of the International Tribunal for Rwanda, 1994; Rome Statute of the International Criminal Court, 1998; Declaration on the Rights of Persons Belonging to National or Ethnic, Religious and Linguistic Minorities, 1992.

when, in the name of emerging egalitarian principles, victims lose their rights and then have to resist egalitarian principles.[185]

However, it is important to recognise that none of the brutalities carried out by the big powers have been addressed and their aggression and atrocities persist. As a result, we can no longer have confidence in the judgements of international criminal courts given that the theory of criminality and international criminal responsibility is decided by the strong, brutal governments. No explanation is needed here because the theory of justice is clearly playing a serious, dangerous game against the rights of the victims. We are therefore no better off than we were before the establishment of the International Criminal Court in The Hague. This is because every single norm of the system of international criminal justice and its judgement depends on higher-ranking decisions in the name of democracy or the international development of the principles of egalitarianism.

2. Invading the Structure of the ICC

The entire system of international criminal justice aims to prevent any infringement on the rights of others. Therefore, the primary theory of international criminal justice can be said to be the prevention of any invasion of the legitimate rights of other populations around the world. In of the event of an invasion, the objectives of criminals are to destroy, kill, massacre, or forcibly seize the properties, land, or sovereign rights of other nations. This is why moral justification becomes crucial and raises numerous questions regarding our criminal actions. Consequently, those who engage in criminal conduct against other nations provide various justifications for their actions and believe they are not violating the systems of international criminal courts—in fact, they argue the opposite. They claim to be fighting for their rights that have been taken away by others and base all their arguments on falsehoods. This form of argumentation kills the notion of international criminal responsibility and grants the criminals the right to massacre other nations, as we have seen in the Middle East.

However, it is overly simplistic to believe that such states will not face any response from the victims and that they will remain silent about the crimes

---

[185] See Farhad Malekian, *The Monopolization of International Criminal Law in the United Nations, A Jurisprudential Approach* (Stockholm: Almqvist Wiksell International, 1st ed., 1993, 2nd ed., 1995).

for several decades. This is why international criminal justice has developed based on the criminal theories of those who brutally manipulate barrels of moral justification in their decisions and actions, only to then call themselves the most moral military powers in the world. This is an irrational attack on the legality of the international criminal responsibility of governments and their states. It indicates that invasion is not a theory for the restoration of rights, but rather a means of taking the rights of others through various forms of violations and the commission of international crimes. Once again, it does not benefit the invaders to issue any declaration or statement that represents a completely erroneous interpretation of the truth and presents lies as the fundamental basis for their claims. This is the current situation facing the systems of international criminal justice and international human rights.

Therefore, there is always a significant contradiction between what is right and what is wrong. The general evidence available to the International Criminal Court merely reflects the lies upon which the Court must base its judgments. This means that the legal authority of the barrel of the Court is automatically seized by the criminals, and there will be so many lies occupying the minds of the judges and influencing the court's response. Problems arise if the Court is able to find evidence that is free from defects and that can help distinguish lies from truth. This precisely mirrors the situation of the Palestinian population, which is fed lies from the governing bodies of the court, the sovereignty of states, and Western governments—all of which promote lies and attempt to criminalise the actions of victims based on said lies. This is exactly the challenge that the system of international law faces within the Security Council and the International Criminal Court.

The truth is that the governments working to perpetuate these lies are so relentless it essentially becomes impossible to reject the lies. This policy, employed by the Israeli, British, Canadian, Australian, French, Dutch, and American governments, has traditionally served to undermine the fundamental premise of hypocrisy in international human rights, international criminal law, and international criminal justice. It is essentially impossible to identify anywhere within the policies of these terrorist governments where a genuine moral truth and legal truth can be discerned. The concepts of the fairness of the barrel of justice and injustice no longer hold significance, and thus the justification for ethical judgments and the ethical truth is corrupted. As a result, there is no wisdom in evaluating the situation, and the paths to justice and righteousness are obstructed by the lies and military power of the invaders.[186] The question then is: how can we uphold the theory of international criminal responsibility while our moral convictions support the hypothesis of hypocrisy without trusting the underlying lies?[187]

When all of the evidence is presented through lies and a state is formed as a result of the criminal policies of the Nazis and the UK/United states, then all theories also become false. Therefore, any perception regarding the decisions and actions of the invaders involves constructing the fundamental structure of the system of international criminal justice with certain lies that do not align with the moral truth of reasoning. Moreover, the moral convictions of governments that merely present lies as the foundation of their morality lack legal validity.[188] Consequently, we face the standards of guns and military power, and wherever we speak, there is a necessity for the presentation of truth. However, the truth is not respected in the slightest. Although we recognise that no plausible case for justice can be overlooked, the reality is that our understanding is merely a narrative of its own, as the justice of lies unfortunately equates to the justice of truth. Any perspective on the consequences of lies undermines the values of truth, resulting in increased suffering for the victims. A clear example of this is the widespread and barbaric genocide of Palestinians in Gaza and the West Bank and the serious violations of the norms of international criminal justice or the responsibility of governments that are kept in the barrel of International Criminal Court.

---

[186] Farhad Malekian, *Gravity of Wisdom in International Criminal Law* (New York: Nova Science Publishers, 2021).

[187] A clear example is the Julian Assange case read Farhad Malekian, *Allegations by Political Laundering* (Cambridge Scholars Publishing, 2019).

[188] Consult P. M. S. Hacker and J. Raz, (eds.), Law, *Morality and Society: Essays in Honour of H. L. A. Hart* (1977); Farhad Malekian, *Classical Morality in International Peremptory Criminal Law* (Newcastle: Cambridge Scholars Publishing, 2021); Raz Joseph, *Ethics in the Public Domain: Essays in the Morality of Law and Politics* (Oxford: Oxford University Press, 1994); Raz Joseph, *The Morality of Freedom* (1986); Robert Vischer K., *Martin Luther King Jr. and the Morality of Legal Practice: Lessons in Love and Justice* (2014); Fuller Lon Luvios, *The Morality of Law* (Virginia: Yale Law University, 2nd, ed., 1969); Duncan A. R. C., *Practical Reason and Morality* (Nelson, 1957); M. J. Detmold, *The Unity of Law and Morality: A Refutation of Legal Positivism* (Canada: Law Book Co. of Australasia, 1984); Lea Brilmayer, *American Hegemony: Political Morality in a OneSuperpower World* (1994); Ahmad Haque Adil, *Law and Morality at War* (2017); Himma Kenneth and Brian Bix (eds), *Law and Morality* (2005); David Lyons, 'Moral Aspects of Legal Theory' in Kenneth Himma and Brian Bix (eds) *Law and Morality* (2005).

3. Moral Justification Refusing Occupied Judgements

Moral justifications require no legal support because they are legal, incomparable norms by nature. Therefore, when discussing the system of international criminal justice in conjunction with the nature of moral justification, we must have a reliable belief in the broad understanding that the system of international criminal justice should not be controlled by the power dynamics of international criminal justice, as they are far removed from any notion of moral justification. Furthermore, justifying a moral judgment or moral truth does not necessitate appealing to unexpected arguments that are presented as the norms of true international criminal justice even though that is not the case. The awareness is that moral justification does not require international criminal justice in the form of miracles that can be empowered and controlled by certain governments. Moral justifications result from the automatic and appropriate implementation of international criminal responsibility without the need for additional jurisdiction over the Court's judgments.

The underlying statements regarding the controlling power of the dominant governments are clear and unquestionable. The rules, norms, provisions, and principles of international criminal law should align with the already-established and documented programs of superior governments under all circumstances. This means that the pursuit of justice is entirely under the control of states employing the theory of criminalisation and criminal condemnation as a foreign policy tool in order to pursue their own wills and interests. This explanation is essential for understanding both the historical and contemporary events of international criminal justice and the reasons why the International Criminal Court have become ineffective.

If the victims of international crimes such as genocide, crimes against humanity, war crimes, aggression, serious sexual violence, and apartheid seek vindication for these grave international offenses, they are generally not supported. This is also true for the judges and prosecutors of the International Criminal Court, indicating that their reactions—whether negative or positive—to the theories of the powertionist system of international criminal justice play a minimal role. It suggests that jurists who embody the true nature of an international criminal court blindly follow the cultivated and discarded plans of terrorist states. The appeals made by the prosecutors or judges of the International Criminal Court to the perceptions presented by the major powers are ultimately empty. All of this indicates an intention to evade the concept of international criminal responsibility on the part of individuals, governments, and their states while presenting different legal and moral values. This is how the moral barrel of international criminal justice is abused as a result of the decisions of various United Nations bodies and the Court.

The logical strength of moral justification against the judgments of terrorist governments is fundamentally based on the serious crimes they commit in their international relations, particularly in connection with the genocide currently being perpetrated against the Palestinians living in Gaza and the West Bank. These crimes are also being committed against the civilians in Lebanon with the most advanced weapons. This crime of genocide, which has been committed against an unarmed population over the course of several decades and has been well-documented, serves as clear evidence that the Israeli government is forcing several million people into exile and preventing access to water, energy, food, and medical treatment. Without any hesitation, the aforementioned suggests that the Zionist government plans to achieve the total annihilation of the population in Gaza. Therefore, moral justification rejects the judgments of the powertionist governments that stem from biased justice and serious violations of the principles of the system of the international criminal responsibility of states positioned in the barrel of justice.

The primary duty of the International Criminal Court is to deliver justice, protect the population of Gaza, and reject the monopolisation of the concept of international criminality by the powertionist international criminal justice system. Consequently, the moral justification of the ICC is undermined by the criminal interventions of the governments that are the root cause of all crimes and the major cause behind economic, political and human rights corruption globally. There is no doubt that the crimes committed in Gaza violate the provisions of international criminal justice and reflect the intentions of the Israeli military power to seize control of Palestinian sovereignty. The rejection of moral justification against aggressive armed attacks illustrates that the various explanations used to justify the underlying claims of the powertionist terrorist governments are fundamentally false. This falsification primarily aims at the destruction of Palestinian civilisation and thus presents a distorted version of the sound of the barrel of justice. Here, the reference to the Palestinian case is just one contemporary example and does not limit the very serious violations of the system of international criminal justice by powertionist governments in other parts of the world.

4. Invading Procedures of Implementation

The arguments I have examined in this book may not align with what most readers expect from a discussion about the theory of international criminal responsibility. The length and foundational basis of these arguments may not cater to those seeking insight into the potential functions of the international criminal law system regarding responsibility or the specifics of its norms and provisions. However, I am not presenting the provisions of international criminal responsibility as a straightforward list of principles. Such lists have already been compiled by numerous authors, and as such, I believe it is not necessary to present the list here again. Instead, my intention is to address the challenges that these lists of provisions may prompt. In other words, I aim to approach the theory of moral justification within the framework of international criminal law by focusing on the substantive violations of its core principles and the implications of these serious breaches of moral law.

However, I am also aware that moral judgments are essentially predictions of sentiment based on specific cases, particularly in light of the serious violations of established principles of international criminal law by powertionist governments. Any opposition to the official implementation of the provisions of the International Criminal Court reflects a powertionist government's mentality that undermines the rule of law and the presentation of moral judgments within that framework. Our argument is that violations of international criminal principles significantly impact, and are influenced by, moral judgments under the procedures of an international criminal court. This implies that any resistance to holding criminals accountable for international crimes leads to either definitive or ambiguous moral judgments. This is why court procedures delve deeper into the evidence presented.

This situation mirrors the current case involving the Palestinian population, for which the prosecutor requested that Pre-Trial Chamber I issue arrest warrants for two Israeli individuals accused of crimes. After deliberately delaying the issuing of arrest warrants, Judge Iulia Motoc, the Presiding Judge, Judge Reine Alapini-Gansou, and Judge Nicolas Guillou made their final decision. It is particularly distressing to comprehend that opposition to the ICC's policies could also come from within the Court itself, in collaboration with powerful criminal governments. My perspective emphasises a substantive moral justification rooted in the legitimate legal basis of the Palestinian case, which is both essential and customary for any state. This implies that it is impossible to deny the international legal personality of the

Palestinian people.[189] It possesses the characteristics of Jus Cogen's international law.[190]

Views regarding international legal personality suggest that a state's population possesses an unequivocal legal right to seek justice from the International Criminal Court (ICC). There is no definitive answer to the delays on the part of Chamber I in addressing the case concerning the grave genocide against the population of Gaza. There have been serious flaws in the Chamber policy at most times, which have concerned powertionist governments. Numerous legal and moral judgments issued by various temporary, unofficial international criminal tribunals clearly highlight the severity of the atrocities being committed against the Palestinians. Consequently, the Pre-Trial Chamber I of the ICC cannot assert that it has been actively working on the case and evaluating evidence for a long time for the condemnation of Israeli criminal government.

The phenomenon is that the system of international criminal justice and the framework of international human rights principles should not continue to be treated as they currently are within the ICC. It is important to acknowledge that an appealing legal or moral approach may not be favourable to powerful governments, and may not effectively address the systematic and egregious violations of international criminal justice.[191] *We all recognise that apartheid,*

---

[189] https://www.icj-cij.org/node/204172.

[190] Examine M. W. Janis, 'The Nature of *Jus Cogens*' 3 *Connecticut Journal of International Law* (1988), p. 359; A. Kawasaki 'A Brief Note on the Legal Effects of *Jus Cogens* in International Law in International Law' 34 *Hitotsubashi Journal of Law and Politics* (2006), p. 27; A. J. J. de Hoog, 'The Relationship between *Jus Cogens, Obligations Erga Omnes* and International Crimes: Peremptory Norms in Perspective' 42 *Österreichische Zeitschrift für öffentliches Recht und Völkerrecht* (1991), p. 18; M. Byers, 'Conceptualising the Relationship Between *Jus Cogens and Erga Omnes* Rules' 66 *Nordic Journal of International Law* (1997), p. 211; A. Cassese, 'For an Enhanced Role of *Jus Cogens*' in A. Cassese (ed.), *Realizing Utopia* (2012); C. Chinkin, '*Jus Cogens*, Article 103 of the UN Charter and other Hierarchical Techniques of Conflict Solution' *Finnish Yearbook of International Law* (2008), p. 63.

[191] For the concept of justice and its violations see Farhad Malekian, 'Mutilating the Philosophy of Justice in the Time of Armed Conflicts', *Contemporary Journal of International Criminal Law* (2007); Farhad Malekian, *The Concept of Islamic International Criminal Law, A Comparative Study* (1994); Farhad Malekian, 'The Miserable Wedding of Naturalism into Positivism,' 2 *ID EST Journal* (2009). Immanuel Kant, *Religion within the Limits of Bare Reason* (1795), p. 87. Launched by Jonathan Bennett, Available online at http://www.earlymoderntexts.com/pdfs/kant1795part4.pdf; Alf Ross, *On Law and Justice* (London: Stevens & Sons Limited, 1958); Vagn Greve, 'Sheep or Wolves' 4 *European Journal of Crime, Criminal Law and Criminal Justice* (2005), 515-552; Hans Kelsen, 'What is Justice?' *Justice, Law and Politics in the Mirror of Science* (1957); Farhad Malekian, 'The Functions of International Criminal Law and the Problem of Positivism and Neutralism Philosophy', *Contemporary Journal of International Criminal Law* (2007).

slavery, and the genocide of thousands of civilians are all wrong. Therefore, anyone who believes that genocide is not occurring, and that the Palestinian population is not being deprived of their homeland, must not fully understand the principles of international human rights law and international criminal justice.[192] *When an international crime is widely perpetrated and recognised by various international organisations, including the International Court of Justice in The Hague, denying such criminal acts clearly undermines the dignity and integrity of the relevant society. Those who dismiss these crimes are thus exhibiting a troubling detachment from reality.*

This position suggests that the concept of international criminal responsibility does not adequately address the rights of populations living under occupation and sanctions imposed by powertionist governments. To what extent can we disregard the rights of ancient populations and the principles of international human rights? How long should the international community tolerate such injustices? *While we are not specifically discussing the ongoing crimes in the Middle East, we must consider the rights of any nation occupied by the dominant powers of the world. There must be a limit to the level of cruelty that both moral and legal truths can no longer accept. Although we may encounter various arguments and disagreements within the framework of international human rights law, it is important to recognise that the sheer volume of crimes is enough for a genocide to be declared. Genocide involves the perpetration of egregious acts without any regard for the limits of such crimes.*

---

[192] The problem is that terrorist governments use religious ideologies to create war and success. Consult also Farhad Malekian, *Corpus Juris of Islamic International Criminal Justice* (Cambridge Scholars Publishing, 2017), p. 17; M Abdel Haleem (ed.), *Criminal Justice in Islam: Judicial Procedure in the Sharīah* (2000); Abdelkader, Deina, *Social Justice in Islam* (Herndon, VA: IIIT, 2000); Mohamed Elewa Badar, 'Islamic Criminal Justice in the 21st Century,' *International Criminal Law Review*, Vol. 9, Number 4, 2009, pp. 591-595; M. Cherif Bassiouni, *The Islamic Criminal Justice System* (London: Oceana Publications, 1982); M. Cherif Bassiouni, 'Protection of Diplomats under Islamic Law', *74 American Journal of International Law* (1980), pp. 609-655;, M. Cherif Bassiouni, '*Islam: Concept, Law and Word Habeas Corpus,*' 2 *Rutgers Camden Law Journal* (1970); M. Cherif Bassiouni, *Sources of Islamic Law, and the Protection of Human Rights in the Islamic Criminal Justice System*, see Bassiouni, pp. 5-55;, M. Cherif Bassiouni, *Studies in Early Hadith Literature* (Indianapolis, 1978); Richard Bell, *Introduction to the Quran,* (Edinburgh University Press, 1955).

5. Moral Comparison Facing Contradictions

Contradictions surrounding the moral implications of the international criminal justice system are not a new phenomenon. This system continually grapples with the atrocities committed by authoritarian governments, which forces moral judgments to either defend or challenge the barbarity of these powerful regimes. As a result, the theory of international criminal responsibility has often been overlooked and hindered in judicial proceedings, and its legal barrel of justice has been satisfied by the conditions of big criminals. It is an intimidating reality that the concept of international criminal responsibility may not be applied to significant offenders, especially given the numerous procedural requirements that must be established and approved for the prosecution of criminals. Consequently, the value of criminalisation diminishes, thereby making it even more difficult to restore the rights of victims.

I do not believe that the system of international criminal justice could disappear due to the moral contradictions posed by powerful criminal governments. However, the question remains: what is the purpose of the Statute of the International Criminal Court when its outcomes are so disheartening? Consequently, the value it is supposed to provide for the victims of international crimes also faces contradictions as it concerns the inherent worth of human life. This implies that no substantial value will be recognised in the establishment of international criminal jurisdiction, nor in the support for the victims. Naturally, through moral comparison, we expect that the effective implementation of international criminal law and human rights will be upheld, and that justice for gross violations of criminal law will be pursued in court.[193]

We do not support the undermining of the most significant international criminal justice legislation by those who, according to the provisions of the United Nations Charter, are fundamentally responsible for preventing aggression, the use of force, international crimes, and maintaining international peace through peaceful means of resolution. However, the reality is that it is not only justice and peace that are compromised by the most accountable members of the Security Council. The rights of victims, along with issues such as murder, rape, torture, and immorality, have become the subjects of unjust and immoral resolutions of the Council, where the veto is

[193] Human Rights in Palestine and Other Occupied Arab Territories: Report of the United Nations Fact-Finding Mission on the Gaza Conflict, GA. A/HRC/12/48 (25 September 2009).

itself unjust and immoral. This indicates that the ethical foundation of the international criminal justice system faces negative moral judgments in practice.

The system of international criminal justice is often viewed negatively thereby leading to a lack of trust among the international public and in the minds of dissenting protesters. Consequently, the trust that victims place in the process of seeking justice becomes a form of defence. The critical question of whether victims should resist injustice or endure their suffering not only weighs heavily on their minds, it also poses a significant challenge for established international criminal justice systems that strive for the universal respect of human rights. It is not without reason that the principle of universality in international criminal justice is generally regarded as an alternative to injustice in the practice of states. When the international criminal justice system fails to uphold the rights of victims, legal judgments falter, and moral restitution becomes nearly impossible to achieve.

Once again, I must address the current state of the international criminal justice system in relation to the ongoing genocide and the systematic erasure of identity. This situation leaves little room for an objective assessment of the atrocities being committed against the Palestinian children, including those of a sexual nature. The harm being inflicted is not only physical but also psychological, and it will have a lasting impact on the victims' personal dignity. It is unlikely that a just decision or a satisfactory answer will emerge from the compromised body of international criminal justice. Consequently, it might be futile to compare the capabilities or achievements of other international criminal tribunals or the previous rulings of the International Criminal Court with the current situation.

The rationale behind this is straightforward: the earlier judgments of the Court focused on African leaders, whom Western governments have historically regarded as inferior. Therefore, any comparison inherently contradicts the fundamental realities that shape the roles, challenges, and context of the current situation. Here, we ought to once again go to the moral barrel of international criminal justice, centred in the office of the prosecutor of the International Criminal Court (ICC). This system has been orchestrated and directed by the political agendas of two dominant nations—the United States and the United Kingdom. I am not exaggerating the brutal actions of these governments.[194] A straightforward investigation into the numerous crimes committed over the course of several centuries by these two states provides more than sufficient evidence of their criminality.[195]

6. Indeterminacy of the Barrel of the ICJ

There are various responses regarding the notion of international criminal responsibility of states. One may offer both positive and negative perspectives on this seemingly simple, yet complex question, depending on how we interpret serious violations within the framework of international criminal law and the collective authority of the relevant state bodies. Our responses may also be influenced by different political constitutions and the prevailing political theories that shape the constitutional frameworks of both national and international criminal justice. Consequently, the concept of indeterminacy within the international criminal justice system highlights the unpredictability of decisions and the disparities in achieving sound moral judgments that are grounded in both moral and legal truths.

There exist indeterminate judgments within the system of international criminal jurisprudence that reflect the quality of the decisions and actions taken by the prosecutor or the Pre-Trial Chambers. These judgments may fail to enforce the provisions of international criminal justice for various reasons, thereby resulting in uncertainty or vagueness in the court's decisions. Even if we adopt a more sceptical perspective regarding the future impact of the Court's judgments on its authority, the underlying issue persists due to the subjective nature of victims' rights in relation to the decisions made by different departments of the International Criminal Court. Despite efforts to seek a viable alternative, we often encounter a problematic approach that fails to uphold the rights of victims when most vital.

The term "indeterminacy" refers to the uncertain position from which parties involved in a case may express differing opinions. Additionally, the term deals with cases that are wilfully overlooked due to negative moral judgments. This implies that judges or prosecutors may feign engagement in certain cases. When the timeframe for issuing a simple arrest warrant exceeds

---

194 Read also David William Pear, 'The US-Led Genocide and Destruction of Yemen', https://www.unz.com/article/the-us-led-genocide-and-destruction-of-yemen/ (October 12, 2019).

195 Furthermore, the perspectives of esteemed scholars, such as Noam Chomsky, Richard Falk, and David Jeffrey from the United States, support these assertions.

reasonable limits and the commission of international crimes is clearly evident, it raises concerns about the accountability of those responsible for making just decisions because they are hesitant to act. Consequently, certain arguments or analogies regarding indeterminate judgments may appear artificial and fail to adequately address the serious implications of criminal conduct by governments.

In the case concerning Palestine before the International Criminal Court (ICC), the prosecutor holds full responsibility for initiating cases against the governments of the United States and the United Kingdom. However, this is unlikely to happen. As previously mentioned, initiating a case could threaten the prosecutor's position, potentially leading to severe condemnation from his own government. This concern underscores the importance of supporting his legal stance. The responsibility for the barrel of international criminal justice is temporarily entrusted to the prosecutor, provided that he adheres to the directives he is given and does not violate his well-known commitments. I reiterate my earlier point: *the judgments and decisions of the prosecutor's office must be politically informed rather than strictly legally informed. In reality, the prosecutor's decisions must align with the values of those in power.*

In this context, the term "indeterminacy" refers to a default judgment that acknowledges the truth of a given fact. However, due to the circumstances surrounding the case and the relationship between the decision and the individual affected by that decision, the judgment does not align with the truth. Consequently, any persuasive argument can be valid for both sides of the case, owing to the significant influence and control one side exerts over the other. *This suggests that for dominant powers, the only correct decisions are the ones they themselves make. The prosecutor's decision often fails to effect change, leaving victims marginalised and unrecognised as such. We must therefore acknowledge that we lack a genuine mechanism that would enable international criminal justice to be capable of addressing cases impartially. This deficiency undermines not only the rights of victims, but also the fundamental principles necessary for the authentic and effective application of justice and judgment.*

My approach to the issues of justice and the concept of international criminal responsibility within the Office of the Prosecutor of the International Criminal Court (ICC) and the Court as a whole, does not present purely positive or negative arguments. This is due to the fact that the commission of international crimes in Gaza can be observed and reported on by anybody in the United Nations or by members not affiliated with the Office of the Prosecutor. The intentional inaction of certain members of the Security

Council is in and of itself sufficient to perpetuate the indeterminate situation regarding the judgments of the Prosecutor, including any chamber of the Court responsible for issuing arrest warrants against perpetrators of crimes. Consequently, the uncertainty created by the influential members of the Security Council generates confusion and anxiety within the framework of international human rights law. This situation undermines the established rights of nations concerning independence and sovereignty. Therefore, any arguments based on monopolisation and authoritarian dominance would contradict the fundamental jurisdiction of a court.[196]

7. Ringleader of International Crimes

The reason why the system of international criminal justice does not work does not rest in the nature of the provisions in the Statute of the ICC. Instead, it results from the fact that we left the Statute in the hands of the perpetrators and instigators of international crimes. This indicates that the ringleader of this group does not allow the idea of international criminal responsibility to be applied against themselves, and the only way to prevent it is to control the dominance of the Court by any means available to them. This could even threaten the prosecutor or the entire ICC itself. Both international courts in The Hague were threatened by the United States government in the past to prevent a case against them from being initiated concerning the crimes they committed in Afghanistan. That is why the ICC modified its stance and did not open an investigation into the terrorist governments engaged in the commission of international crimes in Afghanistan, Libya, and Iraq. The exceptions concerning the prosecution and punishment of criminals were not only minimal, but merely an ornamental procedure in the system of international criminal justice.

Even if the system of international criminal justice were strong enough to bring criminals under its procedures of prosecution and punishment, such a notion of international criminal responsibility would not work due to the strong connections between criminals and the governments of the judges on the court, such as those from the United Kingdom, South Korea, Japan, Canada, France, Romania, and Hungary. This means that the procedures of

---

[196] See Farhad Malekian, *The Monopolization of International Criminal Law in the United Nations, A Jurisprudential Approach* (Stockholm: Almqvist Wiksell International, 1st ed., 1993, 2nd ed., 1995).

international criminal justice cannot solely rely on evidence to accurately present the grave barbarity perpetuated by the criminals of the Israeli, American, and British governments. These states not only make sure to destroy the majority of the evidence relating to their criminality, they also hinder the potential for growth in the countries of their victims. Therefore, the origins of international criminal justice in the prosecutor's office cannot be considered sound, especially given the current Holocaust being committed against unarmed civilians in Gaza and massive murder of civilians in Lebanon. This highlights the formidable challenges faced by an international criminal justice system that has been confronted with Zionist crimes against the civilisation of humanity in Palestine for over eight decades.

Accordingly, the integrated metaphysics of the Statute of the International Criminal Court regarding the rights of justice and the rights of victims cannot guard against the tyranny aggressively perpetuated by authoritarian powertionist governments. The humanitarian intention of international criminal justice has, as a result, been replaced with the aggravated provocation of norms that empower the nation of powertionist governance, international criminal justice, and the concept of powertionist governance in international criminal courts.[197] This situation is clearly detrimental to the essence of equal international criminal justice and consequently supports violations of the already-established system of equal justice.

Adherence to certain brutal discrete convictions becomes the norm of an informal or improvised principle for the ICC, and because those who work in the Court hold dependent positions, justice replaces its platform with injustice, while powertionist governments announce the falsified orders of the powertionist international criminal court. This means that powertionist governments violate the legal personalities of other governments or powertionist governments' ideologies beyond any legitimate political power of other governments. This is why we present the principle of moral justification as one of the fundamental pillars of the international criminal justice system and of the ongoing struggle for the respect of victims within the framework of human rights and the rejection of powertionism in international criminal justice.

My arguments are not intended to deny the authority of the International Criminal Court in our discussions—rather, they aim to affirm it. Nonetheless,

---

[197] Thomas G. Weiss, *Military-Civilian Interactions: Humanitarian Crises and the Responsibility to Protect* (2nd ed., Rowman & Littlefield Publishers Inc, Lanham (MD), 2005).

we are compelled by the force of authentic and imperative truth to seek justice and examine whether the principles of justice are being upheld within the corridors of the Court. Thus, I am not making moral claims here, although some moral assertions may be objectively true in relation to the Court, which is meant to uphold justice and not violate it. The concept of justice, as understood and practiced by those engaged with justice-related issues, should differ from that of those who have not occupied the seats of the Court. This implies that individuals working in the Court must not only possess legal expertise, but also moral integrity, which is essential for the pursuit of truth and respect of the principles of international human rights law.

These human rights are upheld by the body of international criminal justice, which operates under the concept of individual, governmental, and state responsibility for international crimes. This concept is not only grounded in legal positivism, it also embodies a moral truth. While we are not required to strictly adhere to moral justifications, it is evident that legal positivism cannot effectively serve its purpose when it is being manipulated and directed negatively by oppressive governments. Such coercion should not override the rights of victims whose rights have been egregiously violated through international crimes, including war crimes, crimes against humanity, genocide, rape, and apartheid. This argument indicates that with all these individualist presentations, deductions, and implementations, we violate the merit of international criminal justice—the primary intention of which is accountability of individuals, groups, governments, and states for infringements on positive and moral law.

8. Serious Violations of Human Rights Principles

My discussion may not seem necessary, as any lawyer or politician well-versed in international law should recognise that the concept of international responsibility is fundamental to any subject within this field. Law cannot be discussed effectively without addressing the notion of responsibility. This is particularly significant within human rights law and international criminal justice. Any violation of legal systems prompts a re-evaluation of our ethical reasoning regarding the specific case, particularly when it involves serious breaches of international human rights that amount to criminal offenses. We are addressing the values inherent in our human rights and criminal law norms, as well as the obligation for all individuals and authorities to respect these values. This underscores the fact that our arguments possess established legal characteristics and should not be overlooked.

The imperative function of international human rights law and international criminal justice cannot be selectively applied and it must be upheld consistently at all times. When discussing the international criminal responsibility of a government or state, we must not diminish the rights of certain victims while emphasising the rights of others. Our arguments in the courtroom must therefore be grounded in a legal theory or framework that cannot be easily dismissed, regardless of the powerful positions held by the perpetrators. There are more complex and compelling legal arguments rooted in the established norms of international human rights that must be given due consideration, especially when the rights of victims have been egregiously violated during armed conflicts.

I cannot comprehend the current situation and the ongoing massacre of the Palestinian population in their homeland. It is essential to uphold the principles of international human rights, which must be respected at all times. The evidence supporting the claim of ongoing genocide is significantly stronger than any arguments that could be presented by the International Criminal Court or by members of the Security Council. We should not draw false comparisons between the actions of those committing these barbaric crimes and the realities of the atrocities being committed. The horrific crimes perpetrated by Hitler against *innocent Jews* were undeniably barbaric, and any rationale he offered for his crimes was not only misguided, but fundamentally lacking in moral justification. This remains true regardless of our engagement with the barrel of criminal justice and whether or not we recognise Hitler as a criminal. Those who are corrupt, surly bear the flags of Nazism permanently. A similar theory is valid about the Obama, Biden, Bush (both), Boris Johnson, Rishi Sunak, Tony Blair, Keir Starmer, to name but a few. Millions have perished because of them.

How can a further claim regarding international crimes be defended when the orchestration of fruitful barrels of the proceedings of the International Criminal Court is no longer essential? The awareness is that when principles of international human rights are egregiously violated, discussions about the rights of victims in the Court become imperative. It would be absurd and dogmatic to argue that the perpetrators of the most heinous and inhumane crimes are seeking to identify those who are striving for self-determination. Our intention here is not to undermine the authority of the ICC. Rather, we seek to emphasise that international legal norms cannot function effectively and ethically if they compromise the moral justification for the actions taken against victims. The only reasonable and logical argument that warrants the attention of the International Criminal Court is the recognition of the crimes committed through military trade and the application of the concept of international criminal responsibility to the offenders.

Moreover, according to the United Nations Arms Trade Treaty of 2013, exporting firearms not only undermines the international criminal justice system under specific circumstances, it is also regarded as a serious violation of human rights norms. Article 7 of the Treaty establishes the most significant norms for preventing serious violations of international criminal justice. Interestingly, one of the most important concepts within the treaty encompasses not only various forms of legal infractions, but also refers to both moral and legal truths. [198] This implies that terms such as "violations", "systematic violations", and other similar phrases are condemned under the Treaty Proviso.[199] Furthermore, the veto power held by the permanent members undermines the system of international human rights and international criminal law, potentially constituting serious violations of the principles of international criminal justice.

Deceptions presented as truth by criminals during wartime and within the halls of the Security Council reflect a malevolent mind-set. Consequently, a substantive moral argument forms the foundation of the conscience of lawyers, judges, prosecutors, politicians, and all those involved in matters of justice and politics.[200] While I recognise that identifying a righteous individual is indeed complicated for lawyers and even more challenging for politicians, we must not abandon hope. We should remember that justice thrives on hope rather than security, and this is the most crucial reason why the hopes of victims must not be extinguished by the malevolent actions of brutal criminals.[201]

---

[198] Article 7.

[199] Examine also E. Cannizzaro, 'A Higher Law for Treaties?' in E. Cannizzaro (ed.),The Law of Treaties Beyond the Vienna Convention (2011); Emerson DeAnna, Mars/Earth Enigma: A Sacred Message to Mankind (1996), 238Danilenko G. M., 'International *Jus cogens*: Issues of Law Making,' *European Journal of International Law* (1991).

[200] Farhad Malekian, *Conscience of Judges in International Criminal Law, the Heart of Judgements* (New York: Nova Science Publishers, 2021); Farhad Malekian, *Conscience of Lawyers in International Criminal Law, the Burden of Doppelgängers* (New York: Nova Science Publishers, 2021); Farhad Malekian, *Conscience of Prosecutors in International Criminal Law, the Heart of the Matter* (New York: Nova Science Publishers, 2021).

[201] https://www.thearmstradetreaty.org/hyper-images/file/TheArmsTradeTreaty1/TheArmsTradeTreaty.pdf.

Chapter 8

Conclusion

The body of international criminal responsibility cannot function with dishonoured hands and ruined minds violating the system of international law of jus cogens.[202] In this brief work, I have discussed the system of international criminal responsibility, not by detailing where to find the relevant provisions concerning the criminal accountability of individuals, governments, or states, but rather by exploring the emergence of their applications as the system of *erga omnes*.[203] Furthermore, a reader who only engages with my conclusion may miss the broader context of my arguments. Conclusions in works addressing justice serve to guide readers in the appropriate direction to effect

---

[202] On *jus cogens* consult Czaplinski, Wladyslaw 'Concepts of *Jus Cogens* and Obligations Erga Omnes in International Law in the Light of Recent Developments' 23 *Polish Yearbook of International Law* (1997–1998), p. 87; G. Danilenko, 'International *Jus Cogens*: Issues of Law-Making' 2 (1) *European Journal of International Law* (1991), p. 42; A. D'Amato, 'It's a Bird, It's a Plane, It's *Jus Cogens*' 6 *Connecticut Journal of International Law* (1990), p. 1; AJJ de Hoog, 'The Relationship between *Jus Cogens*, Obligations Erga Omnes and International Crimes: Peremptory Norms in Perspective' 42 *Österreichische Zeitschrift für öffentliches Recht und Völkerrecht* (1991), p. 183; E de Wet, '*Jus Cogens* and Obligations Erga Omnes' in de Wet, E and J. Vidmar (eds.), *Hierarchy in International Law: The Place of Human Rights* (2012); P Dupuy, 'Some Reflections on Contemporary International Law and the Appeal to Universal Values: a Response to Marti Koskenniemi' 16 *European Journal of International Law* (2005), p. 131; C. Focarelli, 'Promotional *Jus Cogens*: A Critical Appraisal of *Jus Cogens*' Legal Effects' 77 *Nordic Journal of International Law* (2008), p. 429; M. J. Glennon, 'De l'Absurdité du Droit Impératif (*Jus Cogens*)' 110 *Revue Générale de Droit International Public* (2006), p. 529; Robledo Gómez, A El Ius Cogens Internacional (Estudio Histórico Crítico) (1982); A. Gómez Robledo 'Le *Jus Cogens* International: Sa Genése, sa Nature, ses Fonctions' 9 *Recueil des Cours de l'Académie de Droit International de la Haye* (1982), p. 172; L. Hannikainen, *Peremptory Norms (Jus Cogens) in International Law: Historical Development, Criteria, Present Status* (1988).

[203] E. de Wet, '*Jus Cogens* and Obligations Erga Omnes' in, E de Wet and Vidmar (eds.), J *Hierarchy in International Law: The Place of Human Rights*, (2012). A. J. J. de Hoog, 'The Relationship between *Jus Cogens*, *Obligations Erga Omnes* and International Crimes: Peremptory Norms in Perspective' 42 *Österreichische Zeitschrift für öffentliches Recht und Völkerrecht* (1991); A. de Hoogh, *Obligations erga omnes and International Crimes: A Theoretical Inquiry into the Implementation and Enforcement of the International Responsibility of States* (Kluwer The Hague, 1996). See also Erika de Wet, 'The Prohibition of Torture as an International Norm of *Jus Cogens* and its Implementation for National and Customary Law,' 15 (1) *European Journal of International Law* (2014), Vol. 15, No. 1, 97-121.

change; thus, conclusions do not encapsulate the entirety of any book but rather only provide guidelines on how to achieve objectives of the relevant book. I acknowledge that I have not fully addressed the entire philosophy of this subject, as each word can spark endless debates and discussions. Consequently, what we write about justice worldwide often amounts to mere phrasal play. This suggests that our statements are often repetitions of words and explanations used to persuade one another.

However, despite what I have stated in the previous paragraph, there are certain matters that no longer distort the reality of the truth. Theories surrounding words and phrases cannot alter or misrepresent their established legal nature. In other words, it would be more prudent for me to align with the writings of the significant majority of authors who support politicians or other writers. This confirms that I do not need to engage in new arguments to justify providing moral or legal support for the rights of victims. It would be easier and less controversial to present a novel approach to these discussions. Such an approach would not only satisfy the reader, but also appease the ruthless politicians of our time, who are averse to hearing any new arguments regarding their criminal activities. However, none of this would fulfil my mind or my soul, as a soul that does not seek a new and controversial approach to combatting the criminal activities of major offenders is no longer a free soul. Instead, such a soul becomes a slave to the theories of those who have influenced the international community and directed it toward the condemnation of victims. This is not my personal character, and furthermore, I cannot support those who barter away the rights of victims.

The reality is that my convictions regarding the international criminal responsibility of states and governments are not mere bargaining words or phrases; rather, they are fundamentally unyielding. I have not, and will not, relinquish my pursuit of justice under any circumstances. I am acutely aware of how international human rights lawyers and authors of international criminal justice negotiate with their subjects, i.e., often with a misplaced sense of confidence and conscience. They seem to believe that their actions, thoughts, and intentions remain just and noble, akin to a gilded representation of justice. However, this perspective starkly contrasts with the true essence of justice, which is often overshadowed by malevolent intentions. In truth, these individuals appear to be deaf to the anguished cries of victims, whose suffering is drowned out by the symphonies of international human rights being orchestrated by powertionist governments within the frameworks of the International Criminal Court and the United Nations, as well as by the vetoed resolutions of the Security Council. The voices of the victims are conspicuously absent when we observe and analyse the human rights frameworks embedded in various solutions. This absence signifies a profound moral failure, akin to the erasure of the very concept of morality itself.

These central conclusions may seem unusual and inadequate for a comprehensive understanding of the international criminal justice system and its legal jurisdiction. The limited scope of many authors' texts and the conclusions they support do not address the issue of moral strength; instead, they emphasise the form of legal strength that is favoured by their superiors. However, it is the legal interpretation that is significant, not the flawed interpretations and deductions derived from relevant laws. The validity of a moral claim is inconsequential as long as the complete truth lies with the jurisdiction of the Security Council, the International Court of Justice (ICJ), or the International Criminal Court (ICC). Many international lawyers, judges of the Court, authors of international human rights law, and even experts in international criminal justice aspire to find solutions that satisfy both parties, as they are eager to avoid losing financial support. The essence of sound reasoning in any matter, particularly within the domain of international criminal justice and accountability, forms the foundation of genuine moral or legal theory. It is not important whether or not the advocates are the victims or the perpetrators. Rather, what matters is that the ultimate advocate must promote the truth to the system of justice and its process of jurisprudence. This is why we established the United Nations, the International Court of Justice, and the International Criminal Court.

As a fundamental imperative principle of justice, we should avoid becoming trapped in a cycle that results in a hollow victory. A victory that is not grounded in a truthful representation of all relevant matters—both visible and invisible—cannot adequately convey the extent of the suffering experienced by victims. *We cannot obscure the profound truth with grandiose lies. Otherwise, the moral barrel of truth will swell and ultimately burst. My moral convictions regarding international criminal justice are not based on personal judgments, but rather on how the victims of international crimes confront the realities of war crimes, crimes against humanity, genocide, sexual abuse, torture, and apartheid.* My concerns about the moral barrels of justice under the influence of the Security Council extend beyond the Council itself and the decisions it vetoes. Furthermore, I am aware that the barrels of justice are indirectly undermined by the International Criminal Court (ICC) as well. This is because the veto decisions made by certain members of the Security Council effectively serve to veto the judgments of the ICC.

If manipulating and vetoing the system of criminal responsibility is deemed to be acceptable in the name of justice, then we are compelled to uphold similar standards for all future judgments and not prevent any barbaric acts of murder. Moreover, the current distinction being made between various subjects of international criminal justice with similar international legal personalities is fundamentally flawed and should be avoided. This suggests that the United Nations Security Council should be abolished, and accountability for all entities involved in the commission of international crimes should be firmly established within the International Criminal Court (ICC).

A further dimension of this is that the foundations of international criminal justice must be established at the heart of the General Assembly. This entails achieving consensus concerning the identification of criminals and the prevention of heinous crimes perpetrated by terrorist regimes. I am not imposing my own beliefs about right and wrong here and instead aim to uphold the value of the truth over falsehoods. While my judgments may appear personal, they are not in essence. While forming convictions is certainly permissible, it does not justify allowing our judgments—whether based intentionally or unintentionally on falsehoods—to serve as mere embellishments on the fabric of justice. This holds true regardless of the colour of the fabric or the intentions behind it. Justice must always confront the truth, not lies, and must not be influenced by those with power.

If we believe that our reasons for accepting the arguments of powerful nations are valid and should be concealed, we must recognise that we are confronting the core of deception and following falsehoods that masquerade as the truth within the system of international criminal justice. My arguments do not imply that I intend to diminish the intellect of my readers or steer them toward my own interpretations and understanding of international criminal justice and the scope of international criminal responsibility. While some individuals are capable of recognising and articulating the truth regarding serious violations within the international criminal justice system, others may still be convinced that the issues within international criminal justice have been caused by the victims themselves. When a criminal case is addressed through the procedures of the International Criminal Court we may encounter additional facets of the case that have been overlooked due to the significant influence of perpetrators on the ICC and its judges.

Nonetheless, the situation described above should not diminish our moral and legal responsibilities as advocates for justice, particularly within the framework of international criminal justice. We must confront the reality of how the current circumstances are being engineered with the explicit goal of annihilating the Palestinian nation, occupying their territories, and erasing their longstanding sovereignty. I cannot absolve myself of the responsibility for the barbaric conditions perpetuated by Western colonial powers through the use of force and egregious violations of the rights of a historic nation. Conversely, how can the systems of international criminal justice and international human rights remain silent and allow these serious violations to go unaddressed? It is essential for readers to reflect on the concept of justice and, more importantly, on the foundational principles that underpin appropriate justice.[204] These facts are crucial to understanding the present violations and the ongoing genocide in Palestine.

We must consider the crucial question of how moral justifications and legal truths can be undermined, not only by authoritarian or powertionist governments, but also by the International Criminal Court (ICC), which has ostensibly addressed the most serious violations of international criminal law and justice since the establishment of international criminal courts. However, the reality is that the ICC has been largely ineffective. This indicates a pressing need for more comprehensive moral perspectives regarding the values of international criminal norms and the importance of upholding those norms despite a wide array of moral challenges faced by the Court and every government within the General Assembly. My interpretation weaves together values for every member of the international legal and political community, uniting them in their purpose. We bear moral responsibility to the extent that our numerous concrete interpretations of the international human rights system confront the central issues and ensure that the crimes of totalitarian governments do not go unpunished. It is not my intention within the international legal community to evaluate or dismiss the ICC's decisions based on the perceived weaknesses of its prosecutor. Nonetheless, it is undeniable that the three judges of Chamber I, who delayed issuing arrest warrants for Israeli perpetrators, also share significant responsibility for failing to fulfil

[204] Issues in Contemporary Legal Philosophy: The Influence of H. L. A. Hart (Ruth Gavison, ed., 1987); Heidi Hurd, Challenging Authority, 100 Yale Law Journal 1611 (1991); G. Hughes, Validity and the Basic Norm, 59 California Law Review695 (1971); H. L. A. Hart, Essays in Jurisprudence and Philosophy (1983); Joseph Raz, The Morality of Freedom (1986); J. W. Harris, Legal Philosophies, 2ndedn. (1997); John Austin, The Province of Jurisprudence Determined and the Uses of the Study of Jurisprudence (1954);, Gerald J. Postema, Bentham and the Common Law Tradition (1986); Julie Dickson, Evaluation and Legal Theory (2001); H. L. A. Hart, The Concept of Law (1961); H. L. A. Hart, The Concept of Law, 2ndedn., (P. A. Bulloch and J. Raz eds., 1994).

their duties in a timely manner. Presiding Judge Iulia Motoc,[205] Judge Reine Alapini-Gansou,[206] and Judge Nicolas Guillou[207] have not been managing the moral and legal obligations of the case appropriately. They have acted as the puppets of the owners of the ICC. However, they chose a very harsh policy regarding the Russian and Ukraine case.

If moral reasoning is absent in the administration of the International Criminal Court (ICC), then the issue of justice becomes purely subjective, as we see today. How can we discuss the concept of international criminal jurisdiction when, in the context of interpretive moral concepts, we hide behind the passage of time? In other words, when we indirectly reject the notion of international criminal responsibility and permit heinous crimes to be committed against the children of Gaza, we are complicit in the massacre and exploitation of human civilisation. It is essential to remember that the concept of responsibility is a fundamental principle within the framework of human rights and morality.[208] Furthermore, it is the inherent duty of all international criminal tribunals and courts to act responsibly and acknowledge their obligations concerning the prosecution and punishment of offenders. When the judges of Chamber I of the International Criminal Court neglect to timely pursue the arrest of Israeli leaders, they are not only permitting impunity but also facilitating, aiding, cooperating with, supporting, and colluding in the commission of the international crime of barbarism.

The powertionist governments that start wars with other nations and kill innocent individuals with the intention of seizing their sovereignty, resources, oil, and gas cannot claim that they are acting irresponsibly. The same applies to the International Criminal Court (ICC), which has been authorised by the international legal and political community to prevent international crimes and enforce penalties, and yet fails to do so. This means that regardless of the assertions made by judges of the International Court of Justice, they bear responsibility for crimes being committed against civilians or individuals within international criminal jurisdiction. It is essential to remember that all nations are subject to the authority of the International Criminal Court. This implies that the court has a duty to protect victims when their rights have been

---

[205] The nomination was made by the Romanian government.

[206] The Benin government, a former French colony.

[207] The nomination was made by the French government.

[208] Michael J. Perry, A Global Political Morality: Human Rights, Democracy, and Constitutionalism (Cambridge University Press, 2017); Farhad Malekian, *Tour de force of Moral Virtue in International Criminal Justice* (New York: Nova Science Publishers, 2022), p. 103. Consult also Farhad Malekian, *The Mirage of International Criminal Law, Kant Metaphysics of Mens Rea* (Cambridge Scholars Publishing, 2018).

criminally violated. How can the Pre-Trial Chamber and judges of the Court fail to act in the face of crimes being committed against the Palestinian population under the guise of searching for hostages? All offenses perpetrated against victims impose a significant responsibility upon the judges of the Court, irrespective of whether they are serving in a Chamber or within the office of the Prosecutor. The entire Palestinian nation has effectively been held hostage by Israel for over eighty years. However, this situation has not been acknowledged by any entity in the world, and now the ICC is also neglecting the enduring suffering of the Palestinians on top of it.

The judges of the Court are clearly not naive. They take pride in their international titles and are deeply committed to their roles. The judges, including the Chief Justice of the Court, bear the responsibility for upholding the principles of international criminal justice, which includes protecting the law, ensuring justice, delivering fair judgments, and advocating for victims' rights. While the Israeli government is responsible for starting the conflict, the Court must also be held accountable for its failure to act decisively as it concerns bringing perpetrators under its jurisdiction. The framework of international criminal justice has not been mistakably placed under the control of the International Criminal Court (ICC), despite the fact that the Security Council oversees its operations. The ICC is tasked with the implementation of international criminal justice, and this duty should not be disregarded by any judge of the Court. In fact, all ICC judges have a critical responsibility to ensure that their judgments meet established criteria. They must choose between ignoring prosecutable crimes or imposing appropriate penalties.

Moreover, it is imperative that all of the judges of the International Criminal Court, in addition to their established duties and obligations, assume a judicial responsibility to acknowledge the crimes that are occurring, identify any intentional misconduct or deficiencies among their colleagues, and observe the significant suffering endured by the children of Palestine as well as the broader population. They must ensure that the provisions of the ICC are diligently applied in every case presented before its jurisdiction. While they may continue to overlook and temporarily disregard the position of the victims and fail to promote their rights, this does not absolve them of their potential personal and ethical-legal duties and responsibilities. Various interpretations of responsibility can be cited to explain why the Court fails to take the necessary actions when necessary. Nevertheless, the essence of the judicial responsibility of ICC judges, both as judges and as individuals, remains unchanged. It is true that morally responsible judges of the Court act according to their personal moral principles and do not evade their personal accountability in relation to their professional roles. *These judges act in accordance with the universal principle of humanity, regardless of the requirements of their duties. This means that their responsibility is irrevocable.*

In order to serve as a judge or prosecutor at the International Criminal Court, one must possess a comprehensive understanding of the law and its moral implications. At first glance, it may appear that moral responsibilities and obligations are immutable; however, judges often fail to safeguard the rights of victims within the justice system. The laws of nature do not heed to the whims and self-serving interests of authoritarian governments, nor can they ignore the cries of those suffering from torture or sexual violence at the hands of oppressive regimes. Unfortunately, such governments have officially permitted their operatives to seize humanitarian aid intended for victims. Consequently, the question of what constitutes brutality becomes irrelevant when the principles of justice, peace, security, and judgment confront the same injustices, even within the framework of natural law.[209] Self-preservation has become the primary face of injustice, serving as the catalyst for atrocities such as the Holocaust and the annihilation of entire nations. Such self-serving motives, often rooted in utilitarianism, also drive wars and the erosion of the traditional rights of nations. Fundamentally, the rationale behind utilitarianism and self-preservation poses a significant threat to the foundation of morality and the ethical application of criminal justice. This indicates that even though the system of international criminal law holds individuals accountable for violations and the framework of international human rights is tasked with preventing such violations, the power of the enforceability of all laws is still monopolised by the strong, brutal governments.

[209] Examine Mark J Osiel, *Obeying orders: Atrocity, Military Discipline, and the Law of War* (Transaction Publishers, 1999); Timothy L. H McCormack, *The Law of War Crimes: National and International Approaches* (Brill, 1997); Rene Provost, *International Human Rights and Humanitarian Law* (2002); William A. Schabas, *War Crimes and Human Rights: Essays on the Death Penalty, Justice and Accountability* (Cameron May, 2008); Steven R. Ratner, Jason S. Abrams, and James L. Bischoff, *Accountability for Human Rights Atrocities in International Law: Beyond the Nuremberg Legacy*, (3rd ed., Oxford Press, 2009); Eric Stover, *My Neighbour, My Enemy: Justice and Community in the Aftermath of Mass Atrocity* (Cambridge University Press, 2004); Benjamin B. Ferencz, *New Legal Foundations for Global Survival: Security Through the Security Council* (Oceana Publications,1994). See also Farhad Malekian, 'Judging International Criminal Justice in the Occupied Territories,' 12 *International Criminal Law Review* (2012), 827–869; Farhad Malekian, *Trading Virginity of International Criminal Justice* (Nova Sciences Publishers, 2020).

Bibliography*

Albanese Francesca P. and Lex Takkenberg, *Palestinian Refugees in International Law* (2nd Edition, 2020).

Albanese Francesca, Anatomy of a Genocide: Report of the Special Rapporteur on the situation of human rights in the Palestinian territories occupied since 1967, p.3, https://www.ohchr.org/sites/default/files/documents/hrbodies/hrcouncil/sessions-regular/session55/advance-versions/a-hrc-55-73-auv.pdf (visited 03/11/2024).

Alexy R., *'Effects of Defects - Action or Argument? Thoughts about Deryck Beyleveld and Roger Brownsword's Law as a Moral Judgment'* (Ratio Juris, 2006), pp. 169–79.

Alexy R., 'The Dual Nature of Law, *Ratio Juris'* (2010), pp. 167–82.

Alexy R., 'The Reasonableness of Law' in *Reasonableness and Law* Ed. Giorgio Bongiovanni, Giovanni Sartor, and Chiara Valentini (Dordrecht: Springer, 2009), pp. 5–15.

Alexy R., Discourse Theory and Fundamental Rights' in *Arguing Fundamental Rights* Ed. Agustín José Menéndez and Erik Oddvar Eriksen (Dordrecht: Springer, 2006), pp. 15–29.

Alexy R., *On the Concept and the Nature of Law* (Ratio Juris, 2008), pp. 21: 281–99.

Allison H., *Kant's Theory of Freedom* (Cambridge University Press, 1990).

Amato A. D., 'It's a Bird, It's a Plane, It's *Jus cogens*' 6 *Connecticut Journal of International Law*, (1990).

Ambion B. C., Organisation of a Court of International Criminal Jurisdiction, 29 *Philippine Law Journal* 345 (1954).

Andreopoulos G. J., (ed.), *Genocide: Conceptual and Historical Dimensions* (Philadelphia, 1994).

Annacker C., 'The Legal Régime of erga omnes Obligations in International Law' 46 *Austrian Journal of Public International Law*, (1994), pp. 131–66.

Aquila R. E., *Matter in Mind: A Study of Kant's Transcendental Deduction* (Indiana University Press, 1989).

Arts K., Vesselin Popovski. (eds.), *International Criminal Accountability and the Rights of Children* (Heidelberg: Springer, 2006), pp. 37–52 and 53–65.

Austin J., *The Province of Jurisprudence Determined and the Uses of the Study of Jurisprudence* (1954).

Baderin M. A., *International Human Rights and Islamic Law* (New York, NY: Oxford University Press, 2005).

Baderin M., A., 'A Comparative Analysis of the Right to a Fair Trial and due Process under International Human Rights Law and Saudi Arabian Domestic Law,' 10 (3) *The International Journal of Human Rights*, (2006).

Bantekas I., Susan Nash, *International Criminal Law*, (2007).

* Mention here neither includes nor excludes in the text. It neither confirms nor rejects the work.

Barron A., (Legal) Reason and its "Others": Recent DevelopmentinLegal Theory, in *Introduction to Jurisprudence and Legal Theory: Commentary and Materials* (Schiff Penner, and Nobles, eds., 2002), 1038-63.

Bartlett E., *'What's Happening in Syria? The Media 'Kills the Truth,' 'Terrorism' is Described as 'Moderate Opposition.'* (Global Research, February 05, 2017).

Bartlett E., *How We Were Mislead about Syria.*

Bartlett E., *Is Eva Bartlett Credible?* https://www.quora.com/Is-Eva-Bartlett-credible (Accessed: 14th 2016).

Bassiouni C., 'International Crimes: Jus cogens and Obligatio Erga Omnes' 59 *Law and Contemporary Problems*, (1996).

Bassiouni M. Cherif and Benjamin B. Ferencz, The Crime Against Peace and Aggression: From Its Origins to the ICC, in *International Criminal Law,* vol. I, (M. Cherif Bassiouni, ed. 2008), pp. 207-242.

Bassiouni M. Cherif, (ed.), *International Criminal Law* (US: Ocean Publication, 3 vols., 1999).

Bassiouni M. Cherif, (ed.), *International Terrorism and Political Crimes* (1975).

Bassiouni M. Cherif, 'A Comprehensive Strategic Approach on International Cooperation for the Prevention, Control and Suppression of International and Transnational Criminality, Including the Establishment of an International Criminal Court,' 15 *Nova Law Review*, 353, (1991).

Bassiouni M. Cherif, 'The Discipline of International Criminal Law,' in M. cherif Bassiouni (ed.), *International Criminal Law*, Vol. 1, (2008), pp. 5-40.

Bassiouni M. Cherif, 'The Subjects of International Criminal Law: Ratione Personae' in M. Bassiouni Cherif (ed.), *International Criminal Law*, Vol. 1, (2008), pp. 41-70.

Bassiouni M. Cherif, Benjamin B. Ferencz, *The Crime Against Peace and Aggression: From Its Origins to the ICC, in International Criminal Law*, vol. I, (M. Cherif Bassiouni, ed. 2008).

Bassiouni M. Cherif, *Crimes Against Humanity in International law*, (1999).

Bassiouni M. Cherif, *Criminal Justice in the Time of War and Peace* (Cambridge University Press, Cambridge, 2014).

Bassiouni M. Cherif, *Introduction to International Criminal Law*, (2005).

Bassiouni M. Cherif, The Discipline of International Criminal Law, in *International Criminal Law,* Vol. I (M. Cherif Bassiouni, ed., 2008).

Bassiouni M. Cherif, *The Shariah and Islamic Criminal Justice in the Time of War and Peace* (Cambridge University Press, Cambridge, 2014).

Baum L. M., 'Pursuing Justice in a Climate of Moral Outrage: An Evaluation of the Rights of the Accused in the Rome Statute of the International Criminal Court,' 19 *Wisconsin International Law Journal* (2001).

Beccaria C., *On Crimes and Punishments*, (1764).

Bellamy A., *Responsibility to Protect: the Global Effort to End Mass Atrocities* (Polity Press, Cambridge, 2009).

Bellamy R. (ed.), *C Beccaria, On Crimes and Punishments*. (1995).

Benneh E. Y., 'Sovereignty Immunity and International Crimes,' 22 *Ghana Law Journal*, (2002–2004), 112.

Bennett J., *Kant's Analytic* (Cambridge University Press, 1966).

Bennett J., *Kant's Dialectic* (Cambridge University Press, 1974).

Bennoune K., 'As-Salamu 'Alykum? Humanitarian Law in Islamic Jurisprudence,' 15 *Michigan Journal of International Law*, (1994), pp. 605-643.

Berman S. (ed.), *The Oxford Handbook of Legal Pluralism* (Oxford University Press, 2019).

Berman S., *Global Legal Pluralism: A Jurisprudence of Law Beyond Borders Global* (2012).

Bermann G. A. Roger J. Goebel, William J. Davey, Eleanor M. Fox et al., *Cases and Materials on European Community Law* (1993).

Bernstein R. J. *Radical Evil: A Philosophical Interrogation* (New York: Blackwell Publisher, 2002).

Bianchi A., 'Human Rights and the Magic of Jus cogens,' 19 *European Journal of International Law*, (2008), pp. 491-508.

Bigi G., 'Joint Criminal Enterprise in the Jurisprudence of the International Criminal Tribunal for the former Yugoslavia and the Prosecution of Senior Political and Military Leaders: The Krajišnik Case' 14 Guyer Paul, *The Cambridge Companion to Kant,* (1992).

Bigi G. 'Joint Criminal Enterprise in the Jurisprudence of the International Criminal Tribunal for the former Yugoslavia and the Prosecution of Senior Political and Military Leaders: The Krajišnik Case' 14 *Max Planck United Nations Yearbook*, (2010), pp. 51-83.

Bird G., *Kant's Theory of Knowledge*, (Humanities Press, 1962).

Bix B., 'Natural Law: The Modern Tradition' in Jules Coleman and Schott Shapiro (eds.), *The Oxford Handbook of Jurisprudence and Philosophy of Law*, (2002).

Bloxham Donald, *Genocide on Trial: War Crimes Trials and the Formation of Holocaust History and Memory* (2001).

Boas G., *International Criminal Justice: Legitimacy and Coherence*, (2012).

Boas G., William A. Schabas (eds.), *International Criminal Law Developments in the Case Law of the ICTY* (2005).

Boot M., *Genocide, Crimes against Humanity, War Crimes: Nullum Crimen Sine Lege and the Subjective Matter of Jurisdiction of the International Criminal Court*, (2002).

Brilmayer L., *American Hegemony: Political Morality in a One Superpower World* (1994).

Broomhall B., *International Justice and the International Criminal Court: Between Sovereignty and the Rule of Law* (2003).

Browning C., *The Path to Genocide: Essays on Launching the Final Solution*, (2002).

Browning D. (eds.), *Universalism vs. Relativism: Making Moral Judgements in a Changing, Pluralistic, and Threatening World* (Rowman and Littlefield Publishers, United Kingdom, 2006).

Brownlie I., *International Law and the Use of Force by States* (Oxford: Oxford University Press, 1996).

Brownlie I., *Principles of Public International Law* (Oxford: Clarendon Press, 5th ed., 1998).

Brunnée J., 'The Prohibition on Torture: Driving *Jus cogens* Home?' 104 *Proceedings of the Annual Meeting of the American Society of International Law*, (2010).

Buchanan A., 'Toward a Drone Accountability Regime,' 29 (1) *Ethics and International Affairs*, (2015), pp. 15–70.

Burke-White W. W, 'Implementing a Policy of Positive Complementarity in the Rome System of Justice,' 19 *Criminal Law Forum*, (2008), 59-89.

Burns P. 'An International Criminal Tribunal: The Difficult Union of Principle and Politics,' 5 *Criminal Law Forum*, (1994).

Byers M. 'Conceptualising the Relationship Between *Jus cogens* and *Erga Omnes Rules*' 66 *Nordic Journal of International Law*, (1997).

Caenegem R. C., Van, *European Law in the Past and the Future: Unity and Diversity over Two Millennia* (Cambridge: Cambridge University Press, 2001).

Cançado T., A. '*Jus cogens* in Contemporary International Law,' *UN Audiovisual Library*, (http://www.un.org/law/avl).

Carvin S., 'Getting Drones Wrong,' 19 (2) *International Journal of Human Rights*, (2015), pp. 127–141.

Cassese A. and Albin Eser (eds.), *The Rome Statute of the International Criminal Court: A Commentary* (2002).

Cassese A. and Paola Gaeta, *Cassese's International Criminal Law* (3rd, 2013).

Cassese A., (ed.), *The New Humanitarian Law of Armed Conflict* (Naples: Editoriale Scientifica, 1979).

Cassese A., 'First Annual Report of the ICTY,' *Yearbook of International Law Commission*, (1994).

Cassese A., 'For an Enhanced Role of Jus cogens' in Cassese, A (ed.), *Realizing Utopia*, (2012).

Cassese A., Albin Eser, Giorgio Gaja and Robert E. Conor, *Justice at Nuremberg* (1980).

Cassese A., *International Criminal Law* (Oxford: Oxford University Press, 2nd, ed., 2008).

Cassese A., On the Current Trends Towards Criminal Prosecution and Punishment of Breaches of International Humanitarian Law, 9 *European Journal of Internaitonal Law* 2 (1998).

Chinkin C., '*Jus Cogens*, Article 103 of the UN Charter and Other Hierarchical Techniques of Conflict Solution,' 17 *Finnish Yearbook of International Law* (2008), pp. 63-90.

Chomksy N. and Barsamian D., *Keeping the Rabble in Line.* Boston: Common Courage Press (1994).

Chomsky N., *Media Control: The Spectacular Achievements of Propaganda.* New York: Seven Stories Press (2004).

Chossudovsky M., *War and Globalisation: The Truth Behind September 11* (Global Outlook, 2002).

Christian P., Scherrer, *Iraq: Genocide by Sanctions* (2011).

Clark M., *Nietzsche on Truth and Philosophy* (1991).

Clark R. S., 'The Crime of Apartheid,' in M. Cherif Bassiouni (ed.), *International Criminal Law*, vol. I (1986), pp. 299-323.

Clark R., *War Crimes – A Report on United States War Crimes against Iraq* (Maisonneuve Press, 1992).

Claus K., 'Aggression and the Use of Force in International Law,' *Proceedings of the 108th Annual Meeting of the American Society of International Law,* No. 108, 2014, pp. 325–346.

Cohen M., 'Moral Aspects of the Criminal Law,' 49 *Yale Law Journal* (1949), pp. 987-1026.

Crawford J., Olleson S., 'The Continuing Debate on a UN Convention on State Responsibility,' 54 *ICLQ*, (2005), 959–71.

Cryer R., 'The Doctrinal Foundations of International Criminalisation,' in M. cherif Bassiouni, ed., *International Criminal Law*, Vol. 1, (2008), pp. 107-128.

Cryer R., *Prosecuting International Crimes, Selectivity and the International Criminal Law Regime* (Cambridge University Press, Cambridge, 2005).

D'Amato A., 'It's a Bird, It's a Plane, It's *Jus cogens'* (1990) 6 *Connecticut Journal of International Law*.

D'Amato A., 'The Moral Dilemma of Positivism,' 20 *Valparaiso University Law Review*, (1985-86), 43-53.

D'Amato A., 'The Moral Dilemma of Positivism,' 20 *Valparaiso University Law Review* (1985-86), 43-53.

Danilenko G., 'International Jus cogens: Issues of Law-Making,' 2 *European Journal of International Law* (1991).

Dautricourt J. The Concept of International Criminal Court Jurisdiction-Definition and Limitations of the Subject, in *A Treatise on International Criminal Law* 636 (M. C. Bassiouni & V. P. Nanda eds., 1973).

Davis M. C., Dietrich Wolfgang, Bettina Schoolman and Sepp Dieter, *International Intervention in the Post-Cold War World: Moral Responsibility and Power Politics* (M. E. Sharpe, Inc., 2003).

de Hoog A. J. J., 'The Relationship between *Jus cogens, Obligations Erga Omnes* and International Crimes: Peremptory Norms in Perspective,' 42 *Österreichische Zeitschrift für öffentliches Recht und Völkerrecht* (1991).

de Hoogh A., *Obligations Erga Omnes and International Crimes: A Theoretical Inquiry into the Implementation and Enforcement of the International Responsibility of States* (Kluwer The Hague, 1996).

de Wet E., 'The Prohibition of Torture as an International Norm of *Jus cogens* and its Implementation for National and Customary Law,' 15 (1) *European Journal of International Law* (2014), Vol. 15, No. 1, 97-121.

de Wet, E., '*Jus Cogens* and Obligations Erga Omnes' in de Wet, E and Vidmar (eds.), J *Hierarchy in International Law: The Place of Human Rights*, (2012).

Delmas-Marty M., 'The Contribution of Comparative Law to a Pluralist Conception of International Criminal Law,' 1 *Journal of International Criminal Justice*, (2003), pp. 13-25.

DeSon J. S., 'Automating the Right Stuff? The Hidden Ramifications of Ensuring Autonomous Aerial Weapon Systems Comply with International Humanitarian Law,' 72 *Air Force Law Review*, (2015), pp. 85–122.

Detmold M. J., *The Unity of Law and Morality: A Refutation of Legal Positivism* (Canada: Law Book Co. of Australasia, 1984).

Dhanapala J., *Under-Secretary-General for Disarmament Affairs United Nations, International Law, Security, and Weapons of Mass Destruction*, (New York, 9 May 2002).

Dhokalia. 'Problems Relating to *Jus Cogens*,' in S. Agrawala (ed.), *Essays on the Law of Treaties*, (1972).

Dickson J., *Evaluation and Legal Theory*, (2001).

Don P., Jim Hoffman, *Waking Up from Our Nightmare, the 9/11/01 Crimes in New York City* (New York: I/R Press, 2004).

Douzinas C., Peter Goodrich and Yifat Hachamovitch, *Politics, Post modernity and Critical Legal Studies* (1994).

Drost P. N., *The Crime of State: Genocide* (Original from Indiana University, 1959).

Dryer D. P, *Kant's Solution for Verification in Metaphysics* (Allen and Unwin, 1966).

Duffett J., *Against the Crime of Silence* (New York, London, 1968).

Dugard J., 'Lifting the Guise of Occupation and Recourse to Action before the ICJ and ICC,' *Palestine Yearbook of International Law,* Vol. 17, 2013–14, pp. 9–27.

Duncan A. R. C., *Practical Reason and Morality* (Nelson, 1957).

Dupuy P., 'Some Reflections on Contemporary International Law and the Appeal to Universal Values: a Response to Marti Koskenniemi' 16 *European Journal of International Law,* (2005).

Duţu M., *Vespasian V. Pella*. (1897-1952) Founder of International Criminal law, Promoter of the Unification of the Criminal Law, *Architect of the International Criminal Justice* (Universul Juridic, Bucharest, 2012).

Eric D., *Principes de Droit des Conflits Armés*, (2nd, ed. 1999).

Ewald F., 'Unger's Philosophy: A Critical Legal Study,' 5 *Yale Law Journal* 665(1988).

Ewing A. C., *A Short Commentary on Kant's 'Critique of Pure Reason'* (Methuen, 1978).

Falk R. A. & Burns H. Weston, The Relevance of International Law to Palestinian Rights in the West Bank and Gaza: In Legal Defense of the Intifada, 32 *Harvard International law Journal* (1991), pp. 129-157.

Falk R., 'The Accountability of Leaders: A Challenge to Civil Government and Society' in Jeremy Brecher, Jill Cutler, Smith Brendan, *In the Name of Democracy: American War Crimes in Iraq and Beyond* (American Empire Project), (New York: Metropolitan Books, Henry Holt and Company, 2005).

Falk R., *Slouching Toward a Palestinian Holocaust,* www.transnational.org/Area.../Falk Palestine Genocide.html, 20 October 2010.

Falk R., *The Vietnam War and International Law (*Princeton University Press, 1968).

Farmer J., *The Ground Truth: The Story Behind America's Defense on 9/11* (New York: Riverhead Books, 2009).

Feimpong J. K. & S. Azadon Tiewel, 'Can Apartheid Successfully Defy the International Legal System?' 5 *The Black Law Journal* (1977), pp. 287-311.

Fein B., *'Hillary Clinton's 5 lies about Syria, Terror Threat,'* The Washington Times (25 October, 2016).

Feld W., *The Court of the European Communities: New Dimension in International Adjudication* (1964).

Ferencz B. B. 'Ending Impunity for the Crime of Aggression,' 41 *Case W. Res. J*, (2009), pp. 281-290.

Ferencz B., 'An International Criminal Code and Court: Why They Stand and Where They're Going,' 30 *Columbia Journal of Transnational Law*, (1992), 375.

Ferencz B., *International Criminal Court* (2 vols. 1980).

Findlay E. por Mark J, *International and Comparative Criminal Justice: A Critical Introduction* (Routledge, London, 2013).

Finnis J. (ed.), *Natural Law*, (1991).

Finnis J., *Aquinas: Moral, Political and Legal Theory* (1998).

Fischer-Lescano A., Teubner G., 'Regime Collision: The Vain Search for Legal Unity in the Fragmentation of Global Law,' 25 *Michigan Journal of International Law*, (2004), pp. 999-104.

Fitzpatrick P. (ed.), *Dangerous Supplements: Resistance and Renewal in Jurisprudence* (1991).

Focarelli C., 'Promotional Jus cogens: A Critical Appraisal of *Jus Cogens*' Legal Effects' 77 *Nordic Journal of International Law*, (2008), 429.

Fouladvand S., *Complementarity and Cultural Sensitivity: Decision-making by the International Criminal Court (ICC) Prosecutor in Relation to the Situations in the Darfur Region of the Sudan and the Democratic Republic of Congo* (DRC), (2012).

Franck T. M., *Fairness in International Law and Institutions* (1997).

Fuller L. L., *The Morality of Law* (Virginia: Yale Law University, 2nd, ed., 1969).

Fuller S., "Playing Without a Full Deck: Scientific Realism and the Cognitive Limits of Legal Theory," 97 *Yale Law Journal* 549 (1988).

Gebrehana T., *Duty to negotiate: An Element of International law* (1978).

Gebrehana T., T *Arbitration - An Element of International Law* (1984).

George J. Andreopoulos, (ed.), *Genocide: Conceptual and Historical Dimensions* (Philadelphia, 1994).

George R. P. (ed.), *The Autonomy Of Law: Essays On Legal Positivism*, (1995).

George R. P., *Natural Law Theory: Contemporary Essays*, (1994).

Gerhard O. W. Mueller & Edward M. Wise (eds), *International Criminal Law* (1965).

Ginsberg Benjamin., *The Dark Side of Politics: Essays on the Unpleasant Realities of Political Life* (2023).

Glennon M. J., 'De l'Absurdité du Droit Impératif (Jus cogens)'/*On the Absurdity of Imperative Law (Jus cogens)* 110 *Revue Générale de Droit International Public*, (2006), 529.

Goldstone R. J., *For Humanity: Reflections of a War Crimes Investigator* (2000).

Gómez R., *A., El Ius Cogens Internacional* (Estudio Histórico Crítico), (1982).

Goodrich P., *Languages of Law* (1990).

Gracia-Amador, 'The Crime of Apartheid: Responsibility and Reparations,' *Review of Contemporary Law* (1981), pp. 31-38.

Gray C., *International Law and the Use of Force*, (2000).

Grayeff F., *Kant's Theoretical Philosophy* (Barnes & Noble, 1970).

Green P. J. and Ward, T., State crime, Human rights, and the Limits of Criminology, 27 *Social Justice* (2000), pp. 101–120.

Greenawalt A. K. A., 'The Pluralism of International Criminal Law,' 86 *Indiana Law Journal*, (2011), 1063-1130.

Grover S., *Prosecuting International Crimes and Human Rights Abuses Committed Against Children – Leading International Court Cases*, (2010), pp. 169–279.

Haas J. De, *History of Palestine - The Last Two Thousand Years* (USA: Macmillan, 1934).

Hannikainen L., *Peremptory Norms (jus cogens) in International Law: Historical Development, Criteria, Present Status* (1988).

Haque A. A., *Law and Morality at War* (2017).

Harees L., *The Mirage of Dignity on the Highways of Human 'Progress': the Bystanders Perspective*, (2012).

Harle V., *Ideas of Social Order in the Ancient World* (1998).

Harris J. W., *Legal Philosophies*, 2 edition (1997).

Harris W., *Tyranny on Trial* (Dallas: Southern Methodist University Press, 1999).

Hart H. L. A., *The Concept of Law,* 2nd ed., (P. A. Bulloch and J. Raz, eds., 1994).

Hartnack J., *Kant's Theory of Knowledge* (Harcourt, Brace and World, 1967).

Heller K. Jon, 'The Shadow Side of Complementarity: The Effect of Article 17 of the Rome Statute on National Due Process,' 17 *Criminal Law Forum* (2006), available at file:///C:/Users/admin/AppData/Local/Temp/SSRN-id907404.pdf.

Heller K. Jon, *The Nuremberg Military Tribunals and the Origins of International Criminal Law* (2010).

Hickey J. E., *Challenges to Security Council Monopoly Power over the Use of Force in Enforcement Actions: The Case of Regional Organisations*, 10 Ius Gentium 75 (2004).

Hitchens C., *The Trial of Henry Kissinger* (London: Verso Books, 2001).

Hoffe O., *Immanuel Kant* (State University of New York Press, 1994).

Hoover J. *Moral Practices: Assigning Responsibility in the International Criminal Court,* 76 *Law and Contemporary Problems* (2014), pp. 263-86.

Hughes G., Validity and the Basic Norm, 59 *California Law Review* 695 (1971).

Huntington C., 'Plato's Theory of Law,' 56 *Harvard Law Review*, (1942), pp. 559-587.

Hurd H., Challenging Authority, 100 *Yale Law Journal* 1611 (1991). https://www.gordogan.com.hr/gordogan/wp-content/uploads/2011/10/2001-Hitchens-The-Trial-of-Henry-Kissinger.pdf.

Hurlock W. L., "The International Court of Justice: Effectively Providing a Long Overdue Remedy for Ending State-Sponsored Genocide (Bosnia-Herzegovina v. Yugoslavia)," 12 *American University Journal of International Law and Policy* (1997).

Husabø E. J., Ingvild Bruce, *Fighting Terrorism through Multilevel Criminal Legislation: Security Council Resolution 1373, the EU Framework Decision on Combating Terrorism and their Implementation in Nordic, Dutch and German Criminal Law* (Martinus Nijhoff Publishers, 2009).

Huskey K. with Aleigh Acerni, *Justice at Guantanamo: One Woman's Odyssey and Her Crusade for Human Rights* (2009).

Ineke B. 'Towards a Strong System of Supervision: The Human Rights Committee's Role in Reforming the Reporting Procedure under Article 40 of the Covenant on Civil and Political Rights,' *Human Rights Quarterly*, 17. 4, (1995), pp. 766-793.

Jacovides A., *Treaties Conflicting with Peremptory Norms of International Law and the Zurich-London 'Agreements,'* (1966).

James P., Jonathan Friedman, Globalisation and Violence, Vol. 3: *Globalizing War and Intervention* (London: Sage Publications, 2006).

Janis M. W., 'The Nature of *Jus* Cogens' 3 *Connecticut Journal of International Law*, (1988), 59.

Jevons W. S., *The Theory of Political Economy* (London: Macmillan and Co., 1871).

John C. and John R. Pritchard (eds.), *International Humanitarian Law: Origins, Challenges and Prospects* (2000).

Jørgensen, *The Responsibility of States for International Crimes* (OUP Oxford 2000).

Jori M. (ed.), *Legal Positivism* (1992).

Jori M. (ed.), *Legal Positivism,* (1992).

Kairys D.(ed.), *The Politics of Law: A Progressive Critique* (1982).

Kant I., *Answering the Question: What is Enlightenment?* (1784).

Kant I., *Critique of Judgment* (1790).

Kant I., *Critique of Pure Reason* (1781).

Kant I., *Groundwork of the Metaphysic of Morals* (1785).

Kant I., *Metaphysical Foundations of Natural Science* (1786).

Kant I., *Opus Postumum* (1995).

Kant I., *Perpetual Peace, and Other Essays on Politics, History, and Morals* (1784).

Kant I., *Perpetual Peace: A Philosophical Sketch* (1795).

Kant I., *Practical Philosophy* (editor: Mary J. Gregor, 1999).

Kant I., *Prolegomena to Any Future Metaphysics* (1783).

Kant I., *Religion within the Bounds of Bare Reason* (1793).

Kant I., *The Critique of Practical Reason* (1788).

Kant I., *The Metaphysics of Morals* (1797).

Kant I., *The Only Possible Argument in Support of a Demonstration of the Existence of God* (1763).

Kant I., *The Science of Right* (1790).

Kawasaki K., 'A brief Note on the Legal Effects of *Jus Cogens* in International Law,' 34 *Hitotsubashi Journal of Law and Politics* (2006), pp. 27-43.

Kelman M., *A Guide to Critical Legal Studies* (1987).

Kelsen H., 'Will the Judgement of the Nürenberg Trial Constitute a Precedent in International Law,' 1 *International Law Quarterly* (1947), 153.

Kelsen H., 'Will the Judgement of the Nürenberg Trial Constitute a Precedent in International Law,' 1 *International Law Quarterly* (1947), 153.

Kelsen H., *What is Justice? Justice, Law and Politics in the Mirror of Science* (1957).

Kelsen H., *What is Justice? Justice, Law and Politics in the Mirror of Science* (1957);

Kemal S., *Kant's Aesthetic Theory: An Introduction* (St. Martin's Press, 1992).

Khadduri M., *Major Middle Eastern Problems in International Law*, (1972).

Kitcher P., *Kant's Transcendental Psychology* (Oxford University Press, 1990).

Klein D., F., 'A Theory for the Application of the Customary International Law of Human Rights by Domestic Courts,' 13 (2) *Yale Journal of International Law* (1988), pp. 332-365.

Kolb R. 'Jus cogens, Intangibilité, Intransgressibilité, Dérogation 'Positive' et 'Négative' 109 *Revue Générale de Droit International Public* (2005), 305.

Koskenniemi M. 'Solidarity Measures: State Responsibility as a New International Order?' 72 *BYIL*, (2001), pp. 337–56.

Koskenniemi M., "The Politics of International Law," *European Journal of International Law* (2011).

Kos-Rabcewicz-Zubrowski L., The Creation of an International Criminal Court, in *International Terrorism and Political Crimes* 519 (M. Cherif Bassiouni ed., 1975).

Kramer R. C., Michalowski, R. and Kauzlarich, D., 'The origins and development of the concept and theory of state-corporate crime,' 48 *Crime and Delinquency* (2002), pp. 263–282.

Kress C., 'Aggression and the Use of Force in International Law,' *Proceedings of the 108th Annual Meeting of the American Society of International Law* (2014), pp. 325–346.

Kuper L., *International Action against Genocide* (Minority Rights Group Report No. 53, London, 1982).

Kuper L., *The Prevention of Genocide* (New Haven and London, 1985).

Lefenya K., 'Use of Explosive Weapons in Densely Populated Areas: Implications for International Humanitarian Law,' *African Yearbook on International Humanitarian Law* (2014), pp. 68–86.

Leonetti. 'Interprétation des traités et rêgles impératives du droit international général (jus cogens),' 24 *ÖZÖR*, (1973).

Linderfalk U., 'The Creation of Jus cogens – Making Sense of Article 53 of the Vienna Convention,' *Max-Planck-Institut für ausländisches öffentliches Recht und Völkerrecht* (2011), pp. 259-278.

Lippman M., 'Genocide,' in *International Criminal Law*, Vol. I (M. Cherif Bassiouni, ed., 2008) pp. 405-455.

Luper-Foy S., 'Introduction: Global Distributive Justice' in Steven Luper-Foy (ed.), *Problems of International Justice* (London: Westview Press, 1988), pp. 1-24.

Lyons D., 'Moral Aspects of Legal Theory,' in Kenneth Himma and Brian Bix (eds) *Law and Morality* (2005).

MacGregor 'State Immunity and *Jus cogens,*' 55 *International & Comparative Law Quarterly* (2006), 437.

MacGregor D., 'September 11 as 'Machiavellian State Terrorism,' in Paul Zarembka, *The Hidden History of 9-11-2001* (New York: Seven Stories Press, 2008).

MacIntyre A., *A Short History of Ethics: a History of Moral Philosophy from the Homeric Age to the Twentieth Century* (1965).

MacIntyre A., *After Virtue: A Study in Moral Theory* (University of Notre Dame Press, 1982).

Madsen W., Jean-Charles, Guillaume Dasquie. *Forbidden Truth: U.S.-Taliban Secret Oil Diplomacy,* Saudi Arabia and the Failed Search for bin Laden, (2002).

Majd Mohammad Gholi, *The Great Famine & Genocide in Iran 1917-1919* (2nd edition, University Press of America, 2013).

Majd Mohammad Gholi, *A Victorian Holocaust: Iran in the Great Famine of 1869–1873* (Hamilton Books, 2017).

Majd Mohammad Gholi, *Iran Under Allied Occupation In World War II: The Bridge to Victory & A Land of Famine* (University Press of America, 2016).

Malekian, F., 'Armenian Genocide and the Questions of Responsibility of the Turkish Government,' *House of Commons Conference on the Armenian Genocide, Armenian Solidarity, British-Armenian All-Party Parliamentary Group, No Security Publication* (2007), pp. 31-9.

Malekian, F., *Barrels of Justifications Violating International Criminal Responsibility* (New York: Nova Science Publishers, 2025).

Malekian, F., 'Comparative Substantive International Criminal Justice,' in Ronald Slye (ed.), *The Nuremberg Principles in Non-western Societies: A Reflection on their Universality, Legitimacy and Application* (2017), pp. 10-44.

Malekian, F., 'Conundrums of *Jus Cogens:* In Case Law' (Part II), No. 13 *Вісник Південного регіонального центру Національної академії правових наук України,* (No. 13 *Journal of the South regional Center of National Academy of Legal Sciences of Ukraine)* (2017), pp. 12-21.

Malekian, F., 'Conundrums of *Jus Cogens*: in International Criminal Law' (Part I), *Вісник Південного регіонального центру Національної академії правових наук України (No.12 Journal of the South regional Center of National Academy of Legal Sciences of Ukraine)* (2017), pp. 8-16.

Malekian, F., 'Emasculating the Philosophy of International Criminal Justice in the Iraqi Special Tribunal,' *Cornell International Law Journal*, 58/5 (2005), pp. 675-725.

Malekian, F., *Hypocrisy in International Criminal Justice* (New York: Nova Science Publishers, 2025).

Malekian, F., *International Crime of Blackboard-Barbarism* ((New York: Nova Science Publishers, 2025).

Malekian, F., 'International Criminal Responsibility,' in *International Criminal Law* (M. Cherif Bassiouni, 2ed, ed., 1999).

Malekian, F., 'International Criminal Responsibility: International Criminal Responsibility of Individuals' in M. Cherif Bassiouni, *International Criminal Law,* Vol. *Crimes* (2ed, ed., New York: Transnational Publishers, 1999).

Malekian, F. and Kerstin Nordlöf, 'International Legal Status of Children' in Jay S. Albanese (ed.), *The Encyclopaedia of Criminology & Criminal Justice* (United States: Wiley-Blackwell (5 volumes, 2013), vol. III, pp. 1173-1178.

Malekian, F., 'Islamic Law Justice Systems' in Jay S. Albanese, *The Encyclopaedia of Criminology and Criminal Justice* (United States: Wiley-Blackwell (5 volumes, 2013), vol. III, pp. 1220-1225.

Malekian, F., 'Judging International Criminal Justice in the Occupied Territories,' 12 *International Criminal Law Review* (2012), pp. 627-869.

Malekian, F., 'Mutilating the Philosophy of Justice in the Time of Armed Conflicts,' *Contemporary Journal of International Criminal Law* (2007).

Malekian, F., 'The Canon of Love against the Use of Force in Islamic and Public International Law: Part II: The Anatomy of Love Against Violations,' 15 *International Criminal Law Review*, 2015), pp. 861-895.

Malekian, F., 'The Canon of Love against the Use of Force in Islamic and Public International Law: Part I: The Chamber of Love within Legal Discipline,' 15 *International Criminal Law Review*, 2015), pp. 591-628.

Malekian, F., 'The Child as an Autonomous Subject of Justice' in Farhad Malekian and Kerstin Nordlöf, *Sovereignty of Children in Law* (Cambridge: Cambridge Scholars Publishing, 2012), pp. 2-55.

Malekian, F., 'The Functions of International Criminal Law and the Problem of Positivism and Neutralism Philosophy,' *Contemporary Journal of International Criminal Law* (2007).

Malekian, F., 'The Heaven of Justice with Love,' *The Journal of the Henry Martyn Institute* (2017), pp. 5-29.

Malekian, F., 'The Homogeneity of International Criminal Court with Islamic Jurisprudence,' 9 (4) *International Criminal Law Review* (2009), pp. 595-621.

Malekian, F., 'The Laws Governing Crimes against Women Constituting *Obligatio Erga Omnes*' in David Wingeate Pike, *Crimes Against Women* (2011).

Malekian, F., 'The Miserable Wedding of Naturalism into Positivism,' 2 *ID EST Journal* (2009).

Malekian, F., *Allegations by Political Laundering* (Cambridge Scholars Publishing, 2019).

Malekian, F., *Classical Morality in International Peremptory Criminal Law* (Newcastle: Cambridge Scholars Publishing, 2018).

Malekian, F., *Classical Morality in International Peremptory Criminal Law* (Newcastle: Cambridge Scholars Publishing, 2021).

Malekian, F., *Concreting Righteousness in International Criminal Justice* (New York: Nova publishers, 2024).

Malekian, F., *Condemning the Use of Force in the Gulf Crisis* (Almqvist & Wiksell International, 1st ed., 1992).

Malekian, F., *Conscience of Judges in International Criminal Law, the Heart of Judgements* (New York: Nova Science Publishers, 2021).

Malekian, F., *Conscience of Lawyers in International Criminal Law, the Burden of Doppelgängers* (New York: Nova Science Publishers, 2021).

Malekian, F., *Conscience of Prosecutors in International Criminal Law, the Heart of the Matter* (New York: Nova Science Publishers, 2021).

Malekian, F., *Conundrums of Paternalism in International Criminal Justice* (New York: Nova Science Publishers, 2024).

Malekian, F., *Corpus Juris of Islamic International Criminal Justice* (Newcastle: Cambridge Scholars Publishing, 2017).

Malekian, F., *Documents on the Principles of International Human Rights* (Stockholm: Norstedts Juridik AB, 2007).

Malekian, F., *Exploitation of Christian Islamic International Criminal Justice* (New York: Nova Science Publishers, 2024).

Malekian, F., *Gravity of Wisdom in International Criminal Law* (New York: Nova Science Publishers, 2021).

Malekian, F., *Imperative Philosophy of International Criminal Justice: Visible Power – Invisible Essence* (Nova Sciences Publishers, 2022).

Malekian, F., *International Criminal Law of Children* (New York: Nova Science Publishers, 2021).

Malekian, F., *International Criminal Law, the Law of Somebodiness, the Law of Nobodiness* (New York: Nova Science Publishers, 2021).

Malekian, F., *International Criminal Law: The Legal and Critical Analysis of International Crimes* (Almqvist & Wiksell International, 2 vols. 1991).

Malekian, F., *International Criminal Responsibility of States: A Study on the Evolution of International Responsibility of States with particular Emphasis on the Concept of Crime and Criminal Responsibility* (Stockholm, 1985).

Malekian, F., *International Criminal Vacations: Tears of Justice* (New York: Nova Science Publishers, 2024).

Malekian, F., *Judgments of Love in Criminal Justice* (Switzerland: Springer: 2017, 2018).

Malekian, F., *Jurisprudence of International Criminal Justice* (Introduction by Professor Benjamin B. Ferencz, the former Prosecutor of the Nuremberg Tribunal (Cambridge: Cambridge Scholars Publishing, 2014).

Malekian, F. and Kerstin Nordlöf, *Prohibition of Sexual Exploitation of Children Constituting Obligation Erga Omnes* (Cambridge: Cambridge Scholars Publishing, 2013).

Malekian, F. and Kerstin Nordlöf, *The Sovereignty of Children in Law* (Cambridge: Cambridge Scholars Publishing, 2012).

Malekian, F. and Kerstin Nordlöf, *The Basic documents with Analysis (*Cambridge: Cambridge Scholars Publishing, 2012).

Malekian, F., *Orchestrating Diversity in International Criminal Justice* (New York: Nova Science Publishers, 2021).

Malekian, F., *Paralysing International Criminal Justice* (New York: Nova Science Publishers, 2021).

Malekian, F., *Powertionism in International Criminal Justice* (Nova Sciences Publishers, 2022).

Malekian, F., *Principles of Islamic International Criminal Law: A Comparative Search* (Netherlands: Brill & Nijhoff, 2011).

Malekian, F., *Prohibition Governing Child Soldiers Constituting an Integral Part of Jus Cogens and Obligatio Erga Omnes*, XVII *World Congress of the International Association of Youth and Family Judges and Magistrates*, Belfast, Northern Ireland, 27 August – 2 September (2006).

Malekian, F., *System of International Law: Formation, Treaties, Responsibility* (Uppsala, 1987).

Malekian, F., *The Concept of Islamic International Criminal Law, A Comparative Study* (Netherlands: Brill, 1994).

Malekian, F., *The Mirage of International Criminal Law*: Kant Metaphysics of *Mens Rea* (Cambridge: Cambridge Scholars Publishing, 2018).

Malekian, F., *The Monopolisation of International Criminal Law in the United Nations, A Jurisprudential Approach* (Stockholm: Almqvist Wiksell International, 1st ed., 1993).

Malekian, F., *The Monopolisation of International Criminal Law in the United Nations, A Jurisprudential Approach* (Stockholm: Almqvist Wiksell International, 2nd ed., 1995).

Malekian, F., *Tour de force of Moral Virtue in International Criminal Justice* (Nova, Science Publishers, 2022).

Malekian, F., *Trading Virginity of International Criminal Justice* (New York: Nova Science Publishers, 2020).

Malekian, F., *Utipolitianist International Criminal Court* ((New York: Nova Science Publishers, 2025).

Manacorda S., 'Cesare Beccaria e la pena dell'ergastolo' *Jus* (2015), pp. 165–182.

May L., 'Habeas Corpus as *Jus cogens* in International Law' 4 (3) *Criminal Law and Philosophy* (2010), 249–265.

May L., *Aggression and Crimes Against Peace* (New York: Cambridge University Press, 2008).

May L., *Crimes against Humanity: A Normative Account* (New York: Cambridge University Press 2004).

May L., *War Crimes and Just War* (New York: Cambridge University Press, 2007).

Mendus S., 'The Importance of Love in Rawls's Theory of Justice' 29 (1) *British Journal of Political Science* (1999), pp. 57-75.

Meron T., 'On Hierarchy of International Human Rights' 80 *American Journal of International Law*, (1986), 1.

Meron T., *The Humanisation of International Law* (Netherlands: The Hague Academy, 2006).

Meyssan T., *11 September 2001: L'effroyable Imposture*, (2002).

Mokhtar A., '*Nullum Crimen, Nulla Poena, Sine Lege*: Aspects and Prospects,' 26 *Statute Law Review*, pp. 41-55.

Morten B., Emiliano J. Buis, *Philosophical Foundations of International Criminal Law* (2018).

Mosaddeq A., N. (2006), "Terrorism and Statecraft: Al-Qaeda and Western Covert Operations after the Cold War," Zarembka, P. (Ed.) *The Hidden History of 9-11-2001. (Research in Political Economy, Vol. 23)*, Emerald Group Publishing Limited, Bingley, pp. 149-188. https://doi.org/10.1016/S0161-7230(06)23005-0.

Moyn S., *Not Enough: Human Rights in an Unequal World*, (2018).

Muchnik P., *Kant's Theory of Evil: An Essay on the Dangers of Self-love and the Aperiodicity of History* (Lexington Books, 2010).

Mueller G. O. W., 'International Criminal Law: Civitas Maxima,' 15 *Case Western Reserve Journal of International Law* (1985).

Mullins Christopher W., Kauzlaric David, Rothe Dawn, "The International Criminal Court and the Control of State Crime: Prospects and Problems," 12(3) *Critical Criminology* (2004), pp. 285-308.

Naiman A. *'9/11: The Simple Facts — Why the Official Story can't Possibly be True,'* (US: Soft Skull Press, 2011).

Nieto C., Chris Brandt, Howard Zinn (Foreword), *Masters of War: Latin America and U.S. Aggression From the Cuban Revolution Through the Clinton Years* (2003).

Nietzsche F. W., *The Will to Power,* https://en.wikisource.org/wiki/The_Will_to_Power.

Nietzsche F., *The Genealogy of Morals: A Polemic* (translated J. M. Kennedy, Vol. 8th, 1913).

Nozary F., *Unequal Treaties in International Law* (Stockholm, 1971).

O'Connor Susan, 'Up in Arms: A Humanitarian Analysis of the Arms Trade Treaty and Its New Zealand Application,' 11 *New Zealand Yearbook of International Law* (2013), pp. 73–105.

O'Neill O., *Constructions of Reason: Explorations of Kant's Practical Philosophy* (Cambridge University Press, 1989).

Ogunfolu A., Oludayo Fagbemi, 'I Have a Drone: The Implications of American Drone Policy for Africa and International Humanitarian Law,' 23 (1) *Revue Africaine de Droit International et Comparé* (2015), pp. 106–128.

Olivecrona K. 'The Imperative Element in Law,' *Rutgers Law Review* (1964).

Olson Peter M., 'The Lawfulness of Russian Use of Force in Crimea,' 53 (1) *Revue de Droit Militaire et de Droit de la Guerre* (2014), pp. 17–40.

Orakhelashvili A., 'The Impact of Peremptory Norms on the Interpretation and Application of United Nations Security Council Resolutions' 16 (1), *The European Journal of International Law* (2005), pp. 59-88.

Orakhelashvili A., *Peremptory Norms in International Law* (2006).

Osiel M. J., Why Prosecute? Critics of Punishment for Mass Atrocity, 22 *Human Rights Quarterly* 118 (2000).

Osiel M., *The End of Reciprocity* (Cambridge University Press, 2009).

Otterman M., *American Torture: From the Cold War to Abu Ghraib and Beyond* (Pluto Press, 2007).

Pardo P. V. S., 'Is International Criminal Law a living discipline?,' 3:4 *The International Journal of Human Rights* (1999), pp. 92-100.

Paris Declaration, International Conference on Sanctions Against South Africa (And Special Declaration on Namibia), 27 May1981, Published by the United Nations Center Against Apartheid.

Parish M., *International criminal law – Justice or Mirage? Transonflict* (2013).

Paton H. J., *Kant's Metaphysic of Experience* (Humanities Press, 1961).

Patrides C. A., Joseph Anthony Wittreich. *The Apocalypse in English Renaissance Thought and Literature: Patterns, Antecedents, and Repercussions* (Manchester University Press, 1984).

Patterson D.(ed.), *Postmodernism and Law* (1994).

Paulus A., 'Jus cogens in a Time of Hegemony and Fragmentation,' 74 *Nordic Journal of International Law* (2005), pp. 297-334.

Paust J. 'The Reality of Jus cogens,' 7 *Connecticut Journal of International Law* (1991), 83.

Pellet A., 'Comments in Response to Christine Chinking and in Defense of Jus cogens as the Best Bastion against the Excesses of Fragmentation,' 83 *Finnish Yearbook of International Law* (2006).

Pellet A., 'Vive le crime! Remarques sur les degrés de l'illicité en droit international' in United Nations/International Law Commission (ed.), *International Law on the Eve of the Twenty-first Century: Views from the International Law Commission* (United Nations New York 1997), pp. 287–315.

Penrose M. M.'Lest We Fail: The Importance of Enforcement in International Criminal Law An Essay on the Nature and Immutability of Truth,' 15 (2) *American University International Law Review* (1999), pp. 321-394.

Perelman C., *The Idea of Justice and the Problem of Argument* (1963).

Peterson J., 'Unpacking Show Trials: Situating the Trial of Saddam Hussein,' 48 *Harvard International Law Journal* (2007).

Postema G. J., *Bentham and the Common Law Tradition* (1986).

Potter R. B., *War and Moral Discourse* (Richmond, Va., John Knox Press, 1969).

Power J., *Conundrums of Humanity: The Quest for Global Justice* (2007).

Protector J. H.., *Islam and International Relations* (New York, 1965).

Ragazzi M., *The Concept of International Obligations erga omnes* (Clarendon Press Oxford 1997).

Rahmdel M., 'Money Laundering in Iranian Law: Present and Future,' *Journal of Money Laundering Control* (2002).

Rahmdel M., 'The *Ne Bis In Idem* Rule in Iranian Criminal Law,' *Journal of Financial Crime* (2004).

Rahmdel M., The Role of the Courts in the Reform of Iranian Criminal Law Policy,' *Criminal Law Forum*, (2006).

Rawls J., *A Theory of Justice* (1999).

Raz J., 'Why the State?' in N. Roughan and A. Halpin (eds) In *Pursuit of a Pluralist Jurisprudence* (CUP 2017).

Raz J., *Ethics in the Public Domain: Essays in the Morality of Law and Politics* (Oxford: Oxford University Press, 1994).

Raz J., *The Morality of Freedom* (1986).

Reddy E. S., 'India and the Struggle Against Apartheid,' 26 *Indian Journal of International Law* (1986), pp. 551-567.

Reddy E. S., *Apartheid: The United Nations and the International Community* (1986).

Rehman J. *International Human Rights Law* (London and New York: Longman Pub Group, 2nd ed., 2010).

Reisman W. M., 'Legal Responses to Genocide and Other Massive Violations of Human Rights,' 59 *Law and Contemporary Problems* (1996), 75.

Reiss H. S., *Kant: Political Writings*, (2003).

Report of the Independent Inquiry into the actions of the United Nations during the 1994 genocide in Rwanda, UN Doc S/1999/1257, (1999) [Rwanda Report].

Rinceanu J., 'Criminal Liability of Legal Persons in Romania' in Riccardo Borsari, *Responsabilita` da reato deli enti* (Padova: Padova University Press, 2016). pp. 407–418.

Rinceanu J., 'The principle of legality (Nullum crimen sine lege) in Romania' in U. Sieber, S. Forster, & K. Jarvers (Eds.), *National Criminal Law in a Comparative Legal Context*, vol. 2 (1): Max-Planck-Institute für Ausländisches und Internationals Strafrecht, (2011), pp. 89-101.

Robertson G., *Crimes Against Humanity – The Struggle for Global Justice* (Penguin Books, 3rd ed., 2006).

Robinson M., "Genocide, War Crimes, Crimes Against Humanity," *25 Fordham International Law Journal* (1999), p. 275.

Roht-Arriaza N., State Responsibility to Investigate and Prosecute Grave Human Rights Violations in International Law, 78 *California Law Review* 451 (1990).

Roméo Dallaire's, *Shake Hands with the Devil: The Failure of Humanity in Rwanda* (Carroll & Graf, New York, 2003).

Rorty R., *Philosophy and the Mirror of Nature* (1990).

Rosen A. D. *Kant's Theory of Justice* (Ithaca, London: Cornel University Press, 1996).

Rosenstock R. 'An International Criminal Responsibility of States?,' in United Nations/International Law Commission (ed.), *International Law on the Eve of the Twenty-First Century: Views from the International Law Commission* (United Nations New York, 1997), pp. 265–85.

Ross J. I., *Controlling State Crime* (2nd Edition, New Brunswick, NJ: Transaction Press, 2000).

Ross J. I., *Varieties of State Crime and its Control* (Monsey, NY: Criminal Justice Press, 2000).

Schabas W. A., 'The Banality of International Justice,' 11 *Journal of International Criminal Justice* (2013), pp. 545–551.

Schabas W. A., *An Introduction to the International Criminal Court* (Cambridge University Press, 2011).

Schabas W. A., *Genocide in International Law: The Crimes of Crimes* (Cambridge University Press, 2000 and 2009).

Schabas W. A., Justice, 'Democracy and Impunity in Post Genocide Rwanda: Searching for Solutions to Impossible Problems,' 7 *Criminal Law Forum* (1996).

Schabas W. A., Sentencing by International Tribunals: For a Human Rights Approach, 7:2. *Duke Journal of Comparative & International Law* (1997), pp. 461-518.

Schabas W. A., *The Abolition of the Death Penalty in International Law*, (2002 and 2005).

Schachter O., *International Law in Theory and Practice* (1991).

Schwarzenberger G. 'The Problem of an International Criminal Law,' 5 *Current Legal Problems* (1950).

Schwarzenberger G., *International Jus Cogens?* 43 *Tax. L. Rev* (1965), p. 476.

Schwelb E., *Crimes against Humanity, British Yearbook of International Law* (1946) 178.

Seltzer G., 'The Rule of the South Africa Criminal Code in Implementing Apartheid,' 8 *Georgia Journal of International and Comparative Law* (1978), pp. 176-194.

Sevrine K., 'State Immunity and the Promise of *Jus Cogens*,' *Northwestern Journal of International Human Rights* (2011), Vol. 9, No. 2, pp. 149-183.

Shaffer T. L., 'The Legal Ethics of Radical Individualism,' 65 *Texas Law Review* (1997).

Shelton D., 'Normative Hierarchy of International Law,' 80 *American Journal of International Law* (1986), 1.

Simmonds N., *Law as a Moral Idea* (2008).

Sliedregt E. van., Pluralism in International Criminal Law, 25 *Leiden Journal of International Law* (2012), 847.

Smith N. K., '*Commentary to Kant's 'Critique of Pure Reason'* (Humanities Press, 1962).

Smith T. S., *Lecture Delivered over the Remains of Jeremy Bentham*, Esq., in the Webb-Street School of Anatomy & Medicine, on the 9th June, 1832 (London: Effingham Wilson, 1832).

Sowilet A., *The Problem of the Creation of a Permanent International Criminal Court* (1951).

Spiermann 'Humanitarian Intervention as a Necessity and the Threat or Use of *Jus Cogens*' 71 *Nordic Journal of International Law*, (2002), 523.

Spooner L., *Natural Law; or the Science of Justice: A Treatise on Natural Law, Natural Justice, Natural Rights, Natural Liberty, and Natural Society; showing that all Legislation whatsoever is an Absurdity, a Usurpation, and a Crime.* Part First. [1882], available at http://oll.libertyfund.org/titles/spooner-natural-law-or-the-science-of-justice-1882 (Accessed: on 18 December 2017).

Stern R., *Understanding Moral Obligation: Kant, Hegel, Kierkegaard* (Cambridge, Cambridge University Press, 2012).

Stone J. and Robert Woetzel, *Toward a Feasible International Criminal Court* (1970).

Sugarman D. ed., *Legality, Ideology and the State* (1985).

Sugarman D., (ed.), *Legality, Ideology and the State* (1983).
Svaček O., 'The Human Rights Dimension of the ICC's Complementarity Regime,' *Czech Yearbook of Public and Private International Law,* 2015, Vol. 6, pp. 273-288.
Tunnell K., *Political Crime in Contemporary America* (New York: Garland, 1993).
Unger R., The Critical Legal Studies Movement, *96 Harvard Law Review 561* (1983).
van Schaack B., "The Crime of Political Genocide: Repairing the Genocide Convention's Blind Spot," 106 *Yale Law Journal* (1997).
Van Schaack B., Ronald C. Slye, *International Criminal Law: Intersections and Contradictions* (2020).
Van Schaack B., Ronald C. Slye, *International Criminal Law: The Essentials* (2008).
Van Schaack B., Ronald Sly. (ed.), *International Criminal Law and Its Enforcement* (University Casebook Series, 2nd).
Vanhullebusch M. 'The Arab League and Military Operations: Prospects and Challenges in Syria,' 22 (2) *International Peacekeeping* (2015), pp. 151–168.
Vasilijevic V. A., Crimes against Peace: Between the Past and the Future, 43 *Jugoslovenska Revija Za Medunarodno Pravo* 425 (1996).
Verdross A., 'Forbidden Treaties in International Law: Comments on Professor Garner's Report on 'The Law of Treaties,'' 31 *American Journal of International Law*, (1937), 571.
Verdross A., 'Jus Dispositivum and *Jus Cogens* in International Law' 60 *American Journal of International Law* (1966), 55.
Vespesian P. V., 'Plan for World Criminal Code,' 17 *Revue Internationale de Droit Penal* (1946).
Vespesian P. V., 'Towards an International Criminal Court,' 44 *American Journal of International Law* (1950), 57.
Vespesian P. V., *La criminalité collective des états et le droit pénal de l'avenir, Bucarest : Imprimerie de l'état* (1925).
Vespesian P. V., *La Guerre-Crime et les Criminels de Guerre/War-Crime and War Criminals* (Paris, 1946).
Vespesian P. V., Plan d'un Code Répressif Mondial, 6 *Rewe International de Droit Pénal* 1948, (1955).
Vespesian P. V., *Revue Internationale de Droit Penal* (1928).
Virally M., 'Réflexions sur le Jus cogens' 12 *Annuaire Français de Droit International* (1966), 5.
Vischer K. R., *Martin Luther King Jr. and the Morality of Legal Practice: Lessons in Love and Justice* (2014).
Vyver J. D. van der, 'Prosecution and Punishment of the Crime of Genocide,' 25 *Fordham International Law Journal* (1999).
Waldock H., 'General Course on Public International Law,' 106 *Recueil Des Course* (1962), pp. 39-103.
Ward I., *An Introduction to Critical Legal Theory* (1998).
Weatherhall T., *Jus cogens International Law and Social Contract* (2015).
Weil P., 'Towards Relative Normativity in International Law,' 77 *American Journal of International Law* (1983).

Weisburd M., 'The Emptiness of the Concept of *Jus Cogens*, As Illustrated by the War in Bosnia-Herzegovina,' 17 *Michigan Journal of International Law* (1995-1996), pp. 1-51.

Weiss, T. G., *Military-Civilian Interactions: Humanitarian Crises and the Responsibility to Protect* (2nd ed., Rowman & Littlefield Publishers Inc., Lanham (MD), 2005).

Weller M., *Iraq and the Use of Force in International Law* (Oxford: Oxford University Press, 2010).

Wet D., 'The Prohibition of Torture as an International Norm of *Jus Cogens* and Its Implications for National and Customary Law,' 15 *European Journal of International Law* (2004).

Wright Q., Proposal for an International Criminal Court, 46 *American Journal of International Law* 60 (1952).

Whiteman M. M., '*Jus Cogens* in International Law: With a Projected List,' 7 *Georgia Journal of International and Comparative Law* (1977), p. 609.

Wilkes F. Klein & Daniel, United Nations Draft Statute for an International Criminal Court: An American Evaluation, in *International Criminal Law 526* (Gerhard O. W. Mueller & Edward M. Wise eds., 1965).

Schabas W. A., *Genocide in International Law, the Crime of Crimes* (2000).

Wippman D., Atrocities, Deterrence, and the Limits of International Justice, 23 *Forham International Law Journal* 473 (1999).

Czaplinski W., 'Concepts of *Jus Cogens* and Obligations Erga Omnes in International Law in the Light of Recent Developments,' 23 *Polish Yearbook of International Law* (1997–1998).

Wood A., *Kant's Ethical Thought* (Cambridge University Press, 1999).

Wright Q., 'The Scope of International Criminal Law: A Conceptual Framework,' 15 *Virginia Journal of International Law*, (1975).

Zaman R., 'Playing the Ace? *Jus Cogens* Crimes and Functional Immunity in National Courts,' 17 *Australian International Law Journal*, (2010), 53.

Zarembka P., *The Hidden History of 9-11-2001* (New York: Seven Stories Press, 2008).

Index

B

D

E

F

G

H

I

R

S

T